T0214038

Lecture Notes
in Business Information Processing **374**

Series Editors

Wil van der Aalst ⓘ
  RWTH Aachen University, Aachen, Germany
John Mylopoulos ⓘ
  University of Trento, Trento, Italy
Michael Rosemann ⓘ
  Queensland University of Technology, Brisbane, QLD, Australia
Michael J. Shaw
  University of Illinois, Urbana-Champaign, IL, USA
Clemens Szyperski
  Microsoft Research, Redmond, WA, USA

More information about this series at http://www.springer.com/series/7911

David Aveiro · Giancarlo Guizzardi ·
José Borbinha (Eds.)

Advances in Enterprise Engineering XIII

9th Enterprise Engineering Working Conference, EEWC 2019
Lisbon, Portugal, May 20–24, 2019
Revised Papers

 Springer

Editors
David Aveiro (iD)
University of Madeira
Funchal, Portugal

Giancarlo Guizzardi
Free University of Bozen-Bolzano
Bolzano, Italy

José Borbinha (iD)
University of Lisbon
Lisbon, Portugal

ISSN 1865-1348   ISSN 1865-1356 (electronic)
Lecture Notes in Business Information Processing
ISBN 978-3-030-37932-2   ISBN 978-3-030-37933-9 (eBook)
https://doi.org/10.1007/978-3-030-37933-9

This Springer imprint is published by the registered company Springer Nature Switzerland AG
The registered company address is: Gewerbestrasse 11, 6330 Cham, Switzerland

Preface

This book contains the revised papers of the 9th Enterprise Engineering Working Conference (EEWC 2019), held in Lisbon, Portugal, in May 2019, by the CIAO! Enterprise Engineering Network (CEEN), a community of academics and practitioners who strive to contribute to the development of the discipline of enterprise engineering (EE), and to apply it in practice. The aim is to develop a holistic and general systems theory-based understanding on how to (re)design and run enterprises effectively. The ambition is to develop a consistent and coherent set of theories, models, and associated methods that: enable enterprises to reflect, in a systematic way, on how to realize improvements; and assist them, in practice, in achieving their aspirations.

In doing so, sound empirical and scientific foundations should underlie all efforts and all organizational aspects that are relevant should be considered, while combining already existing knowledge from the scientific fields of information systems, software engineering, management, as well as philosophy, semiotics, and sociology, among others. In other words, the (re)design of an enterprise and the subsequent implementation of changes should be the consequence of rationalized decisions that: take into account the nature and reality of the enterprise and its environment; and respect relevant empirical and scientific principles.

Enterprises are considered to be systems whose reality has a dual nature by being simultaneously, on one hand, centrally and purposefully (re)designed, and, on the other hand, emergent in a distributed way, given the fact that its main agents, the humans that are the "pearls" of the organization, act with free will in a creative and responsible (or sometimes not) way. We acknowledge that, in practice, the development of enterprises is not always a purely rational/evidence-based process. As such, we believe the field of EE aims to provide evidence-based insights into the design and evolution of enterprises and the consequences of different choices irrespective of the way decisions are made.

The origin of the scientific foundations of our present body of knowledge is the CIAO! Paradigm (Communication, Information, Action, Organization) as expressed in our Enterprise Engineering Manifesto and the paper "The Discipline of Enterprise Engineering." In this paradigm, organization is considered to emerge in human communication, through the intermediate roles of information and action. Based on the CIAO! Paradigm, several theories have been developed, and are still being proposed. They are published as technical reports.

The CEEN welcomes proposals of improvements to our current body of knowledge, as well as the inclusion of compliant and alternative views, always keeping in mind the need to maintain global systemic coherence, consistency, and scientific rigor of the entire EE body of knowledge as a prerequisite for the consolidation of this new engineering discipline. Yearly events like the EEWC and associated Doctoral Consortium are organized to promote the presentation of EE research and application in practice, as well as discussions on the contents and current state of our body of theories and methods.

Since 2005, the CEEN has organized the CIAO! Workshop and, since 2008, its proceedings have been published as *Advances in Enterprise Engineering* in the Springer LNBIP series. From 2011 on, this workshop was replaced by the EEWC.

This volume contains the proceedings of the 9th EEWC that received 22 submissions. Each submission was reviewed (double-blind) by three Program Committee members and the decision taken was to accept eight full papers and three short papers which were carefully reviewed and selected for inclusion in this volume. Following the spirit of ours being a working conference, we decided to publish post-proceedings after the event, where the papers that were presented and made available to conference participants were revised and extended by the authors taking into account the discussions hapening at the conference, the feedback of the reviewers, and new developments that might have taken place in the research during/after the conference.

EEWC aims at addressing the challenges that modern and complex enterprises are facing in a rapidly changing world. The participants of the working conference share a belief that dealing with these challenges requires rigorous and scientific solutions, focusing on the design and engineering of enterprises. The goal of EEWC is to stimulate interaction between the different stakeholders, scientists, as well as practitioners, interested in making EE a reality.

This year's event was organized in Lisbon in honor of José Tribolet becoming Emeritus Professor at the end of 2019. We remember his vast contribution to the development of the EE discipline and the highly valuable support given to our community.

We thank all the participants, authors, and reviewers for their contributions to EEWC and hope that you will find these proceedings useful to your explorations on current EE challenges.

May 2019

David Aveiro
Giancarlo Guizzardi
José Borbinha

Organization

EEWC 2019 was the ninth working conference resulting from a series of successful EEWC conferences over the past few years. These events are aimed at addressing the challenges that modern and complex enterprises are facing in a rapidly changing world. The participants in these events share the belief that dealing with these challenges requires rigorous and scientific solutions, focusing on the design and engineering of enterprises.

This conviction has led to the effort of annually organizing an international working conference on the topic of enterprise engineering, in order to bring together all stakeholders interested in making enterprise engineering a reality. This means that not only scientists are invited, but also practitioners. Moreover, it also means that the conference is aimed at active participation, discussion, and exchange of ideas in order to stimulate future cooperation among the participants. This makes EEWC a working conference contributing to the further development of enterprise engineering as a mature discipline.

The organization of EEWC 2019 and the peer review of the contributions to the conference were accomplished by an outstanding international team of experts in the fields of enterprise engineering. The following is the organizational structure of EEWC 2019.

General Conference Chair

José Tribolet   IST/INESC and Transformer Lda, Portugal

Conference Chair

José Borbinha   IST/INESC ID, Portugal

EEWC Forum Chair

Pedro Sousa   IST/Link Consulting Lda, Portugal

Program Chairs

David Aveiro   University of Madeira and Madeira Interactive
                                  Technologies Institute, Portugal
Giancarlo Guizzardi   Free University of Bozen-Bolzano, Italy

Organization Chairs

Carlos Mendes   IST/DIGIPRISE Lda, Portugal
Sérgio Guerreiro   IST/INESC ID, Portugal

Advisory Board

Antonia Albani   University of St. Gallen, Switzerland
Jan Dietz   Delft University of Technology, The Netherlands

Program Committee

Alberto Silva   INESC and University of Lisbon, Portugal
Carlos Mendes   University of Lisbon and DIGIPRISE Lda, Portugal
Carlos Pascoa   University of Lisbon, Portugal
Duarte Gouveia   University of Madeira, Portugal
Eduard Babkin   Higher School of Economics, Nizhny Novgorod,
                               Russia
Florian Matthes   Technical University Munich, Germany
Frederik Gailly   Ghent University, Belgium
Geert Poels   Ghent University, Belgium
Gil Regev   Ecole Polytechnique Fédérale de Lausanne,
                               Switzerland
Graham McLeod   University of Cape Town and Inspired.org,
                               South Africa
Hans Mulder   University of Antwerp, Belgium
Henderik Proper   Luxembourg Institute of Science and Technology,
                               Luxembourg
Jan Dietz   Delft University of Technology, The Netherlands
Jan Verelst   University of Antwerp, Belgium
Jens Gulden   University of Duisburg-Essen, Germany
Jose Tribolet   INESC and University of Lisbon, Portugal
Joseph Barjis   Institute of Engineering and Management,
                               San Francisco, USA
Julio Cesar Nardi   Federal Institute of Espírito Santo, Brazil
Junichi Iijima   Tokyo Institute of Technology, Japan
Marcela Vegetti   INGAR (CONICET/UTN), Brazil
Marcello Bax   Federal University of Minas Gerais, Brazil
Martin Op 't Land   Capgemini, The Netherlands,
                               and University of Antwerp, Belgium
Mauricio Almeida   Federal University of Minas Gerais, Brazil
Miguel Mira Da Silva   INESC and University of Lisbon, Portugal
Monika Kaczmarek   University Duisburg Essen, Germany
Niek Pluijmert   INQA Quality Consultants, The Netherlands
Peter Loos   University of Saarland, Germany
Petr Kremen   Czech Technical University in Prague, Czech Republic

Contents

On Blockchain

On Processes

Business Process Compliance in Partially Observable Environments

Isabel Esperança[1](✉), Pedro Sousa[1,2,3](✉), and Sérgio Guerreiro[1,2](✉)

[1] Instituto Superior Técnico, University of Lisbon,
Av. Rovisco Pais 1, 1049-001 Lisbon, Portugal
{isabel.esperanca,pedro.manuel.sousa,sergio.guerreiro}@tecnico.ulisboa.pt
[2] INESC-ID, Rua Alves Redol 9, 1000-029 Lisbon, Portugal
[3] Link Consulting SA, Av. Duque de Avila 23, 1000-138 Lisbon, Portugal

Abstract. This paper addresses how to design and implement business process compliance through observing the business process instances and controlling the business process models, considering environments that are only partial observable. An organization is a dynamic system where actors assume roles and produce results and decisions autonomously, changing the overall state of the system. These decisions often occur in environments that are not fully observable. The business process models are intended to represent an organizational reality and restrict the freedom of design to allow common understanding between stakeholders and to define the roles of the actors. Therefore, organizations need to ensure that operational processes are performed in a controlled way to meet predefined requirements, complying with regulations, laws and agreements established between internal and external stakeholders. The solution is implemented using an enterprise simulation environment, named as Enterprise Cartography (EC). The results obtained demonstrated the ability to observe and control the process instances as a contribution to improving the compliance of business process.

Keywords: Compliance · Enterprise Cartography · Business process models · Development process · Observation · Control

1 Introduction

An organization includes a network of people and machines that work and communicate in an integrated way. While organizations operate to meet optimization requirements to increase their effectiveness and efficiency, unexpected endogenous and exogenous situations occur continuously. The control and management functions are responsible for optimizing the use of runtime resources. These functions, which must conform to predefined restrictions on individual and collective runtime observations. This organizational activity can be divided into three intervals: ex-ante: what happens before execution of business process; ex-dure: what happens during execution; and ex-post: after the executions. This phase includes decision-making processes to estimate future behaviour from the data

© Springer Nature Switzerland AG 2020
D. Aveiro et al. (Eds.): EEWC 2019, LNBIP 374, pp. 3–14, 2020.
https://doi.org/10.1007/978-3-030-37933-9_1

available from past executions. Integration of these three time intervals provides a complete description of control of organizational behaviour and leads to the problem that organizations have an incomplete understanding of the facts and yet, have to make ex-post organizational decisions based on information collected in partially observable environments. This occur when not all transaction states information is available. This problem is recognized with high impact in the health industries, financial, public administration, etc. The problem addressed by this paper - to design and implement business process compliance through observing the business process instances and controlling the business process models, considering environments that are only partial observable - will be solved taking into account the scientific contributions of EC. The solution consists in enforcing observation and control business process instances using Atlas tool and a business process model, modelled in BPMN. The outline of the rest of the paper is as follows. In Sect. 2, we present the methodology. Section 3 deals with theoretical concepts and in particular EC, which we apply to build the solution. Section 4 present the Solution Proposed in order to explain the problem to be solved using Atlas tool and Blueprint. Section 5 contain Case Study and Results Obtained in this research. Concluding remarks are given in the last section.

2   Design Science Resources Methodology

This investigation use Design Science Resources Methodology (DSRM). DSRM consists of an interactive process with six steps and includes rigorous methods for the creation and evaluation of the proposed artefacts [11]. The following DSRM steps are demonstrated in Fig. 1.

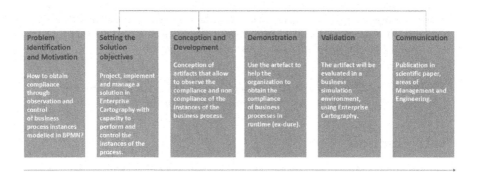

Fig. 1. DSRM process adapted from Peffers et al. [11]

3   Background

3.1   Enterprise Cartography

An organisation can be abstracted as a dynamic system where a network of actors collaborate and produce results that can be depicted using cartographic maps [2]. Actors collaborate with each other over time, creating a dynamic network and produce autonomous behaviours that can change the overall state of system, only be observed after actions end. EC is fundamental to managing the transformation processes of an organization. Transformation is seen as the set of initiatives that change the current state to an intended state. The two states span organizational variables at different points in time. The as-is status represent variables that have changed due to past events, the to-be state represents an expected state configuration of the organizational variables. Between these two states the organization reacts to other events triggered by the operation of the transformation processes. It is important to observe and manage the organization during the transition of states, even if some of the events may not be related to the transformation activity because it can condition the transformation process by diverting the organization from the objectives. Cartography is an abstraction process that systematically and consistently transforms an observation of reality into a map or a graphical representation. EC denotes the discipline that deals with the conception, production, dissemination and study of the maps of an enterprise to support its analysis and collective understanding [2].

3.2   Business Process Compliance

Compliance verification is a very current issue of great importance in communities to management and auditing business process, due to the availability of event data on one hand and by the other hand, due to changes in legislation [4]. Compliance means to ensure that business practice and processes are aligned at commonly accepted norms [5]. Organizations need to continually check whether processes, supported by information systems, are executed within a set of limits. The deviations can be pointed out as negligence, frauds, risks and inefficiencies. Increasingly, organizations are subject to laws and regulations, in compliance with contractual standards and obligations and there is a need to optimize response times for processes subject to these guidelines. At the same time technological advances offer an increasing opportunity to systematically observe processes at a detailed level, with a record of all relevant events in the process. However, increasing computerization of business processes increases opportunities for alternative solutions. Information systems also increase the risk of illusion of control, which means that information systems present information that does not reflect the actual instances of the process [10].

3.2.1   Actor

Actors of an organization are the fundamental part of a company and are organized in social systems Winograd [18]. An actor is usually associated with a person but can be a machine. For the performance of an activity, an actor explicitly or implicitly fulfils a certain role. These actors are endowed with their own will and freedom of action, acting according to their purpose and orchestrations [16]. They are therefore autonomous in deciding what to do next. In companies, some tasks can be automated by software systems, while others are performed by human actors.

3.2.2 Model and Instance of a Business Process Modelled on BPM

"Business Process Management (BPM) is the art and science of overseeing how work is performed in an organization to ensure consistent outcomes and to take advantage of improvement opportunities. Importantly, BPM is not about improving the way individual activities are performed. Rather, it is about managing entire chains of events, activities and decisions that ultimately add value to the organization and its customers. These chains of events, activities and decisions are called processes." [9]. Business process as a collection of inter-related events, activities and decision points that involve a number of actors and objects, and that collectively lead to an outcome that is of value to at least one customer. Figure 2 depicts the ingredients of this definition and their relations. BPM involve different phases and activities in the life cycle of the business process. It is necessary that the previously designed models be implemented in systems (manual, semiautomatic or automatic) and be contained in the organization, so that they can be instantiated later [16]. The instantiation occurs when actors perform their activities throughout the day. It is the multiple instances of the business process, occurring concomitantly, that reveal the existence of the organization on a day-to-day basis. A business process model defines which roles of the actors are involved in each transaction state. It is these same actors who instantiate the transaction states of the business process. In the same way that business process models can be represented, the instances of business processes can also be represented, making it possible to observe if any of the instances are process is not respecting the prescription of the model. The functions of organizational control should be invoked whenever the model is not observed. IT specialists see BPM as a way of communicating with various parts of the business through a common language.

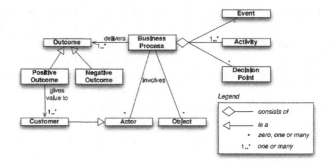

Fig. 2. Ingredients of a Business Process [9]

3.2.3 Observation

Observation is one of the stages of the scientific method and consists in understanding, seeing and not interpreting. And it refers to the action and result of observing something or someone. In control of dynamic systems, Franklin et al. (2009) [19] state that "...a system is completely observable if each system state variable affects some of the outputs. If any of the states cannot be observed from the measurements of the outputs, the state is said to be unobservable and the system is not completely observable or simply unobservable ...".

3.2.4 Control Actions

In a system there are two types of control variables, those who are controllable and those that are not controllable. Franklin et al. (2009) [19] refers "...a process is named fully controllable if each state variable of process is controlled to achieve a certain objective in finite time by a control u(t) without restrictions. If any of state variables are independent from control u(t) meaning that there is no way to act, in finite time from that state variable to the desired state. Therefore, this state in particular is denominated as uncontrollable, so the system is called not totally controllable or simply uncontrollable."

3.2.5 Time

Shewhart (1980) [20] proposes a control cycle of a system, composed of the classical sequence PDCA: (i) intelligence to observe an organizational problem. (ii) the design of potential solutions. (iii) the choose of best solution. (iv) implementation of the solution and verification if it satisfies the fulfilment of the intended objectives. Among the different control activities there are time delays, for example, when a controller decides for a control action u(t) this is based on observations from the past. This means that when the control u(t) is triggered, it may no longer be valid in the operational reality of the system to be controlled. Conceptually, everything that happens before the execution of business processes is called ex-ante, for example, the prescription of business processes. What happens after the execution of business processes is called an ex-post, relating, for example, to the reaction that is needed when something unexpectedly occurs. The decision processes on the most correct action u(t) to be taken consider the ex-ante models of the business processes as a control reference to be followed.

3.2.6 Control Pattern

The goal of the control is to allow the operation of the business process instance(s) to be conducted, using a limited effort to a stable state previously defined by the organization [16]. And being able to react to the exogenous and endogenous changes and disorders that are occurring. In conceptual terms, Kuo (1995) [21] defines the stability of a system as "...considering the response of a system to inputs or perturbations: a system that remains in a constant state, except when it is affected by an external action, but is capable of returning to the initial constant state soon after this external action is removed then can be considered stable...".

4   Solution Proposed

4.1   Atlas

Atlas is a EC tool that supports the organizational transformation of an organization. Atlas is an automation-based solution to enable efficient management of Enterprise Architectures. It enables organizations to: (i) Capture information from enterprise repositories providing a conciliated view of the organization. (ii) Create, customize and analyze repositories. (iii) Time-travel. The proposal for the solution is made using the Atlas tool, a commercial tool that is used in several medium and large corporate architectures (see https://atlas.linkconsulting.com).

4.2   Problem Clarification

In order to explain the problem to be solved, we used the process modeling in BPMN, view Fig. 3. This process was created by the company where our case study focuses, Link Consulting.

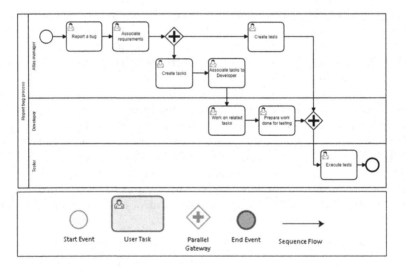

Fig. 3. BPMN Process Report a Bug

Figure 4 shows the Form, produced by the Atlas tool. Whenever an actor find a bug, he must register it through the Bug Form.

An actor in this context can be an Atlas manager, a programmer or a tester. Registration of Bugs allows that the company has a repository of the bugs found and reported by the actors; and give to company the ability to observe at any time current state of a particular Bug by actor.

Fig. 4. Form Report a Bug

4.2.1 Transaction States

When the instances of the Report a Bug process are executed, they go through three states: **ex-ante**, **ex-dure**, and **ex-post**. It is during the ex-dure phase (execution of the process instances) that non-compliance can occur. Non-compliance relate to non-fulfilment of rules or restrictions. The restrictions correspond to the business rules identified by the company and serve to ensure compliance in the execution of the instances of the business process.

4.2.2 Activities of Report a Bug Process

Description of activities of Report a Bug process during transaction states and mapping, according to decision rules, show in Fig. 5.

State ex-ante: an actor identifies a Bug.
State ex-dure: the actor enters in the Atlas tool and accesses the Form to report a new Bug.
The associated activities of the Report a Bug process are:
Activity Report a Bug Restrictions: The actor must fill the properties (fields): Start Date and the field State: On Going.
Activity Associate Requirement Restrictions: The actor must fill the property (field) Requirement.
Activity Create Task Restrictions: The actor must fill the property (field) State: Start.
Activity Associate Tasks To Developers Restrictions: None.
Activity Work On Related Tasks Restrictions: None.
Activity Prepare Work Done For Testing Restrictions: The actor must fill the property (field) Tests.
Activity Create Tests Restrictions: The actor must fill the property (field) State: Validated.
Activity Execute Tests Restrictions: The actor must fill the property (field) State: Finished, if the task is completed; or Rejected if the task is not completed.
State ex-post: after the process instances are executed. The compliance and non-compliance that occur during the execution of the instances of the Report a Bug process, ex-dure, but it's only observable after the execution. From the activities identified above, those in which there are no restrictions are considered as unobservable activities: Associate Tasks To Developers and Work

On Related Tasks. Then we can assume that we are dealing with a partially observable environment because not all state information is available.

		RB_Starte Event	RB_Report Bug	RB_Associate Requirement	RB_Create Tasks	RB_Associate Tasks to Developers	RB_Work on Related Tasks	RB_Prepare Work done for Testing	RB_Create Tests	RB_Execute Tests	RB_Terminate Event
Activity			x	x	x	x	x	x	x	x	
Event		x									x
Property	Name / Assigned to (*)		x	x	x	x	x	x	x	x	
	End Date									x	x
	Owner		x	x	x	x	x	x	x	x	
	Requirement			x	x	x	x	x	x	x	
	Start Date		x	x	x	x	x	x	x	x	
	State — Start					x	x	x	x		
	State — On Going		x	x							
	State — Finished									x/or	
	State — Validated								x		
	State — Rejected									x/or	
	Tests							x	x	x	

Fig. 5. Matrix of Decisions Associated with Report a Bug Activities. In Red: Compliance restrictions (Color figure online)

4.3   Conception and Development

The proposed solution is to create an artifact - Blueprint, which allows to show the compliance and non-compliance that occur during the execution of the instances of the Report a Bug process, by actor.

1. Create Class SystemBPMN (Fig. 6)

Fig. 6. Class SystemBPMN and some instances from process Report a Bug

2. Creation of Blueprint in ERML language, using the Atlas tool.

Algorithm 1: All Instances Algorithm

Data: All Bugs

Result: List of compliance bugs and non-compliance bugs from all instances

begin

    if *(instance = "Report A Bug")* then

        if *(Start Date != NULL)* **and** *(State == On Going)* then

          | Compliance = TRUE;

        else if *(Start Date == NULL)* **and** *(State == 0)* then

          | Compliance = FALSE;

    end

    if *(instance = "Associate Requirements")* then

        if *(Requirement != NULL)* then

          | Compliance = TRUE;

        else if *(Requirement == 0)* then

          | Compliance = FALSE;

    end

    if *(instance = "Create Tasks")* then

        if *(State == Start)* then

          | Compliance = TRUE;

        else if *(State == 0)* then

          | Compliance = FALSE;

    end

    if *(instance = "Create Tests")* then

        if *(State == Validated)* **and** *(Tests != NULL)* then

          | Compliance = TRUE;

        else if *(State == 0)* **and** *(Tests == 0)* then

          | Compliance = FALSE;

    end

    if *(instance = "Prepare Work Donw for Testing")* then

        if *(Tests != NULL)* then

          | Compliance = TRUE;

        else if *(Tests == 0)* then

          | Compliance = FALSE;

    end

    if *(instance = "Execute Tests")* then

        if *(State == Finished* **or** *State == Rejected)* **and** *(End Date != NULL)* then

          | Compliance = TRUE;

        else if *(State != Finished* **or** *State != Rejected)* **and** *(End Date == 0)* then

          | Compliance = FALSE;

    end

end

---

3. Blueprint

In IT domain, Blueprints have always been perceived as an important asset, especially by IT architecture teams or departments. Enterprises would be better understood if they could have a Blueprint (schematic representation) [7]. They represent a common way of communication between people, namely to express an architectural description of things, like a system, an object, a model or in our case, an enterprise [7]. Figure 7 show Blueprint from actor Miguel Correia. Blueprints are automatically generated and represent the compliance and non-compliance of the instances of the process Report a Bug.

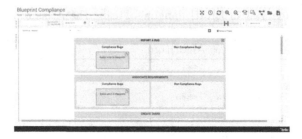

Fig. 7. Blueprint Canvas page

5   Case Study and Results Obtained

In this section we present the case study that follows within a business simulation environment. A solution developed in EC was used to provide observation and control of the instances of the Report a Bug business process. The approach used in the design, development and implementation of the solution was based on the methodology DSRM [11]. The application in real context, from this solution, aims to provide the company with greater compliance in the business process instances, at runtime: ex-dure. The compliance achieved by complying with the predefined restrictions allows the organization to have a better understanding of what is going on in the company, rewarding it in decision making. Memory of the past state (as-was) and the future state (to-be) define the behaviour of an organization. To-be state specifies the goals of transformation projects. Without to-be state the transformation processes cannot be executed or measured since no project goals are defined [2]. During the study period, 80 instances of Report a Bug process were considered. Corresponding to some 480 operations performed by the actors. On these instances, cartographic maps were extracted where it is possible to observe the activities of the Report a Bug process described in Sect. 4.2.2. For the observation and control of the compliance from instances of the process, cartographic maps have been created - Blueprints. The Blueprints were produced by Actor. On a total of 9 Blueprints. In these Blueprints we can observe 78 instances of the 80 contemplated, divided by activity, between compliance and non-compliance. Based on the initial problem - how to design and implement business process compliance through observing the business process instances and controlling the business process models, considering environments that are only partial observable - our investigation concerns the beginning of a solution to find compliance, once that simulation occurs of a just one business process. The goal is to extend this solution to any business process, provided that is modelled in BMPN, and to any organization. Through Blueprints we can observe the compliance and non-compliance based on predefined restrictions and to make error corrections when is verified non-compliance. By assuring the business process instances are executed on a controlled way, the solution can benefit the company because it reduce execution errors on processes and with that assures fulfillment of legal impositions and performs the cost management and risk management.

6 Conclusions

This article presents an innovative solution that allows to observe compliance, ex-dure, during the execution of business process instances using EC. The results obtained through the simulation, show us that through the EC it is possible to observe the compliance and non-compliance associated with each instance of the business process. Thus contributing so an operational improvement in the execution of business processes modelled on BPM. We can more easily identify deviation situations in order to carry out corrective actions to encourage the actors that operate in the instantiation of the business process. When compared with existing solutions, this solution allows the identification of situations of deviation from the prescriptions, ex-dure, during the execution of the instances. In order to achieve greater compliance, is identified the need to: (i) Increase the actors' awareness of compliance with restrictions introducing the concepts explained by Dietz - production acts and coordination acts. (ii) Create an automatism from solution, that allows the observation and controlling the process instances during transaction state, ex-dure.

References

1. Albani, A., Dietz, J.L.G.: Enterprise ontology based development of information system. Int J. Bus. Enterprises Manag. **7**(1), 41–63 (2011)
2. Tribolet, J., Sousa, P., Caetano, A.: The role of enterprise governance and cartography in enterprise engineering. Int. J. Conceptual Modeling (EMISAJ) **9**, 38–49 (2014)
3. Gonçalves, A., Sousa, P., Zacarias, M.: Using DEMO and activity theory to manage organization change. Procedia Technol. **9**, 563–572 (2013). CENTERIS 2013 - Conference on Enterprise Information Systems/Projman 2013 - International Conference on Project Management/HCIST 2013 - International Conference on Health and Social Care Information Systems and Technologies
4. Ramezani Taghiabadi, E., Fahland, D., van Dongen, B.F., van der Aalst, W.M.P.: Diagnostic information for compliance checking of temporal compliance requirements. In: Salinesi, C., Norrie, M.C., Pastor, Ó. (eds.) CAiSE 2013. LNCS, vol. 7908, pp. 304–320. Springer, Heidelberg (2013). https://doi.org/10.1007/978-3-642-38709-8_20
5. Fellmann, M., Zasada, A.: Sate-of-the-art of business process compliance approaches: a survey. In: Twenty Second European Conference on Information Systems (ECIS), Tel Aviv (2014)
6. Becker, J., et al.: Memorandum on design-oriented information systems research. Eur. J. Inf. Syst. **20**, 7–10 (2011)
7. Sousa, P., Lima, J., Sampaio, A., Pereira, C.: An approach for creating and managing enterprise blueprints: a case for IT blueprints. In: Albani, A., Barjis, J., Dietz, J.L.G. (eds.) CIAO!/EOMAS -2009. LNBIP, vol. 34, pp. 70–84. Springer, Heidelberg (2009). https://doi.org/10.1007/978-3-642-01915-9_6

8. Gaaloul, K., Guerreiro, S., Marques, P.: Optimizing business processes compliance using an evaluable risk-based approach. In: 49th Hawaii International Conference on System Sciences (HICSS), Hawaii (2016). https://doi.org/10.1109/HICSS.2016.699

9. Dumas, M., La Rosa, M., Mendling, J., Reijers, H.: Fundamentals of Business Process Management. Springer, Heidelberg (2013). https://doi.org/10.1007/978-3-642-33143-5

10. Röder, N., Schermann, M., Wiesche, M.: A situational perspective on workarounds in it-enabled business processes: a multiple case study. In: Proceedings of the European Conference on Information Systems (ECIS), Tel Aviv, Israel, 9–11 June 2014. ISBN: 978-0-9915567-0-0, http://aisel.aisnet.org/ecis2014/proceedings/track06/6

11. Chatterjee, S., Peffers, K., Rothenberger, M.A., Tuunanen, T.: A design science research methodology for information systems research. J. Manag. Inf. Syst. **24**(3), 45–78 (2007)

12. Guerreiro, S.: Business rules elicitation combining Markov decision process with DEMO business transaction space. In: IEE CBI 2013, Vienna, Austria, pp. 304–320 (2013). https://doi.org/10.1109/CBI.2013.11

13. Guerreiro, S., Tribolet, J.: Conceptualizing enterprise dynamic systems control for run-time business transactions. In: ECIS 2013 Research in Progress, vol. 5 (2013). https://aisel.aisnet.org/ecis2013_rip/5

14. Guerreiro, S., Tribolet, J., Vasconcelos, A.: Enterprise dynamic systems control enforcement of run-time business transactions. In: Albani, A., Aveiro, D., Barjis, J. (eds.) EEWC 2012. LNBIP, vol. 110, pp. 46–60. Springer, Heidelberg (2012). https://doi.org/10.1007/978-3-642-29903-2_4

15. Guerreiro, S., Sousa, P., Tribolet, J.: Enterprise cartography: from theory to practice

16. Guerreiro, S., Marques, R.P.: Mecanismo de controlo para a frente orientado ao risco como garantia da conformidade da execução de processos de negócio. Number 20. In: RISTI - Revista Ibérica de Sistemas e Tecnologias de Informação, Porto, December 2016. http://dx.doi.org/10.17013/risti.20.34-47

17. Ly, L.T., Maggi, F.M., Montali, M., Rinderle-Ma, S., van der Aalst, W.M.: Compliance monitoring in business processes: functionalities, application and tool-support. Inf. Syst. **54**, 209–234 (2015)

18. Winograd, T.: A language/action perspective on the design of cooperative work. In: Proceedings of the ACM Conference on Computer-Supported Cooperative Work, New York, pp. 203–220 (1986). https://doi.org/10.1207/s15327051hci0301_2

19. Franklin, F., Powell, D., Emami-Naeini, A.: Feedback control of dynamic systems. Addison-Wesley Publishing Company (2009). (6th ed.)

20. Shewhart, W.: Economic control of quality of manufactured product / 50th anniversary commemorative issue. American Society for Quality (1980)

21. Kuo, B. C., Golnaraghi, F.: Automatic control systems, Vol. 9. Englewood Cliffs, NJ: Prentice-Hall (1995)

Generation of Stakeholder-Specific BPMN Models

Diogo Cardoso[1][(✉)] and Pedro Sousa[1,2]

[1] University of Lisbon, Av. Rovisco Pais, 1049-001 Lisbon, Portugal
{diogocardoso,pedro.manuel.sousa}@tecnico.ulisboa.pt
[2] Link Consulting, Av. Duque Ávila 23, 1000-123 Lisbon, Portugal

Abstract. A business process model always has a dominant perspective in the detriment of others, motivating the need of different stakeholders to look for different models of the same process. In fact, it is common to see that in different units of an organisation, such as quality, audit, risk or human resources, there are different models of the same processes, each focusing on specific aspects. Unfortunately, these models tend to lack consistency because of the effort required to keep them consistent. To tackle this problem, we are developing an approach that aims to generate stakeholder-specific models on the fly, based on some arbitrary stakeholders' concerns. We derive the generated models from a consolidated business process model, which is previously designed, and its organisational taxonomy, thus ensuring the consistency between the generated models.

Keywords: Business process modelling · Process views · Process repository · BPMN

1 Introduction

Business processes are designed to achieve specific goals and the task of business process modelling is expected to improve the understanding and communication across the different stakeholder groups [9]. However, these goals are difficult to achieve because organisations often have to manage multiple process diagrams that represent the same business process, which can lead to several inconsistencies, such as heterogeneous schemes for naming its activities and entities, usage of different modelling styles and process hierarchies with arbitrary depth and level of detail [4]. We argue that these issues arise due to two main reasons [16,17]:

– On the one hand, business processes often cross multiple organisational units and also tend to cross inter-organisational boundaries. Therefore, process models are often shared among different stakeholders, which have contrasting concerns and focus on distinct perspectives of the same business process, such as performance, auditing, information systems, people or compliance.

© Springer Nature Switzerland AG 2020
D. Aveiro et al. (Eds.): EEWC 2019, LNBIP 374, pp. 15–32, 2020.
https://doi.org/10.1007/978-3-030-37933-9_2

- On the other hand, a business process model is a representation of the modeller's perspective regarding a given process: different modelling teams may choose different ways to model the same business process according to their interests or focus. Thus, they will most likely achieve different specifications for the same process.

Having different models of the same business process is, nonetheless, beneficial for the organisation since each organisational unit has its own concerns and has a process representation that suits these concerns. However, keeping the various models consistent can be a very demanding task. It can be even harder when there are frequent changes to the business process since all the models must be updated accordingly.

To facilitate the consistent modelling of business processes from different perspectives, this paper presents an approach that enables to generate views of a common business process model according to the requirements of its stakeholders. Hence, our approach can be considered an application of ISO 42010 [10] to business process modelling. ISO 42010 states that a view addresses one or more of the concerns of the system stakeholders. A view is a partial expression of a system's architecture with respect to a particular viewpoint. A viewpoint establishes the conventions by which a view is specified, depicted and created.

To ensure that the views are inherently consistent, our approach is limited to the generation of views from a consolidated model that must be previously designed. The design of this consolidated model is out of the scope of this paper but is presented in [6].

The generation of the views is based on arbitrary stakeholders concerns. These concerns, which we call dimensions, are mapped to each of the process activities. For example, one could assign to each activity its level of risk, its actors, location, etc. Furthermore, a hierarchical structure, that we call taxonomy tree, is associated to each dimension and allows the existence of various levels of detail: a possible taxonomy tree for a dimension depicting process participants is an organisational structure. It is the tweaking of these dimensions and respective levels of detail that allows the creation of different views of a business process.

The expected contribution of our work is twofold. First, to provide an approach for the generation of business process views specified in *BPMN 2.0* [13]. Second, to support the stakeholders in the task of business process modelling by proposing a systematic way of representing their concerns.

The remainder of this paper is structured as follows: the next section introduces a scenario that is used to illustrate the problem and the approach. Section 3 reviews relevant background and related work. Section 4 explains our research methodology. Section 5 describes our approach and Sect. 6 shows examples of its application using the developed tool. The research validation is debated in Sect. 7. We discuss conclusions and future work in Sect. 8.

2   Illustrative Scenario

This section describes the research problem by presenting the illustrative example of an automobile repair company, with the intention of promoting the readers' understanding of the problem. This scenario will be used throughout the paper:

"*The ACME automobile repair company specialises in bodywork repairs. When a damaged car arrives at the ACME's garage, its service manager assesses the vehicle damage. Based on the service manager's analysis, a panel beater planishes the damaged parts or goes to the company's warehouse to pick up replacement parts or both. After the body work repair, a painter prepares the car for spraying. The spraying is done on the company's painting greenhouse, where the service manager also inspects the quality of the finished job. If he/she believes the quality is subpar, the painter resprays the vehicle and it is inspected again. Otherwise, the car is ready to be delivered. This process is monitored by two departments: the Human Resources (HR) department and the Facilities Department. To perform this monitoring, each department models their own view of the process focused in the resources that each has to manage: actors for the first and premises for the second department.*"

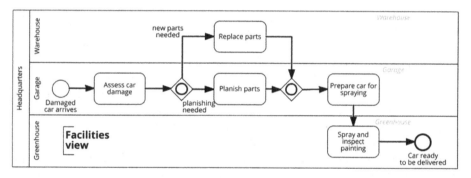

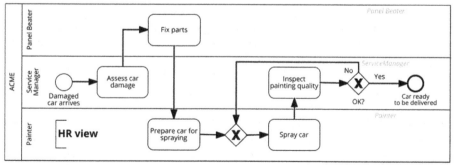

Fig. 1. *BPMN* process views of the car repairing process, designed by the Facilities department (top) and HR department (bottom).

The process is performed by three actors, in three distinct locations and has six activities. Figure 1 shows the business process views designed by the HR and Facilities department. On the one hand, the HR department grouped the "Replace parts" and "Planish parts" activities because they are both performed by the panel beater. On the other hand, the facilities department grouped the "Spray car" and "Inspect painting quality" activities since they are performed in the same location (greenhouse). We refer to the former as the *Who* dimension and the latter as the *Where* dimension.

In the scope of our problem, the question that now arises is: "How do we model additional views of the process or update any of the existing views while maintaining consistency across all views?". In this very simple scenario, a process change would be easy to keep up with. However, in more complex processes (with more decision gateways, exception flows, etc.) it would take a lot of effort to keep consistency across views. To our knowledge, there are no mechanisms to simplify the work of keeping consistency across views nor to assist the creation of new views, thus making these tasks costly and inefficient.

3 Related Work

Our research is closely related with business process variability modelling. [19] shows there have been significant research efforts in the past decade in the area of variability modelling. [19] classifies a process variability modelling approach based on how it captures the relation between a set of elements of a process and the corresponding elements in its variants. This classification resulted in four groups: node configuration, element annotation, activity specialisation and fragment customisation approaches. The approaches that use element annotation and activity specialisation are the ones that most closely resemble the business process view generation approach that we outline in Sect. 5.

On the one hand, element annotation approaches, like [7] and [18], rely on the annotation of model elements with properties of the application domain: in our case, we annotate the stakeholder concerns to the process activities. On the other hand, activity specialization approaches, like [12] and [2], assign variants to the process activities. In our work we use a different, but also hierarchical, abstraction technique: functional decomposition, i.e. recursively breaking down a process as sub-activities.

Regarding business process views, [22] also highlights the existence of conflicting process specifications for the same organisational process, depending on the distinct stakeholders' perspectives and on the modeller's view of that particular process. That work defines the rules for identifying business process activities by applying the Zachman Framework [24]. The Zachman framework describes an architecture using a two-dimensional classification matrix based on the intersection of six contextual dimensions (what, where, when, why, who and how) with six rows according to reification transformation that represents a view of the solution from a particular perspective such as the planner's or the designer's perspective [23,24]. However, [22] does not use such specification but only the six communication questions enumerated above as independent concerns for the decomposition of a business process [4,20]. Thus, each of these six dimensions focuses on a specific and independent concern. The combinations of these concerns characterise aggregate parts of the process or the process as a whole [5]. These criteria for activity decomposition support business process modelling by facilitating the task of different stakeholders consistently modelling the same process. The application of such rules is the basis of our approach.

Pereira [15, pp. 134–137] and later Caetano [3] continued in the same direction of Sousa [22], basing their approach on the use of the contextual dimensions of the Zachman Framework to portray stakeholders' concerns and adding important contributions towards facilitating the generation of process views. Namely, it proposes the arrangement of the concepts associated with each dimension into a hierarchical structure: a taxonomy tree. Our work will fill the gap in knowledge existing in these works because they focus on describing a conceptual tool without formally defining the algorithms that support the generation of the views. Moreover, they do not apply the problem to a specific process modelling notation, like *BPMN*.

Finally, as a complement to our approach, the method proposed by [6] aids process stakeholders in integrating business process views into a process repository, also using the six dimensions. In this case, they are used to guide the annotation of the process elements by the stakeholders. This method is used to populate a process repository which serves as the knowledge base for our approach: we further detail this relation in Sect. 5.

4   Research Methodology

Our research fits in the design science paradigm [8], as we try to solve our problem through the development of new artefacts. Thus, we propose to use the design science research methodology (*DSRM* [14]) to guide our research. The *DSRM* is an iterative research methodology that focus on the creation and validation of artefacts that address a research problem and is divided in six phases.

The first two phases, which consist of identifying the problem, motivation and defining the research objectives, are materialised in the first two sections of this paper. The third phase (design and development) encompasses the definition of the approach that supports the generation of business process views, which is briefly described in the following section. The fourth phase (demonstration) includes the development of a tool that implements the generation algorithm. Example use cases of this tool are shown in Sect. 6. The fifth phase (evaluation) is discussed in Sect. 7 and sees the application of the tool in a real use case with the objective of validating our work. Lastly, the final phase (communication) involves the production of an additional paper to showcase our results.

5   The Approach

As previously stated, this work in progress is complemented by the approach presented in [6]. Thus, we start this section by briefly describing how both works are related and then proceed to explain in more detail our approach.

5.1 The Big Picture

Colaço and Sousa [6] define a method for merging distinct views of a business
process into a single, consolidated business process model. The method also
defines what we call an organisational taxonomy, which is a taxonomy tree for
each dimension. A taxonomy tree is a collection of concepts organised into a hierarchical structure. The method guides the process stakeholders in constructing
these trees by classifying process activities according to the Zachman contextual dimensions. However, other dimensions representing different concerns can
equally be considered in this classification method, as for example risk and security, among others. The resulting mappings are stored in a process repository.

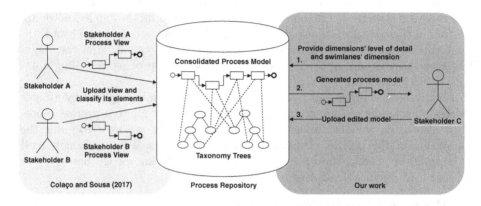

Fig. 2. Illustration of the relation between [6] and our work in progress.

Afterwards, using the approach we are developing, the stakeholders may generate process views, simply by providing the level of detail desired for each
dimension and, if they want to represent swimlanes, the dimension they want
to depict in the swimlanes. Furthermore, the stakeholder can choose to edit the
generated model: rearrange the location of the graphical elements and change
the generated activities' names. This can then be uploaded to the repository to
keep the naming and positioning of the generated activities in future requests.
Such information is cleared whenever the corresponding activities are removed
or changed in the process repository. Figure 2 resumes the relation between both
works.

5.2 The Process Repository

Being the central element of our solution, we describe its content and structure
that is relevant for the work presented here:

– An organisational taxonomy, which holds a hierarchic structure (tree) for
  each dimension. Technically, an unlimited number of dimensions can be
  represented;

– The consolidated *BPMN* process models. At this stage, only basic *BPMN* constructs are supported;
– The mapping between the activities of the consolidated process models and the leaf nodes of the taxonomy trees. This mapping is key for the generation algorithm presented in Sect. 5.3.

The meta-model of the repository is presented in Fig. 3, using an *UML* class diagram. A Process is composed of Flow Elements. A Flow Element can be an Activity, Gateway or Event and is connected to other Flow Elements by sequence flows (represented by the Flow Element class' self-association). A Process also aggregates, for each dimension applied in the generation of views of that process, the root of the dimension's taxonomy tree, which is a Taxonomy Node. Taxonomy Nodes in turn aggregate other Taxonomy Nodes and the leafs of the taxonomy trees classify each Activity of the Process (represented by the association between the Taxonomy Node and the Activity classes).

Regarding the taxonomy trees, they are built using the definition of hierarchy presented in [11]. This definition states that **H** is an hierarchy if and only if it is an ordered triple **(S,b,D)** where **S** is a nonempty set, **b** a distinguished element of **S** and **D** a binary relation over **S** such that:

1. **S** has a single beginner, **b**. That means **H** has one and only one supreme commander.
2. **b** stands in some power of **D** to every other member of S: no matter how low in the hierarchy an element of S may stand, it is still under the command of the beginner.
3. For any given element **y** of **S** except **b**, there is exactly one other element **x** of **S** such that **D(x,y)**, i.e. every member has a single direct boss.
4. **D** is transitive and anti-symmetric.

In the current state of affairs, we only support a small subset of *BPMN* elements, such as non-boundary events, gateways, tasks and swimlanes. Since the *BPMN* standard allows a wide scope for the swimlane elements (i.e. pools and lanes) [13], we derive them from the associations between the taxonomy trees' leaf nodes and the process activities. It is up to the stakeholder to determine which dimension should swimlanes depict in the generated model. This justifies why we chose the definition presented in [11] to build our taxonomy trees: the taxonomy tree root concept is depicted in the pool whereas its descendants in lanes.

As an example of a process model based on the repository meta-model, Fig. 4 presents the information that would be present in the repository for the aforementioned car repairing process. For the sake of simplicity, the associations between Process and Flow Element objects are not represented. In this particular case, the process is only associated with two dimensions: *Where* and *Who*, each with 2 levels of detail. For example, the *Where* dimension has the concept *Headquarters* at level 1 and concepts *Garage*, *Greenhouse* and *Warehouse* at level 2.

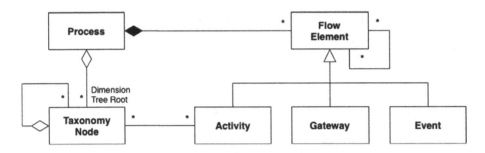

Fig. 3. UML class diagram of the process repository meta-model.

5.3   Generation Algorithm

The algorithm developed to support the generation of views from the repository data is based on the application of a rule derived from one presented in [22]. That rule specifies that an activity α can be decomposed into two or more distinct discrete activities if and only if one of the conditions stated in Table 1 is satisfied.

Table 1. Criteria for activity decomposition presented in [22]

Dimension	Criteria
What	α is composed by two or more activities which receive/create different data entities
How	α is composed by two or more activities which are processed using different applications
Where	α is composed by two or more activities which occur in different locations
Who	α is composed by two or more activities which are managed by different business actors
When	α is composed by two or more activities which are performed in distinct periods of time
Why	α is composed by two or more activities which exist to satisfy different purposes

In [22], there is one aggregation condition for every contextual dimension of the Zachman framework [24], as summarised in Table 1. However, in our approach, the dimensions can be freely defined by the process stakeholders, and there are as many conditions as there are dimensions in the repository. i.e. the set of conditions is not fixed to those six dimensions. Our rule for aggregating process activities is presented below:

Two activities α and β can be aggregated into an activity δ if and only if for every dimension one of the following two conditions applies:

– *the taxonomy concepts mapped to α and β are the same*
– *the taxonomy concepts mapped to α and β are different but their ancestor at the chosen level of detail is the same*

Using the car repairing process as an example, if one chooses the *Where* dimension at level of detail 2 and the *Who* dimension at level of detail 1, two given activities can only be aggregated if they are both performed in the same location (garage, warehouse or greenhouse).

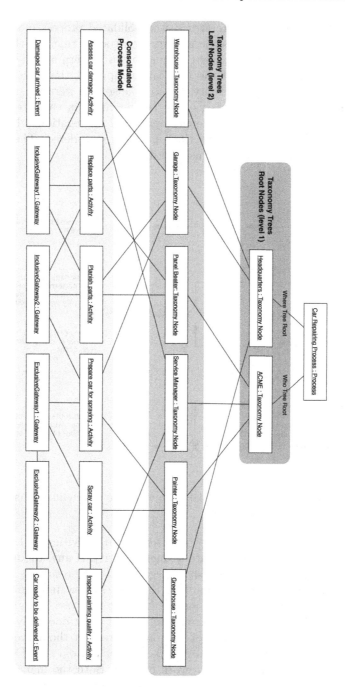

Fig. 4. UML object diagram of the repository content for the car repairing process.

Our generation algorithm iterates the consolidated process model to identify patterns to which it applies the activity aggregation rule. All the activities contained in a piece of process flow that matches a pattern are then evaluated against the aggregation rule. If the rule can be applied, the matched process flow is grouped into a single activity. It can take several iterations to generate the final view because new patterns may be generated in each iteration. The algorithm stops when one can no longer apply any aggregation rule during an entire iteration. Figure 5 shows the three patterns considered. These patterns are composed of some of the patterns identified in [1].

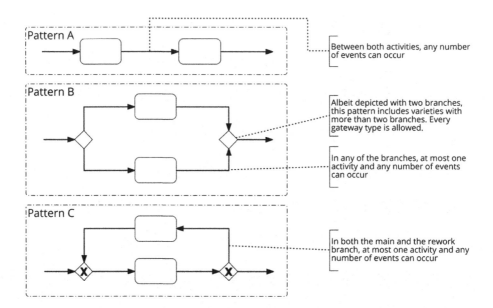

Fig. 5. Patterns that the generation algorithm tries to match during its execution.

Pattern A is the simplest. Any two sequential activities that respect the aggregation rule can be grouped into a single activity. If any, the intermediate events between the activities are also aggregated into the resulting activity.

Pattern B refers to the splitting of the process flow into an unspecified number of branches which must all join at the same gateway. The gateway type is not relevant. The branches must only contain at most one activity and any number of events. If the activities of all branches respect the aggregation rule, then both gateways and the branches can be grouped into a single activity.

Pattern C depicts the classic rework pattern. Both the main branch and rework branch must contain at most one activity and any number of events. If both activities respect the aggregation rule, then both branches and gateways can be grouped into a single activity,

It is expected that not all process flows respect these patterns. When that happens, it is up to the modeller to group the process elements of the generated view as he/she sees fit.

In Fig. 6, a sample execution of the pattern matching is shown reducing the initial process into a single activity in seven iterations: the patterns matched in the first six iterations are represented in different colours and numbered from 1 to 6. Each time a pattern is matched, it is replaced by an activity which in turn may be part of a new pattern to be matched in the next iteration. The iteration stops when there is no further pattern matching. The view generated in this case is simply composed of an activity, preceded by the start event and followed by the end event.

In a final phase, the algorithm assigns a name to each generated activity, which is simply the aggregation of the names of the activities that originated it. Then, it looks for a matching stakeholder defined name and uses it instead, whenever one is found. This mapping between generated names and stakeholder given names is updated whenever the stakeholder changes and uploads a generated model and cleared whenever at least one of the corresponding activities are removed or changed from the process repository.

In what concerns the activities positioning, a similar approach is taken. In the final layout, a stakeholder defined position is searched for each generated activity, and used whenever a position is found. The position information of generated models is cleared whenever one of the corresponding activities in the process model are changed or removed.

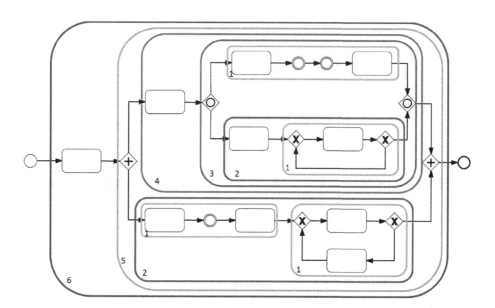

Fig. 6. Sample execution of the view generation algorithm. Pattern matching iterations are numbered from 1 to 6.

6   Demonstration

In this section, we provide a glimpse of the tool developed to support the generation of process views. We also show and explain some examples of generated views of the car repairing process that we believe will further help the reader's understanding of our solution.

The tool was developed extending the *Atlas* [21] tool from Link Consulting[1] with the process view generator. It includes two major components:

– the **Process Repository**, holding the process model and the taxonomy tree for each dimension, is configured in *Atlas*. The construction of organisational taxonomies and the mapping of its concepts to the consolidated model is done solely through the process repository.
– the **Process Modeller**, was developed using the *bpmn.io*[2] library and implements the generation algorithm explained in Sect. 5.3. The modeller integrates with the repository using *REST* services allowing the retrieval and upload of process data (Fig. 7).

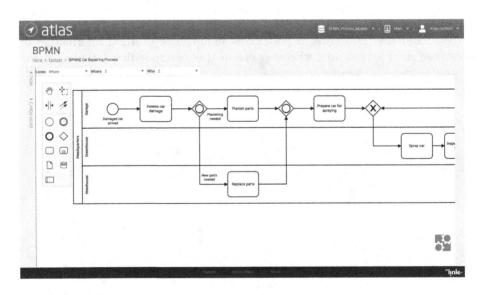

Fig. 7. Screen of the tool after the generation of a view.

Regarding the generation of views, we recall the car repairing process example whose textual description is presented in Sect. 2.

Two stakeholder groups are involved in the modelling of this process and they have diverging perspectives. On the one hand, the HR department is focused on

---

[1] http://www.linkconsulting.com/atlas.
[2] https://bpmn.io.

the employees and organisational units that execute the activities. Thus, their concern can be represented by the *Who* dimension of the Zachman Framework. On the other hand, the Facilities department targets the location where the process activities are performed: buildings, work areas, etc. Applying again the Zachman Framework, this concern can be represented by the *Where* dimension.

As aforementioned, both departments must upload their process views to the process repository using Colaço and Sousa's method [6]. This is not described here in further detail because it is out of the scope of our work. The outcome of applying the view integration method is the process repository content previously portrayed in Fig. 4. Nonetheless, we represent the consolidated process model and the associations between its activities and the taxonomy concepts in Fig. 8. Regarding the organisational taxonomy, we list it below:

- Who dimension
  - ACME (level 1)
    * Service Manager (level 2)
    * Panel Beater (level 2)
    * Painter (level 2)
- Where dimension
  - Headquarters (level 1)
    * Garage (level 2)
    * Warehouse (level 2)
    * Greenhouse (level 2)

With this organisational taxonomy, the stakeholders can generate 12 different process views. Since there are two dimensions, swimlanes can represent either or none (3 options). Moreover, each dimension has two levels of detail (2 × 2 options). We show some of these possible views in Fig. 9.

View (c) clearly focuses on the *Who* dimension as this dimension is represented with the highest level of detail (level 2), whereas the *Where* dimension was set to the lowest level of detail (level 1). Furthermore, swimlanes were used to represent the *Who* dimension. In turn, view (b) was generated from the exact opposite input: the *Where* at the maximum level of detail; the *Who* at the lowest level of detail; and the swimlanes were chosen to represent the *Where* dimension.

Whereas in the previously described views the focus was on one dimension, in views (a) and (d) both dimensions were set to the lowest level of detail and to the highest and swimlanes represent the *Where* and the *Who* dimension, respectively. As expected, the higher the level of detail of the dimensions, the more the process activities are decomposed; if the lowest level of detail is chosen for all dimensions, there is no activity decomposition at all.

The name of a generated activity is simply the aggregation of the names of the activities that originated it. Nonetheless, as previously mentioned, the stakeholder may choose to edit the naming and positioning of the activities. These changes are kept in the repository and used in future generation requests.

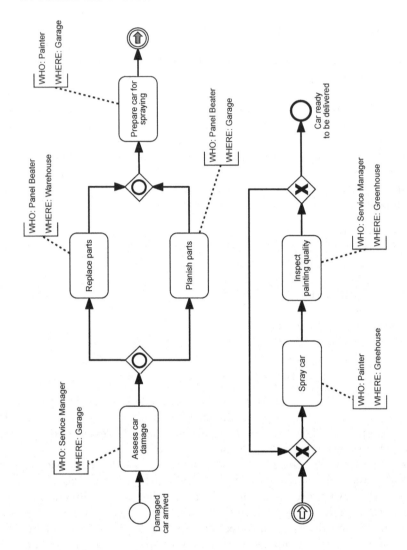

Fig. 8. Consolidated process model of the car repairing process. Notice the associations between the process activities and the taxonomy concepts.

7   Evaluation

To demonstrate and test the applicability and usefulness of our research work, we will apply the view generation approach in real-life cases study performed within real organisations, starting from a company in the automotive retail industry.

In this proof-of-concept, the first step is to select one business process involving several stakeholders and gather information about the chosen process from the various stakeholders, each stating its view. We follow the method proposed in [6] to merge the different process views from the different stakeholders and populate the Atlas process repository. In this process, the dimensions that better

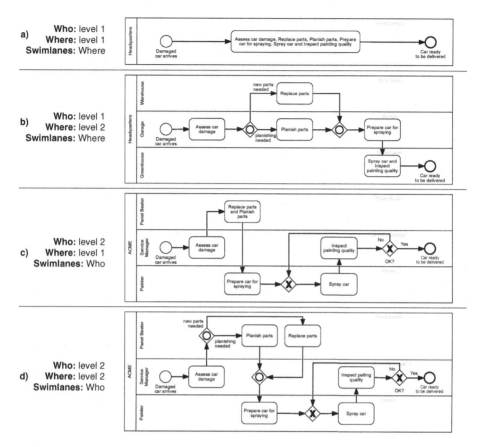

Fig. 9. *BPMN* process views of the car repairing process, as generated by the process modeller from the repository content portrayed in Fig. 4.

address the stakeholder's concerns will become explicit and defined, as well as the taxonomy tree for each dimension.

Afterwards, the participants will be asked to state their concerns and to generate views that better suit such concerns, and comment on the usefulness of the generated views, thus fulfilling the requirement of evaluation of our work.

8   Conclusions and Future Work

This work served the purpose of exposing the difficulties of having consistent process views, with each conveying the concerns of different stakeholders. Our contribution to this problem is grounded on applying a rule for business process activities' aggregation and matching of workflow patterns with the ultimate goal of creating different process views based on existing consolidated models and organisational taxonomies.

Apart from the research work in progress (phases presented in Sect. 4), as future work we intend to eliminate some of the limitations imposed on the consolidated business process model. We are assuming various simplifications on the consolidated models, although they are still compliant with the *BPMN 2.0* standard [13].

First and foremost, we still do not support many *BPMN* constructs, such as data objects and data flows, message flows, boundary events, transactions, compensations and cancellations, etc. The proposal presented here is limited to process models with a single pool with any hierarchy of lanes, which always depict one of the existing dimensions in the process repository.

Secondly, the primary focus of the models generated by our algorithm is to improve communication and documentation of business processes. At this stage, we did not aim to generate executable process models.

Moreover, the proposed aggregation patterns do not cover every possible control flow scenario. We expect that the design of the consolidated process model takes this into account and conforms, as much as possible, to the identified patterns. Additionally, the consolidated models must comply with some modelling constraints: they shall have only one start event; activities and events have exactly one outgoing and one incoming arc (except for the start and end event which do not have, respectively, any incoming and outgoing arc); split gateways have only one incoming arc and arbitrary outgoing arcs while join gateways are the opposite.

Finally, we also aim to improve the view generation algorithm by identifying further patterns and enhance the generation of the aggregated activities' names. Besides that, we aim to generate views in notations other than *BPMN*.

Acknowledgements. This research was supported by the Link Consulting's project IT-Atlas n° 11419, under the IAPMEI 2020 PO CI Operational Program.

References

1. van der Aalst, W., ter Hofstede, A., Kiepuszewski, B., Barros, A.: Workflow patterns. Distrib. Parallel Databases **14**(1), 5–51 (2003). https://doi.org/10.1023/A:1022883727209
2. Acher, M., Collet, P., Lahire, P., France, R.: Composing feature models. In: van den Brand, M., Gašević, D., Gray, J. (eds.) SLE 2009. LNCS, vol. 5969, pp. 62–81. Springer, Heidelberg (2010). https://doi.org/10.1007/978-3-642-12107-4_6
3. Caetano, A., Pereira, C., Sousa, P.: Generation of business process model views. Procedia Technol. **5**, 378–387 (2012). https://doi.org/10.1016/j.protcy.2012.09.042. 4th Conference of ENTERprise Information Systems - aligning technology, organizations and people (CENTERIS 2012)
4. Caetano, A., Silva, A., Tribolet, J.: Business process decomposition - an approach based on the principle of separation of concerns. Enterprise Model. Inf. Syst. Archit. **5**, 44–57 (2010). https://doi.org/10.18417/emisa.5.1.3
5. Caetano, A., Silva, A.R., Tribolet, J.: A role-based enterprise architecture framework. In: Proceedings of the 2009 ACM Symposium on Applied Computing,

SAC 2009, pp. 253–258. ACM, New York (2009). https://doi.org/10.1145/1529282. 1529337

6. Colaço, J., Sousa, P.: View integration of business process models. In: Themistocleous, M., Morabito, V. (eds.) EMCIS 2017. LNBIP, vol. 299, pp. 619–632. Springer, Cham (2017). https://doi.org/10.1007/978-3-319-65930-5_48

7. Czarnecki, K., Antkiewicz, M.: Mapping features to models: a template approach based on superimposed variants. In: Glück, R., Lowry, M. (eds.) GPCE 2005. LNCS, vol. 3676, pp. 422–437. Springer, Heidelberg (2005). https://doi.org/10. 1007/11561347_28

8. Hevner, A.R., March, S.T., Park, J., Ram, S.: Design science in information systems research. MIS Q. **28**(1), 75–105 (2004)

9. Indulska, M., Green, P., Recker, J., Rosemann, M.: Business process modeling: perceived benefits. In: Laender, A.H.F., Castano, S., Dayal, U., Casati, F., de Oliveira, J.P.M. (eds.) ER 2009. LNCS, vol. 5829, pp. 458–471. Springer, Heidelberg (2009). https://doi.org/10.1007/978-3-642-04840-1_34

10. International Organization of Standardization: ISO/IEC/IEEE 42010:2011 - Systems and software engineering - Architecture description (2011)

11. Krogstie, J., Sølvberg, A.: Information Systems Engineering - Conceptual Modeling in a Quality Perspective. Kompendiumforlaget, Trondheim (2003)

12. Moon, M., Hong, M., Yeom, K.: Two-level variability analysis for business process with reusability and extensibility. In: Proceedings of the 2008 32nd Annual IEEE International Computer Software and Applications Conference, COMPSAC 2008, pp. 263–270. IEEE Computer Society, Washington, DC (2008). https://doi.org/ 10.1109/COMPSAC.2008.129

13. Object Management Group: Business Process Model and Notation (BPMN) (2011)

14. Peffers, K., Tuunanen, T., Rothenberger, M., Chatterjee, S.: A design science research methodology for information systems research. J. Manag. Inf. Syst. **24**, 45–77 (2007)

15. Pereira, C.: Using an organizational taxonomy to support business process design. Ph.D. thesis, Insituto Superior Técnico (2011)

16. Pereira, C.M., Caetano, A., Sousa, P.: Ontology-driven business process design. In: Skersys, T., Butleris, R., Nemuraite, L., Suomi, R. (eds.) I3E 2011. IAICT, vol. 353, pp. 153–162. Springer, Heidelberg (2011). https://doi.org/10.1007/978-3-642-27260-8_12

17. Pereira, C.M., Sousa, P.: Business process modelling through equivalence of activity properties. In: Proceedings of the Tenth International Conference on Enterprise Information Systems, pp. 137–146 (2008)

18. Reijers, H., Mans, R., van der Toorn, R.: Improved model management with aggregated business process models. Data Knowl. Eng. **68**, 221–243 (2009). https://doi. org/10.1016/j.datak.2008.09.004

19. Rosa, M.L., Aalst, W.M.P.V.D., Dumas, M., Milani, F.P.: Business process variability modeling: a survey. ACM Comput. Surv. **50**(1), 2:1–2:45 (2017). https:// doi.org/10.1145/3041957

20. Sousa, P., Caetano, A., Vasconcelos, A., Pereira, C., Tribolet, J.: Enterprise architecture modeling with the unified modeling language. In: Rittgen, P. (ed.) Enterprise Modeling and Computing with UML, pp. 67–94. IGI Global (2006)

21. Sousa, P., Leal, R.T., Sampaio, A.: Atlas: the enterprise cartography tool. In: Proceedings of 8th the Enterprise Engineering Working Conference Forum, vol. 2229 (2018)

22. Sousa, P., Pereira, C., Vendeirinho, R., Caetano, A., Tribolet, J.: Applying the Zachman framework dimensions to support business process modeling. In: Cunha, P.F., Maropoulos, P.G. (eds.) Digital Enterprise Technology, pp. 359–366. Springer, Boston (2007). https://doi.org/10.1007/978-0-387-49864-5_42
23. Sowa, J.F., Zachman, J.A.: Extending and formalizing the framework for information systems architecture. IBM Syst. J. **31**(3), 590–616 (1992)
24. Zachman, J.A.: A framework for information systems architecture. IBM Syst. J. **26**(3), 276–292 (1987)

LegalLanguage: A Domain-Specific Language for Legal Contexts

Ambrósio Alves Soares[1(✉)], Paula Ventura Martins[1] ⓘ,
and Alberto Rodrigues da Silva[2] ⓘ

[1] Faculdade de Ciências e Tecnologia da Universidade do Algarve,
Faro, Portugal
a20982@ualg.pt
[2] INESC-ID, Instituto Superior Técnico, Universidade de Lisboa,
Lisbon, Portugal

Abstract. Nowadays legal ontologies have been used in the legal domain, however, being poorly explored in legislative and production processes. This paper analyses the adoption of legal ontologies as a tool to support these processes, in particular, related to activities span from the submission of bills and their subsequent authoring and ratification. This paper introduces the state of the art of legal (or normative) ontologies; and also discusses some application examples. The analysis of this state of the art allows us to identify some problems, namely regarding the activities involving the authoring and validation of laws that tend to be very human-intensive and error-prone. As a consequence of this analysis, we introduce the LegalLanguage, a language particularly suitable for the authoring and specification of law(s) in a more rigorous and systematic way, that would allow to keep track different types of intra and inter-laws relationships (e.g., structural, order or temporal relationships between articles or even between laws). Finally, a simple illustrative example is used and shows the importance of a language like LegalLanguage in the production of normative documents.

Keywords: Legal tech · Legal ontologies · Domain Specific Language

1 Introduction

The need to allow the adequate improvement of practices during the writing phase of normative texts (e.g., laws, regulations) of legal-based organization (e.g., parliamentary, lawyers society), led to the study of legal ontologies as a convenient tool to better support the activities of the production process (e.g., the legislative process) in the period of preparation of proposals of laws that includes a set of phases and acts such as the creation and authoring, but also validation and publishing of such normative texts. The empirical studies found in the literature on legal ontology, like [1–3], present aspects for the understanding and use of the subject in the perspective of legal application (judicial process) and not in the process of legislative production (legislative process). There are few studies [4] on the use of legal ontologies as supporting parliamentary activities, of the legislative process.

© Springer Nature Switzerland AG 2020
D. Aveiro et al. (Eds.): EEWC 2019, LNBIP 374, pp. 33–51, 2020.
https://doi.org/10.1007/978-3-030-37933-9_3

Figure 1 shows the representation of the two top-level legal processes: the process of producing laws (legislative process); and the process of applying or using of such laws (judicial process).

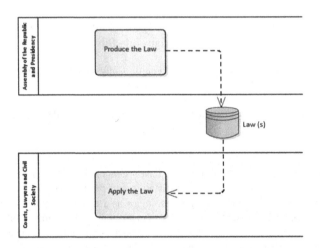

Fig. 1. The two top-level legal processes (in BPMN notation)

The legislative process (production laws) involves the authoring, validation and publication of Laws; while the judicial process (application the law) initiates and receives the final version of the Law (defined from the previous process), giving continuity to the activities related to the use and application of laws. The focus of our research is mainly related to the support of the first process (i.e., the production of laws and other normative texts), which can be considered at the parliamentary scope but also on other levels e.g., at the level of lawyer societies.

Normative legal documents written directly in natural languages (e.g., English, Spanish or Portuguese) present usually coherence failures, as for example (i) at the morphological level, where one deals with the composition of the words and their nature; (ii) at the level of the lexicon, which interprets the individual meaning of words; (iii) at the syntactic level, which focuses on the analysis of the sentence's composition; or (iv) at the semantic level where the meaning of the words or sentences are dealt with.

In the legal domain (in particular parliamentary scope) the responsible for producing laws tend to use common Word Processors tools (like Microsoft Word, OpenOffice or Google Docs) for drafting legal normative acts. However, these software tools do not provide specific support to facilitate such processes. The absence of adequate and specific tools does not help to avoid or mitigate the problems related to the legislative production process, such as: deficiencies in the analysis, navigation, search, traceability and creation of laws; absence of easy navigation between laws and their relationships; absence of traceability mechanisms between laws (e.g., with repealed or in force semantics); lexical and structural ambiguity in words, phrases and expressions; lack of clarity in the text of the body of laws already enacted; or difficulty to automatically check and normalize such laws.

To mitigate some of these problems we propose a legal-specific language, named as "LegalLanguage", that would allow to specify normative texts in a more rigorous and systematic way when compared with the traditional human-intensive and error-prone approaches. This research comes from our previous work on designing languages and tools to improve the rigor of text specifications in disparate domains like privacy policies [5–7] and requirements engineering [8–10]. In addition, recently we have also researched legal ontologies and concluded that the existent proposals are still limited or incomplete [11].

This paper is structured as follows. Section 2 introduces the state of the art on legal ontologies particularly applied in the legislative domain; Sect. 3 introduces and overviews the key aspects of the proposed LegalLanguage; Sect. 4 shows an illustrative example of applying the LegalLanguage; finally, Sect. 5 presents conclusions and overviews future work.

2 Legal Ontologies

The definition of the concept *"ontology"* differs in the context of computer science, and information of reasoning in the philosophical context [12]. According to Gruber, an ontology is a description of concepts and relationships that exist for an individual or a community [13]. The term is borrowed from philosophy, where an ontology is a systematic description of existence. In 2009, Gruber updated the definition of the concept in the context of computer science and information, as a set of representation primitives *(classes, attributes or properties, relations)* with which to model a knowledge domain [14].

Depending on the domain, legal ontologies have several approaches. Figure 2 distinguishes three different approaches, namely: semantic, epistemological and ontological approach. The semantic approach focuses on the meaning of a representation of elements and relationships in a given domain; the epistemological approach is relative

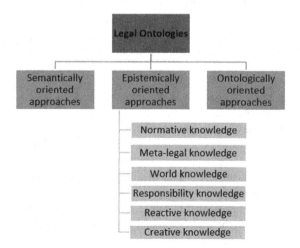

Fig. 2. Different approaches of legal ontologies (source: [12])

to the cognitive knowledge of a domain; the ontological approach gives greater prominence to the entities and relationships that constitute a domain.

The epistemological approach presented in Fig. 2 distinguishes six basic types of knowledge, from an example of this type of approach called functional ontology, that is: normative knowledge, meta-legal knowledge, knowledge of the world, knowledge of responsibility, reactive knowledge, and knowledge creative [12]. Normative knowledge, from the definition of the term "normative" which refers to rules, consists of elements of the legal field which prescribe the behavior of persons in the society in which they are inserted according to certain accepted rules.

Meta-legal knowledge consists of legal rules that govern relationships between different people in society and not directly behavior. World Knowledge does not necessarily mean geographical position, it consists of knowledge of the elements of the world, and how these elements determine how the world looks. Responsibility Knowledge consists in the linking of normative knowledge to reactive knowledge. In the normative case where there are presuppositions to exist of norms, the responsibility is the duty of an agent causing an event to bear the consequences of the own behavior. Reactive knowledge consists of the sanctions imposed if an agent violates a standard and is held accountable for it. Finally, the Creative knowledge of the "creative" concept, which highlights the imagination and ability to create something new, original. It consists of information about created institutions and other entities that arise from law enforcement.

The problems, presented in Sect. 1, related to the improvement in the normative treatment of legal texts, as well as the lack of ontologies related to the structure of legal documents, justify the accomplishment of this work on the normative knowledge type of the epistemological approach, focusing on the normative domain and emphasizing the structure of basic concepts of a law.

The semantic and ontological approaches to the particular domain, presented in Fig. 2, apply in the representation of structural elements of a law and relations, and not as a support for the writing of normative texts, which is the focus of our work.

The following is a brief description of some of the most important legal ontologies. At the conclusion of the chapter, the comparative study of these ontologies is presented based on several criteria, namely the categories of classification presented in Fig. 2, concepts of each ontology and capacity to respond to identified problems.

2.1   LKIF

The Legal Knowledge Interchange Format (LKIF) ontology is based on "basic concepts of law". Terminology issues become the main object of ontology.

LKIF has two main objectives: to allow translation between legal knowledge bases written in different formats and representation formalisms and, secondly, as a knowledge representation formalism that is part of a larger architecture for the development of knowledge systems tool.

Based on the categories presented in Fig. 2, LKIF is identified on the type semantic approach, since it deals with the translation and representation of knowledge, which fits within the principles of the semantic approach.

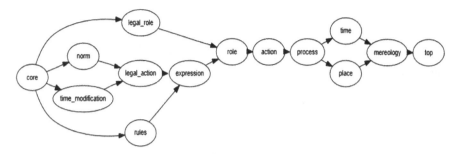

Fig. 3. Dependencies between the main modules of the LKIF ontology (source: [1]).

This ontology defines in five closely related modules the most abstract concepts: top, place, mereology, time, and space-time.

In the top module, LKIF's top ontology is largely based on the upper level of LRI-Core, but has less ontological commitment in that it imposes fewer constraints on subclasses of the major categories. The place module partially implements the theory of relative places in Languages to define and instantiate Web Ontologies (OWL) and based on Description Logics (DL). The mereology module defines theory or logical-mathematical study concepts of the relations between the parts and the whole, and of the relations between the parts within a whole (affiliation, etc.). The time module provides an implementation of the OWL DL of the theory of time [1].

The space-time module consists of basic level concepts that are distributed in four modules: process, role, action and expression.

The process module extends the LKIF top ontology module with a definition of changes, processes (being causal changes) and physical objects. This module introduces a limited set of properties to describe the participants' roles in the processes (see Fig. 3). The role module defines a typology of roles (epistemic roles, roles, personal roles, organizational roles) and the role-linking property. The action module describes the vocabulary to represent actions in general, and does not commit to a particular theory on thematic roles. Actions are processes performed by agents (actor of action). The expression module describes a vocabulary for reporting propositions and propositional attitudes (belief, intention), qualifications, statements, and the media. In addition, it extends the module papers with a number or epistemic roles, and is the basis for the definition of norms.

The remaining basic concepts are extended through three modules that form the legal ontology: legal-action, legal-role and norm. The legal-action module extends the action module with a set of legal concepts related to the action and the agent, such as public acts, public agencies, legal person, natural person, etc. The legal-role module extends the role module with a small number of legal concepts related to roles, legal professions, etc. The norm module is an extension mainly on the expression module, where norms are defined as qualifications. It also defines a number of legal sources, such as legal documents, customary law, etc., and a typology of rights and powers [15]. Further details on the explanation of the ontology can be found in the bibliography in [1].

2.2 CLO

The CLO (Core Legal Ontologies) approach aims to support the construction of legal domain ontologies [16], being classified as an ontological approach (Fig. 2), where the essential concepts of this ontology will be described in Fig. 4.

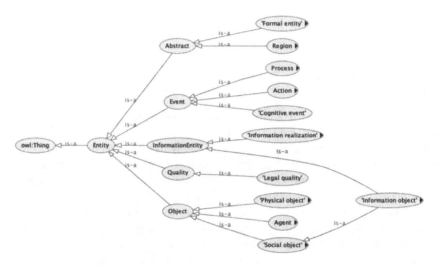

Fig. 4. Context and stated situations (source: [2])

The CLO provides types and relationships for the heterogeneous entities from the legal domain, be it the physical, cognitive, social or legal realm. According to stratification, entities from different layers may be spatially temporally co-located, being completely different and (mutually or unidirectionally) dependent [16].

The role of the CLO is to separate entities/concepts that belong to the general law theory from concepts specific to national legal systems or a specific legal domain. The CLO also aims to fill the gap between domain-specific concepts and abstract categories of formal top-level or foundational ontologies such as DOLCE [2].

2.3 ELTS

The ELTS (European Legal Taxonomy Syllabus) approach describes a tool that has been used to construct multilingual concept dictionaries, allowing the distinction between terms and concepts for the European Union (EU) legislation [3]. The European Union Guidelines (EUDs) constitute a set of legal standards that must be implemented by national legislation and translated into the language of each Member State. The problem of multilingualism in European legislation and the management of the EUDs are complex, since the implementation of a EUD does not correspond to a direct transposition of a law from a member country to another member country.

The ELTS includes different ontologies, one for each national language involved, for example Italian (Ita) and German (Ger), plus one for the European Union

(EU) document language. Each language-specific ontology is related by means of a set of links (association) with the concepts of the UE, as shown in Fig. 5.

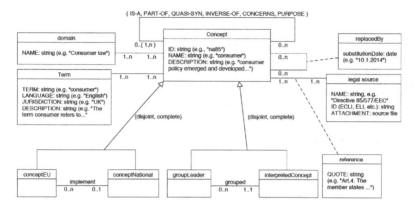

Fig. 5. ELTS ontology schema (UML language, source: [3])

This kind of ontology fits into the type of semantic approach since it deals with the meaning of EU terms coupled with the ontological approach in which it compares two domain-specific ontologies with EU semantic concepts.

2.4 Ontology Reference Model for Normative Acts

The ontological reference model for Normative Acts (NAs) is a modeling approach based on the *OntoUML* ontology [4]. The main objective of this reference model is to represent only the structural elements of NAs.

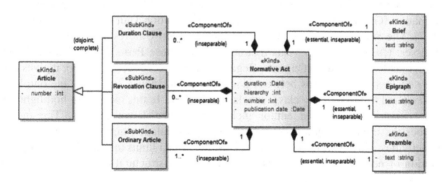

Fig. 6. Compositions of Normative Acts (source: [4])

Figure 6 shows the essential elements of this reference model. Articles may be *Ordinary Articles, Revocation Clauses* or *Duration Clauses. Ordinary articles* also known as regular articles are articles that affirm a new communication. *Revocation*

Clauses consists of articles that revoke other articles. The *Duration Clauses* are articles that affirm a validation time. Every NA must be composed of at least one *Ordinary Article*. All NA has preliminary mandatory elements *Preamble*, *Epigraph* and *Summary*. The *Preamble* is a term that means *introduction, initiation*, or *initial statement* of NA. It is a short text that predates the first chapter and sets out a brief explanation of the content discussed in NA. The *Epigraph* is a title or phrase that serves as a theme or subject introduction. The *Brief* is a collection of information, data collection most relevant to the development of an NA.

This type of approach is classified in the type of normative knowledge since the emphasis is the representation of elements and relations of a law.

2.5   Generic Model of Relationship (GMR)

The GMR (Generic Model of Relationship) approach aims to assist in organizing information with an emphasis on relationships between concepts and information units [17]. GMR consists of three main entities: (i) concept, (ii) information unit and (iii) relationship. Figure 7 illustrates the elementary class hierarchy of the GMR model.

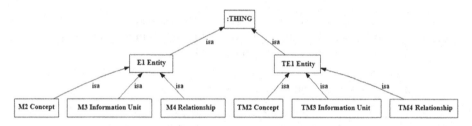

Fig. 7. GMR entities (source:)

The extension of GMR ontology applied in the field of Legal and Juridical Information (GMR-LJI) works on classes M3 Information Unit and M4 Relationship (Fig. 7). The extension applied in class M3 information Unit results in the creation of subclasses: (i) Periods; (ii) Events that start or end these Periods; (iii) Activities and their Agents (Roles) and Participants. Regarding the class M4 Relationship, it gives rise to the subclass Relationships between domain classes. Figure 8 presents the ontology details related to the Activity class (subclass iii of M3). In this model, we highlight the greatest contribution of the author including the legislative process. The model describes the dynamic component through temporal relationships between agent and their activities. However, for legal documents, the model limits to describe the temporal evolution of norms and dispositions, without existing structural or content aspects of legal documents.

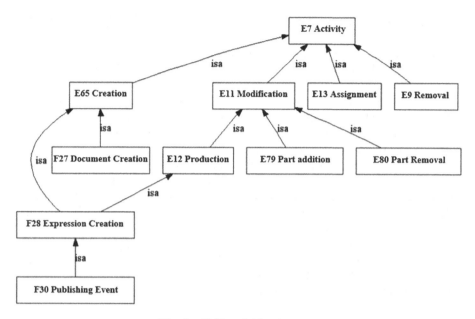

Fig. 8. GMR activities (source:)

2.6   New Developments on Law Content Aspects

The legal domain involves large amounts of concepts, terms and documents. Legal documents are rapidly changing or evolving. New developments in this area must take into consideration syntactic and semantic knowledge [18]. In the legal domain, different ontologies can be defined depending mostly on the task for which they are built.

Several projects involving ontologies dealt with topics such as legal decision support systems, translation and interpretation of legal texts. Sections 2.1 to 2.4 presented different ontologies manually developed from scratch (top-down approach). These approaches were created with a specific domain goal, without paying to legal ontology learning (bottom-up approach). Ontology learning aims to identify terms, concepts, relations or axioms to support ontology building [18].

In the last two decades, different proposals emerged based on Artificial Intelligent techniques to extract concepts and relations among them from unstructured legal texts. In 2005, Lame [19] applied Natural Language Processing (NLP) techniques to create an ontology of French Law dedicated to information retrieval. Saia and Quaresma [20] proposed a methodology to automatically create legal ontologies that allow enriching legal documents. Mezghanni and Gargouri [21] created an approach for ontology learning from Tunisian Legal texts designed for legal information retrieval. Ghosh et al. [22] presented a semiautomatic ontology construction technique (1) reusing existing ontologies to extract similar and complementary information; and (2) capturing relevant legal concepts and relations from textual sources using NLP techniques. Hwang et al. [23] presented a technique for an automatic ontology construction from a structured text (databases). This approach involves NLP and data mining techniques for concept and relationship extraction.

The extraction of rules or conditions from legal texts is a difficult task, so the adoption of a single Natural Language Processing (NLP) approach would not lead to satisfiable results. Considering the limited adoption of current frameworks, Dragoni et al. [24] adopted and combined a set of NLP techniques towards the extraction of rules from legal documents.

In 2019, Fawei et al. [25] presented a methodology that leads to the creation of a legal ontology and a corresponding set of rules. This was the first fine-grained methodology for constructing legal OWL ontologies with Semantic Web Rule Language (SWRL) rules.

Design Engineering and Modelling for Organizations (DEMO) is a theory and method to model interactions between individuals and/or organizations(set of actors) based on a communication-centric approach (social interactions) [26]. The Performance in Social Interactions (PSI) is a component of DEMO that declares how the coordination-acts performed by actors are represented in patterns called transactions. Gouveia and Aveiro [27] present a design of two sources of law based on the transaction axiom of the PSI theory. The authors also analyze the assumptions mismatch between law and DEMO/PSI. In the studied cases, similarities were observed between the main concepts of the previously mentioned ontologies and the essential concepts of DEMO/PSI.

2.7 Discussion

Table 1 summarizes the comparison of the ontologies introduced above. The compared features allow characterizing these ontologies. In addition, it also allows identifying some limitations of these proposals and justifies the motivation for the design of the proposed LegalLanguage.

The LegalLanguage results from the analysis of these ontologies but have a distinct focus: while some concepts are similar, there is a different interest and application domain. Although, the ontological reference model for normative acts proposed by Pedro et al. [4] is also related to the structure of legal documents, it is less flexible since the model details the hierarchical and rigid structure of a NA. This conceptual model was constructed for communication and learning purposes without considering mechanisms to support the writing of normative texts of laws and intra and inter-laws relationships.

In an initial stage of this research work, based on the fact that several ontologies focus semantics of the law, we decide to focus in the structure of a law document. The addition of semantic description will be considered in future work.

3   LegalLanguage Overview

This section overviews the proposed metamodel and the mechanism involved in the construction of law documents. For clarity purposes, Sect. 3.1 presents the LegalLanguage metamodel and provides textual definitions of the elements. Section 3.2 describes the DLS implementation with Xtext [28].

3.1   LegalLanguage Meta-model

As seen in Sect. 2 a legal ontology is an explicit way to represent Laws as rigorous models, which capture and represent common concepts of a generic Law. Figures 9 and 10 present the meta-model (i.e., the abstract syntax as UML class diagrams) of the proposed LegalLanguage. Compared with the ontological reference model for normative acts, the proposed meta-model is more flexible since includes enumerations that only affect the semantics of the respective meta-classes.

Table 1. Comparative analysis of ontologies.

Ontologies	LKIF	CLO	ELTS	ORM for NAs	MGR
Features					
Ontological reference models	N	Y	Y	Y (UML class diag)	Y
Ontological domain of NAs	Europe	Europe	EU	Brazil	Brazil
Concept of					
Law	Y(docs)	Y	Y	Y (NAs)	Y
Legal terms	N	Y	Y	N	N
Legal concepts	Y	Y	Y	N	N
Legal norms	N	Y	Y	NE	Y
Legal texts	Y	Y	Y	N	N
Legal facts	NE	Y	N	N	N
Normative context	N	Y	N	Y	N
Legal situation	N	Y	N	N	Y
Process	Y	Y	N	N	N
Action	Y	NE	NE	N	N
Legal-action	Y	NE	NE	N	N
Role	Y	NE	Y	N	N
Legal-role	Y	NE	Y	N	N
Rules	Y	NE	Y	N	Y
Agent	Y	Y	Y	N	Y
Person	Y	Y	Y	N	Y
Legal-source	Y	Y	Y	N	N
Change	Y	Y	N	N	N
Qualified	NE	Y	NE	N	Y
Approach					N
Semantically oriented	Y	N	Y	N	N
Epistemically oriented					
Normative knowledge	N	N	N	Y	N
Meta-legal knowledge	N	N	N	N	N
World knowledge	N	N	N	N	N
Responsibility knowledge	N	N	N	N	N
Reactive knowledge	N	N	N	N	N
Creative knowledge	N	N	N	N	N
Ontologically oriented	N	Y	N	N	Y

Subtitle: Y (Yes); N (No); NE (Not explicit)

According to this metamodel, the **Law** is composed of several Articles ordered sequentially, which can be further structured in Divisions. The **Law** is the general concept to represent "normative texts" and is classified by a *type* (e.g., Constitution, International Law, Ordinary Law, Public Regulation, Private Regulation), shall be identified by a *unique id* (number) and defined by relevant *dates* (e.g., publication, activation, disactivation). Optionally a Law can be further classified by a *sub*type, for example: Constitution: original or revision; International law: treatise, regulation, directive; Ordinary law: Law, Decree-law, national or regional; Regulation: regulation, contract, tort. It is also possible to define the application domain of the law (e.g., agricultural, aviation, banking, public, civil), and also the possibility to define the current state in which the law can be found (e.g., in edition, submitted to approve, approved, active, suspended, revoked).

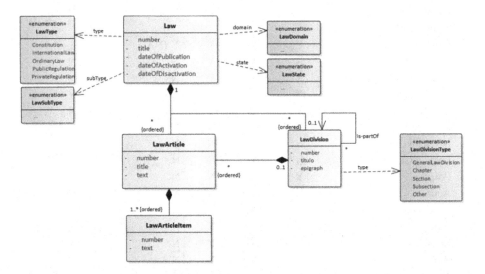

Fig. 9. The meta-model of structural concepts of Law

The **Article** is the basic element of a law, shall be univocally identified by a sequential *number* (e.g., 1, 2, 3), and shall have an optional *title*, a *text* and also a set of *items*.

The **Law** can be structured by a set of **Divisions**, whose properties are *epigraph*, *number*, *type* of division (e.g., Chapter, Section, Sub-section) and *title*. The **Division** may be composed of other divisions, defining hierarchies if relevant. Furthermore, an Article can be assigned to a Division, and on the other hand, a Division may aggregate several Articles.

One may also consider relationships between laws and hierarchies (e.g., order of importance) for the law of laws that assume its subordination to a higher origin. For example, at a country level, laws are hierarchically inferior to the Constitution law. The laws (e.g., ordinary, delegated and complementary) and the regulatory decree, which aims to regulate the provision of the law, follow the same guidelines. Another common relationship between laws (or specific articles of laws) is the revocation: when a new law appears, it may revoke a previous old law, and then the former becomes active and the latter revoked.

Figure 10 shows the LegalLanguage support for the definition of **relations between laws** (inter-law relations) as well as **relations between articles** of the same law (articles intra-law relations) or even from distinct laws (articles inter-law relations). In addition, these relations are typified, which means we may add some semantic to them (e.g., revokes, revoked, depends, specializes).

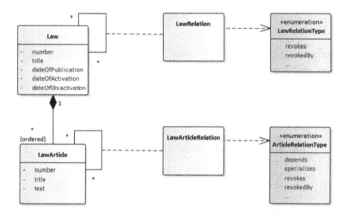

Fig. 10. The meta-model with relations between laws and between articles (same or different laws)

3.2   LegalLanguage Implementation Aspects

The development of a Domain-specific Language (DSL) requires to be aware of two aspects: the characteristics of a DSL and details of the domain to which the language will be contextualized. The particular domain considered is the legal domain, in particular, the scope of parliamentary with activities of the legislative process of drafting laws. To implement the proposed LegalLanguage, we considered the meta-model presented in Figs. 9 and 10.

The Xtext [28], developed as part of the Eclipse Modeling Framework, generates a parser, a serializer, a meta-model and a DSL editor from the grammar of the language.

The code snippet Spec. 1 shows the definition of the LegaLanguage's Law grammar:

```
Law:    'Law' name=ID (nameAlias=STRING)? ':' type=LawType (':' subType=LawSubType)? ('['
                    ('domain' subject=LawDomainType)?
                    ('state' state=LawStateType)?
                    (relationType+= LawRelationType relations+= RefLaw)*
                    ('number' number=INT '/' year=INT)?
                    ('title' title=STRING)?
                    ('dateOfPublication' dateOfPublication=Date)?
                    ('dateOfActivation' dateOfActivation=Date)?
                    ('dateOfDisactivation' dateOfDisactivation=Date)?
                    ('description' description=STRING)?
                    (lawArticles+=LawArticle*)
                    (lawDivisions+=LawDivision*)
            ']')? ;
enum LawType: Constitution | InternationalLaw | OrdinaryLaw | PublicRegulation | PrivateRegulation |...;
enum LawRelationType: revokes | revokedBy;
```

Spec. 1. LegaLanguage's Law grammar

The code snippets Specs. 2 and 3 show the definition in Xtext of the LegaLanguage's Division and Article grammars:

```
LawDivision:
            'Division' name=ID (nameAlias=STRING)? ':' type=LawDivisionType ('['
                    ('partOf' partOf=[LawDivision | QualifiedName] )?
                    ('epigraph' epigraph=STRING)?
                    ('number' number=INT)?
                    ('title' title=STRING)?
                    (divisionArticles+=LawArticle*)
            ']')?;
enum LawDivisionType: Chapter | Section | Subsection | Other;
```

Spec. 2. LegaLanguage's Division grammar

```
LawArticle:
            'Article' name=ID (nameAlias=STRING)?
            ('['
                    (relationType+= ArticleRelationType relations+= RefArticle)*
                    ('number' number=INT)
                    ('title' title=STRING)?
                    ('text' text=STRING)?
                    (itens+=LawArticleItem*)
            ']');
...
enum ArticleRelationType:    depends | specializes | revokes | revokedBy;
```

Spec. 3. LegaLanguage's Article grammar

The Eclipse IDE also includes the LegalLanguage's plug-ins. An editor of laws will be automatically available to assist in the writing of normative texts like laws, and intra or inter-laws relationships. Currently, it is possible to create documents similar to the example presented in the following session.

4   Illustrative Example

The legislative process is crucial in the drafting of a law, it includes a set of phases and acts duly ordered and executed, whose content, form and sequence follow a series of rules specific to each parliament.

```
Package EU_Laws
Law Directive_EC_46_95 "Directive n.° 95/46": InternationalLaw: InternationalLaw_Directive [
         domain IT
         state Revoked
         revokedBy EU_Laws.Regulation_EU_679_2016
         number 95/46
         dateOfPublication 24-Oct-1995
description "DIRECTIVE 95/46/EC OF THE EUROPEAN PARLIAMENT AND OF THE COUNCIL of
24 October 1995 on the protection of individuals with regard to the processing of personal data and on the
free movement of such data. THE EUROPEAN PARLIAMENT AND THE COUNCIL OF THE
EUROPEAN UNION, ..."
```

Spec. 4. Illustrative example. Law header specification in LegaLanguage

Legislative drafting is a complex process, due to the number of copies that are analyzed by the plenary in each ordinary session, and that undergoes constant changes during the phases of the legislative process until the final drafting of the Law. It involves a huge volume of documents in physical format (paper) and many stakeholders.

Spec. 4 illustrates the LegaLanguage specification to instantiate a practical example of the "Directive 95/46/EC" related to the protection of individuals with regard to the processing of personal data and on the free movement of such data.

Spec. 5 illustrates the specification of the article-3 of the Directive 95/46/EC in LegalLanguage. In particular, it is relevant to stress that this article specializes the article-6 (defined in Sect. 1), and also is revoked by article-15 defined in the former EU Regulation 679/2016. The "revokedBy" is an example of an articles inter-law relation, while the "specializes" is an example of an articles intra-law relation.

```
Article Article_3 "Article 3" [
         revokedBy EU_Laws.Regulation_EU_679_2016.SECTION_II.Article_15
         specializes SECTION_I.Article_6
         number 3
         title "Scope"
         ArticleItem Name "..." [ number 1 text "...." ]
]
```

Spec. 5. Illustrative example. Article specification in LegaLanguage

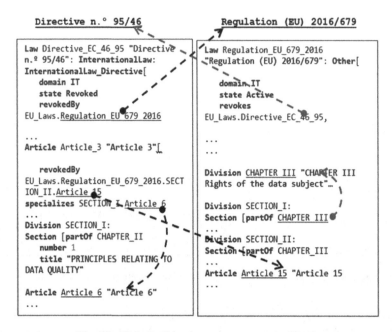

Fig. 11. Relationships between two types of laws

As suggested in Fig. 11, the authors also defined relations between several types of laws, in which each law relates to other(s), also allowing to link articles. Figure 11 illustrates an example where two types of the European Union legislation have relations, namely: Regulation (EU) 2016/679 of the European Parliament and of the Council of 27 April 2016 and Directive 95/46/EC of the European Parliament and of the Council of 24 October 1995. The Regulation (EU) 2016/679 revokes the Directive 95/46/EC (General Data Protection Regulation). On the opposite site, Directive 95/46/EC is revoked by the Regulation (EU) 2016/679. In this example, the relationship between articles is also represented.

5   Conclusion

This paper proposes a DSL for the rigorous specification of normative documents, in particular laws produced in the parliamentary scope. This DSL, named as LegalLanguage, shall support the activities related to the elaboration of laws.

The comparative study of different legal ontologies made it possible to note that some problems, mentioned in Sect. 1, in particular, the activities of laws' elaboration continue prone to several error types. The proposed language allows to represent laws in a more rigorous and explicit form. This language allows the definition of structural patterns, like chapters, articles, sections and subsections, typically found in legal documents.

Although there are some tools to assist in the authoring process of legal ontologies, the selection of a framework for the development of DSLs was the most feasible at the time the problems in this specific-domain were identified. The choice of the development tool required a search for support infrastructures that facilitated an agile and iterative evolution of the domain-specific language, as well as essential resources for its construction. Using the LegalLanguage editor, the normative drafting activities can be improved and less error-prone compared to the actual manual process.

The illustrative examples allow to show the applicability of LegalLanguage in the current drafting of laws. Regarding the main objective of this paper, the LegalLanguage application in the legislative production process was satisfactory, in the sense that it helps in laws elaboration activities.

In the example presented, the LegalLanguage allowed to identify opportunities for future works, such as extend the language to address the remaining identified problems. For example, the realization of empirical studies that will make possible to include improvements on the LegalLanguage. Nowadays, several gaps persist between language and technology, our vision is to establishing a simplified way of working among the various actors in the legislative process. LegalLanguage will act as a facilitator during the writing phase of normative texts (e.g., laws, regulations) of legal-based organization.

Future evaluations will also deliver further input for improving LegalLanguage and eventually to create a supporting tool. Future research will also have to consider applying LegalLanguage in the validation of legal documents in different formats, such has words documents.

References

1. Hoekstra, R., Breuker, J., Di Bello, M., Boer, A.: The LKIF core ontology of basic legal concepts. In: Proceedings of LO A IT 07: II Workshop on Legal Ontologies and Artificial Intelligence Techniques, pp. 43–63 (2007)
2. Francesconi, E., Tiscornia, D.: Building semantic resources for legislative drafting: the DALOS project. In: Casanovas, P., Sartor, G., Casellas, N., Rubino, R. (eds.) Computable Models of the Law. LNCS (LNAI), vol. 4884, pp. 56–70. Springer, Heidelberg (2008). https://doi.org/10.1007/978-3-540-85569-9_4
3. Ajani, G., et al.: European legal taxonomy syllabus: a multi-lingual, multi-level ontology framework to untangle the web of European legal terminology, vol. 3. IOS Press (2006)
4. Pedro, B.P.F., Guizzardi, R.S.S., Garcia, A.S.: An Ontology Reference Model for Normative Acts, Brazil (2013)
5. Caramujo, J., et al.: RSL-IL4Privacy: a domain-specific language for the specification of privacy-aware requirements. Requirements Eng. 24(1), 1–26 (2019)
6. Ribeiro, A., Silva, A.R.: RSLingo4Privacy studio: a tool to improve the specification and analysis of privacy policie. In: Proceedings of ICEIS 2017 (2017)
7. da Silva, A.R., Caramujo, J., Monfared, S., Calado, P., Breaux, T.: Improving the specification and analysis of privacy policies: the RSLingo4Privacy approach. In: Proceedings of ICEIS 2016 (2016)

8. da Silva, A.R.: Linguistic patterns and linguistic styles for requirements specification (i): an application case with the rigorous RSL/business-level language. In: Proceedings of EuroPLOP 2017 (2017)
9. da Silva, A.R., Paiva, A.C.R., da Silva, V.E.R.: A test specification language for information systems based on data entities, use cases and state machines. In: Hammoudi, S., Pires, L.F., Selic, B. (eds.) MODELSWARD 2018. CCIS, vol. 991, pp. 455–474. Springer, Cham (2019). https://doi.org/10.1007/978-3-030-11030-7_20
10. Gonçalves, L.P., da Silva, A.R.: Towards a catalogue of reusable security requirements, risks and vulnerabilities. In: Proceedings of ISD 2018 (2018)
11. Soares, A.A., Martins, P.V., da Silva, A.R.: A systematic literature review of legal ontologies. In: Proceedings of CAPSI 2018 (2018)
12. Mommers, L.: Ontologies in the legal domain. In: Poli, R., Seibt, J. (eds.) Theory and Applications of Ontology: Philosophical Perspectives, pp. 265–276. Springer, Heidelberg (2010). https://doi.org/10.1007/978-90-481-8845-1_12
13. Gruber, T.: A translation approach to portable ontologies. Knowledge Acquisition (1993)
14. Gruber, T.: Toward principles for the design of ontologies used for knowledge sharing. Int. J. Hum.-Comput. Stud. **43**, 907–928 (1995)
15. Rubino, R., Rotolo, A., Sartor, G.: An OWL ontology of fundamental legal. In: Legal Knowledge and Information Systems. JURIX 2006: The Nineteenth Annual Conference. Frontiers, vol. 152 (2006)
16. Gangemi, A., Sagri, M.-T., Tiscornia, D.: A constructive framework for legal ontologies. In: Benjamins, V.R., Casanovas, P., Breuker, J., Gangemi, A. (eds.) Law and the Semantic Web. LNCS (LNAI), vol. 3369, pp. 97–124. Springer, Heidelberg (2005). https://doi.org/10.1007/978-3-540-32253-5_7
17. Lima, J.: Modelo Genérico de Relacionamentos na Organização da Informação Legislativa e Jurídica, Brasilia (2008)
18. Mezghanni, I.B., Gargouri, F.: Towards an Arabic legal ontology based on documents properties extraction. In: 12th International Conference of Computer Systems and Applications (AICCSA), Marrakech, Morocco (2015)
19. Lame, G.: Using NLP techniques to identify legal ontology components: concepts and relations. In: Benjamins, V.Richard, Casanovas, P., Breuker, J., Gangemi, A. (eds.) Law and the Semantic Web. LNCS (LNAI), vol. 3369, pp. 169–184. Springer, Heidelberg (2005). https://doi.org/10.1007/978-3-540-32253-5_11
20. Saias, J., Quaresma, P.: A methodology to create legal ontologies in a logic programming information retrieval system. In: Benjamins, V.R., Casanovas, P., Breuker, J., Gangemi, A. (eds.) Law and the Semantic Web. LNCS (LNAI), vol. 3369, pp. 185–200. Springer, Heidelberg (2005). https://doi.org/10.1007/978-3-540-32253-5_12
21. Mezghanni, I.B., Gargouri, F.: Learning of legal ontology supporting the user queries satisfaction. In: 2014 IEEE/WIC/ACM International Joint Conferences on Web Intelligence (WI) and Intelligent Agent Technologies (IAT), Warsaw, Poland (2014)
22. El Ghosh, M., Naja, H., Abdulrab, H., Khalil, M.: A ontology learning process as a bottom-up strategy for building domain-specific ontology from legal texts. In: 9th International Conference on Agents and Artificial Intelligence (ICAART 2017), New York (2017)
23. Hwang, R.-H., Hsueh, Y.-L., Chang, Y.-T.: Building a Taiwan law ontology based on automatic legal definition extraction. Appl. Syst. Innov. **1**(3), 22 (2018)
24. Dragoni, M., Villata, S., Rizzi, W., Governatori, G.: Combining natural language processing approaches for rule extraction from legal documents. In: Pagallo, U., Palmirani, M., Casanovas, P., Sartor, G., Villata, S. (eds.) AICOL 2015-2017. LNCS (LNAI), vol. 10791, pp. 287–300. Springer, Cham (2018). https://doi.org/10.1007/978-3-030-00178-0_19

25. Fawei, B., Pan, J.Z., Kollingbaum, M., Wyner, A.Z.: A Semi–automated ontology construction for legal question answering. New Gen. Comput. **37**, 453–478 (2019)
26. Dietz, J.L.G.: Enterprise Ontology: Theory and Methodology. Springer, Berlin (2006). https://doi.org/10.1007/3-540-33149-2
27. Gouveia, D., Aveiro, D.: DEMO/PSI theory and the law of the land. In: Aveiro, D., Pergl, R., Guizzardi, G., Almeida, J.P., Magalhães, R., Lekkerkerk, H. (eds.) EEWC 2017. LNBIP, vol. 284, pp. 50–65. Springer, Cham (2017). https://doi.org/10.1007/978-3-319-57955-9_4
28. Bettini, L.: Implementing Domain-Specific Languages with Xtext and Xtend, Second edn. Packt Publishing Ltd., Birmingham (2016)

On DEMO

A Design Evaluation of an Extension to the DEMO Methodology
Five Model and Process Instantiations

M. A. T. Mulder[✉]

Leusden, Netherlands
mark@mulderrr.nl

Abstract. The Design and Engineering Method for Organisations (DEMO) is the principal methodology in Enterprise Engineering (EE). It assists in making so-called essential models of organisations, which are highly abstracted ontological models. Many essential models have been produced in practice, of very different kinds of organisations, and the expressions of these models in diagrams and tables have been presented to various types of stakeholders. It turns out that the ease to understand the models varies significantly, depend on existing knowledge, background and need of the stakeholders. As a consequence, the acceptance of the essential model by these organisations also varies significantly. In this paper, the results of an analysis of the model and model content of five successive iterations are presented and discussed. This has given rise to proposing an extension to the applied OER method (Organisational Essence Revealing), such that the different kinds and levels of foreknowledge among the stakeholders can be accommodated. An iteration of this extension is also briefly presented.

1 Introduction

The Design and Engineering Method for Organisations (DEMO) [1] is the principal methodology in Enterprise Engineering [2]. The first step in applying DEMO is producing the so-called essential model of an organisation. An essential model comprises the integrated whole of four aspect models: the Construction Model (CM), the Action Model (AM), the Process Model (PM) and the Fact Model (FM). Each model is expressed in one or more diagrams and one or more cross-model tables.

Practitioners experience daily the struggle to explain the models to customers, to make them understand the diagrams and tables and to explain the theory of DEMO. While some customers simply refuse to understand, others fail to grasp the abstraction level that is inherent to the methodology. In making DEMO more accessible, various visualising concepts have been used to reduce the complexity, to show the integrity of the model, and to enhance its comprehensiveness. However, most visualisations went beyond the understanding of some of the stakeholders.

© Springer Nature Switzerland AG 2020
D. Aveiro et al. (Eds.): EEWC 2019, LNBIP 374, pp. 55–65, 2020.
https://doi.org/10.1007/978-3-030-37933-9_4

Renovating one's bathroom might serve as a useful example here. When the construction worker explains where the pipes in the walls should be put, one will probably understand the construction. This expert is needed to create this type of model. Management in the building company understands the function of construction models: they enable the construction to run on a daily basis and assure interconnections and smooth operations. To return to our example, project leaders do not need to know where the pipes should be. They only need to know the connections between the associated workers who have to finish the work on time and give them relevant information in the right order. Which brings us to upper management. They do not need to know about the construction model; they are interested in a more efficient business operation seen from a functional perspective. Or, in construction terms, they want to know whether it is possible to build cheaper, faster, and more efficiently. The information that enables these insights starts at the construction of the organisation and needs translation on the way up. It also needs a representation that relates to the construction model and their functionality.

The main research question that we have investigated is, whether the aspect model visualisations of DEMO contain the right properties for explanation to the stakeholders. This paper shares our findings in this search for modelling the construction of the organisation in a way understandable for non-engineers as well as explaining the 'way of working' of creating the model.

The remainder of this paper will consist of the used research method in Sect. 2, the description of the iterations of the artefact in Sect. 3. In Sect. 4, we will formulate the extension of the method and formulate conclusions in Sect. 5.

2   Research Method

The way to answer the main question of this research is to find, based on the existing body of knowledge, the right artefacts to represent the business. This business model will gradually be created from practical cases and leads to improved iterations of the artefact. This makes Design Science Research (DSR) [3,4] an approach that connects with the existing body of knowledge to have the iteration of the artefact that we start with. Then, in subsequent iterations we will find missing aspects of the artefact that needs to be tested in the rigour cycle.

In each practical environment, we have improved the presentation of models and the way of working for creating those models in such a way that it was more complete, based on the information acquired with the previous iteration of the model. Consequently, every iteration has influenced the next ones. The stakeholder types did not change between iterations. When, upon validation, the results of the models were not satisfactory we specified the changes for the next iteration.

3   Model Iterations

Over the past two years, we have created business models for five organisations. The creation and presentation of these models are described as separate iterations which vary in complexity, modelling effort, and modelling purposes. Even though the contexts vary, the descriptions all start with the context of the particular iteration, the way of working of creating the models, their presentation, and the iteration adaptation during the modelling and discussions of these models. DEMO is a non-domain specific methodology which allows us to use the iterations throughout the various domains while the stakeholder types remain stable.

The iterations, which are labelled A-E, have been created in five companies in the Netherlands. Iteration A, D, and E were used at logistic wholesale companies. Iteration B was used at a small property management company whereas iteration C regards a small call centre. We presented the business models to several types of stakeholders which we distinguished in the following way:

- A developer uses models to build a piece of software that follows the functional intention of the model.
- An operational employee is a business user that uses the models to reflect on his or her own work.
- A director is a manager who is responsible for the efficient and effective operation of the organisation itself. He/she uses the models to get an overview.
- A C-level director (e.g. CEO, CFO, CIO...) is a manager who is responsible for parts of the organisation that are managed by a director. He/she uses the models to optimise one particular aspect of information, processes, or finance.
- A project manager is responsible for managing a number of concurrent and interconnected projects. He/she does not use the models directly but needs to understand the concepts.
- A software vendor is the commercial company with developers. He/she needs information to verify that the software complies with the necessary business functionality.

3.1   Iteration A

The company in iteration A was in the process of rebuilding its automation through the implementation of a new software system. At the start of the modelling, a DEMO CM had already been built as a representation of the processes throughout the project. However, the project team responsible for the software implementation only focused on functionality. Moreover, the construction focus of DEMO was not understood by a number of stakeholders. We stepped into the project when it had already been in progress for 18 months. Subsequently, in the next year of the project we tried to embed the constructional philosophy of DEMO into the project but we failed to reach the developers and project leaders while other stakeholders got hold of the concept.

Since the construction philosophy did not stick, the Transaction Kind naming had been changed to accommodate more functional names. In this way the CM became a process oriented model that was understood by many people, including the operational employees.

The CM had been created based on the user input. The model was described at the ontology level but it was insufficiently detailed for implementation. Therefore, in the last six months of the project we extended the CM with the Process Model (PM) and with Transaction Pattern Diagrams (TPDs). In two-hour interviews with two to three employees we captured the information about every step in the process and the connections between these steps. In addition, we followed the complete transaction pattern to add all practical situations that could occur.

The CM and the TPDs were presented to the users. With additional explanation these stakeholders could understand that the diagrams were a representation of their process. However, in the end we felt that they did not grasp the model well enough to increase their understanding of the process.

For completeness, we want to emphasise that no other models were present at the beginning of this project. During the project these models were introduced, causing similar issues as the DEMO models. Therefore, it is not clear from this iteration alone whether the representations, the models, or the lack of understanding of the models is the cause of failing to properly apply DEMO in this project.

Concluding, the findings in this iteration are:

- The default representations of the CM and PM are not understood by operational employees and developers.
- Using process names for Transaction Kinds can help users understand the process. Nevertheless, this subverts the CM because the transaction kinds will be regarded as simple processes or even process steps.
- The models must be constructional to be usable in future tasks.
- The models must be sufficiently detailed for the goal of usage. Although this sounds trivial, methods do not specify the level of detail needed.
- The project must embrace the DEMO methodology to release its full potential. Not only do people have to start with DEMO, they have to maintain this view throughout the entire project to profit from the benefits of the methodology.
- In the end, the understanding of the software system implementation was dogged by many issues which might have been prevented if DEMO was used to its full potential.

3.2   Iteration B

The company in iteration B wanted to start a new software implementation for their property management system. The choice of an implementation partner for the system had to be tendered following government regulations. In preparation for this tender registration, we produced the CM and the FM of the relevant parts of the organisation. They were included in the tender request. Fortunately, the Object Fact Diagrams (OFDs) in the FM were understood, but no participant could fully understand the impact of the Organisation Construction

Diagrams (OCDs) in the CM. This resulted in a presumptuous attitude towards the gathered business information because only the models they were used to, were understandable to them.

In this iteration, we used the CM to describe the processes of the company; the FM to describe the data structure, requirements, and responsibilities. The OFD was extended with the implementation data model of the implemented software. By combining the two models, the theoretical model and the implementation model could be compared (see Fig. 1) and the functionality of the implementation evaluated for proper data structure. In addition an Actor role Function Diagram (AFD) was produced to show the relationship between actor role and organisational functions revealing the mismatch in role and function definitions.

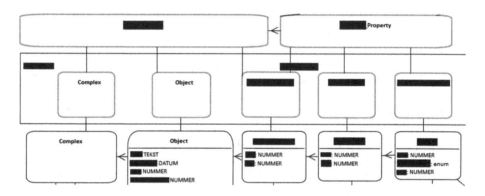

Fig. 1. Iteration B: OFD with implementation (Dutch model)

The execution of DEMO models [6,7] can help to formalise the workflow within an organisation. The software solution of the chosen supplier has a work-flow engine that is based on a Petri net implementation.

The interviews in this company, were recorded. By using these recordings we could capture more information in a single session. This information was used as input for a second session with the interviewee in which we obtained feedback on the model to help understand their own business from the produced model. This approach enabled us not only to achieve model completeness but also to determine the level of understanding of the model by the interviewee.

The CM of the organisation was presented in a layered set of OCDs and Transaction Product Tables (TPTs). From the main diagram, the detailed diagrams were accessible in an interactive visualisation. This first top-down approach was not without challenges: we had to make the CM understandable to the employees. The drill-down visualisation helped to determine the context, but it was not sufficient for the stakeholders to understand the construction perspective on the processes.

The CM and FM, were divided into departments, to get a grip on specialised parts of the model. This proved to increase the enhanced focus on partial models during interviews and feedback sessions. The partial model was particularly helpful to the stakeholders during the feedback sessions.

The findings in this iteration are:

– The software product must be accessible to reverse engineer the product to data and process models in order for it to be verified. The software vendor must be flexible to changes in the new implementation method.

3.3   Iteration C

The Company in iteration C needed to buy (not to build) a new software program to support the business. Therefore, we first analysed its business needs.

We built the DEMO model using interviews. The interviews were mainly aimed at obtaining the transaction kinds, actor roles, and entity types. The feedback on the model was obtained directly by creating the OCD and TPT live with the interviewees. The data model, or FM, was created from other information obtained during the interview. This information was more complex. The main issue in this iteration was the terminology. When terminology is complex and the definitions are not clear or not present, it is difficult to create a correct data model. Therefore, the model was created in a few iterations. The final model was understood by the operational employees as well as by the directors.

The FM was presented to the software vendor in the standard OFD format and was basically understood. However, the vendor only had a data model for the base implementation, including all entity types of the system. This made explanation of the model more difficult.

The CM, as a representation of the process, was not understood by the software vendor. The software vendor had only implemented functionality, divided into software modules, that described the activities that were performed on invocation of a menu option. This functional implementation versus abstract construction mismatch made the CM less usable for explaining to the software vendor. Concluding, our findings comply with those reported in [9].

The findings in this iteration are:

– Data models rely heavily on definitions. Before creating the data model, the list of definitions has to be made. This action should be added to the methodology.
– The OFD can be useful for comparing the match between a theoretical data model and an implementation data model when visualised in the same format.
– The OCD is generally not useful to match implemented functionality with organisation building blocks.

3.4   Iteration D

The company in iteration D wanted to have a scan of the organisation to assess its efficiency. Therefore, we did a full scan of the business processes and the validation of the business data requirements. During the process we concluded that we needed a new approach for this iteration. The Organisational Essence Revealing (OER) method of Design and Engineering Method for Organisations (DEMO), shows how to extract the essence from the implementation by communicating with the people involved. This is a good method to obtain the aspect models in a DEMO analysis including the original, infological and datalogical layers. This allows for re-modelling the green and blue layers when needed. The OER method does intentionally not help with extracting the implementation components themselves (e.g. application components, interfaces). Therefore, we added more models and methods to capture the information.

In company D we created an almost-transcription (called 'statement' that contains the essence of what is said, but not the full literal text) of a recorded interview. This statement was then used as the base of the information analysis. The analysis was done using the following interconnected diagrams: the Organisation Construction Diagram and Transaction Product Table for transaction information, the Application Layer Diagram (ALD) from ArchiMate for application information and interface information, and the Object Fact Diagram (OFD) for the data model.

The main stakeholders for this iteration were an operational employee, a director and a C-level director. The Construction Model (CM) was presented and was comprehensively to the operational employee. The information was clear enough to retrieve unmatched responsibilities that could be added to the model using the Elementary Construction Flaw (ECF) notation [10]. The CM presentation on a company and department level was also good for the director and gave the director insight into ECF issues and the interdepartmental communication. Also, wrongly allocated responsibilities were clearly identified and communicated. For a C-level director the CM was not suitable. The mismatch between the knowledge and abstraction level of the stakeholder and the modeller made communication difficult and reduced the benefits of the modelling effort. We successfully added the Flowchart (FC) viewpoint to reflect the initial knowledge and abstraction level of this stakeholder.

The drill-down reporting, as already initiated in iteration B, Sect. 3.2, was further developed. The mental division between functional processes, constructional models, data or application models and value streams and measurements were added to the drill-down order. Aspects within a diagram were coloured. Now a multi-dimensional set of diagrams can represent each view of a stakeholder. This model construct, despite adding complexity, has a positive impact on the Return On Modeling Effort (ROME) [11]. The modelling effort for creating all elements from different viewpoints is relatively low when starting the creation of the model.

The findings in this iteration are:

– Each stakeholder needs his/her own representation. Although a certain level of abstraction might be good for engineering purposes, it can also hinder the stakeholder's understanding of the complete model.

- The order of building the model may be more important than the DEMO course envisages and re-evaluating information during the modelling is inefficient.
- Finding information and highlighting information in an existing DEMO model is not easy. Marking the highlights when the model elements are created is easier.

3.5   Iteration E

For the company in iteration E we built a model of a single operational process. While this process was relatively small, the modelling depth was very high. The modelling aimed at finding optimisation possibilities.

Based on the changes in the previous iterations, our approach to creating the model was different. First, instead of interviewing all stakeholders upfront, the interviews per stakeholder were directly modelled in thirteen interconnected diagrams before the next interview started. These diagrams are Business Layer Diagram (BLD), ALD, Technology Layer Diagram (TLD), FC, OFD, Organisation Construction Diagram (OCD), Process Structure Diagram (PSD), Organisation Hierarchy Diagram (OHD), Actor role Function Diagram (AFD), Actor role Competence Diagram (ACD) and some combinations of the mentioned diagrams. The BLD, ALD and TLD are existing diagrams of ArchiMate, but are now added as default diagrams in our business model analysis; therefore, expanding the viewpoints of the model. FC is also a standard notation. The OHD is an extension to the DEMO diagrams showing the hierarchical ordering of Composite Actor Roles (CARs).

It has been noted that people tend to think in flows. In the applied approach, which we called the eXtended Organisational Essence Revealing (XOER) method, after notation of the sentence in a statement we reveal the implementation (e.g. flowcharts, Business Process Model and Notation (BPMN)) and move from these implementation models towards abstract, constructional models where we write down every step in the analysis. Moreover, this notation supports the thinking of the analyst and above all, the thinking pattern of the user of the model.

Due to the multiple models at various abstraction levels, it appeared to be possible to accommodate all stakeholders. The Flowchart (FC) accommodated the higher and lower management levels, whereas the OCD and Transaction Pattern Diagram (TPD) of the respective aspect models helped to explain and maintain integrity of the model and the processes. In addition, the data model also helped to reveal missing processes and responsibilities in the master data management process. Next to the diagrams that are used to transfer information, the way of presenting these diagrams to the stakeholders also matters. The completeness of the models and the multiple media used to communicate the diagram increased the understanding of the model. Further research is needed to rule out other variables that influence the stakeholders.

The findings in this iteration are:

- Multiple viewpoints accommodate multiple stakeholders with the same information.
- The modelling effort of multiple diagrams is not significantly higher than modelling a single aspect. When more diagrams and aspects are created, they support thinking about the modelling steps. Therefore, only the action needed to create the elements and connections takes up more time. After creation, the extra modelling supports the reproduction of the thoughts.
- The modelling effectiveness towards stakeholders of using multiple viewpoints during modelling is higher when compared to only modelling the two or three DEMO aspect models. When multiple stakeholders receive modelling support, they are able to see the connection between their thoughts and the DEMO models.
- The modelling integrity and completeness of the models is higher when all the models are used at the same time. When using a depth first approach, one might miss model elements when revisiting a process than when handling the entire issue at once.
- Using the breadth first approach gives modelling teams a better chance to work together on the complete model.

4   Extending OER

Where the Organisational Essence Revealing (OER) method does help to reveal the essence, we need to extend the method to reveal more aspects of the current implementation in a single pass. In the last iteration we have practised this extended method and found promising results. The extension of OER to multiple modelling allows for addressing more types of stakeholders with minimal extra effort. This approach eXtended Organisational Essence Revealing (XOER) will be written into a method in our research (Table. 1).

Table 1. Added aspects in iterations

Iteration	0	A	B	C	D	E
Viewpoints (added)	OCD, PSD, OFD, TPT	TPD, Testscript	AFD, SRD	Definitions	ALD, FC, ARD	BLD, TLD, OHD
Process	OER	interactive		interview	written interview	XOER

This multi method approach leads to the question how to integrate these models in a (single) metamodel. As all viewpoints originate from the same information these model components are connected. Though not all viewpoints are found in every iteration, all viewpoints seem to be relevant in certain context. Therefore, we can conclude that the metamodel must be extendible for new elements, relations and viewpoints (Table. 2).

Table 2. Stakeholders and the found representations

Stakeholders	Viewpoints and conventions output	Modelling input
developer	OCD, PSD, SRD, definitions, ALD, TLD	
operational	functional names, definitions, BLD	interview
director	definitions , OCD, BLD	interview
C-level	functions, FC, High level OCD	
manager	definitions, OCD, FC, BLD	interview
vendor	methodology, OFD, OCD, ALD, TLD	data model, process model

5 Conclusions and Future Research

The big challenge in Design and Engineering Method for Organisations (DEMO) visualisation is to be found in the variety of stakeholders. The more types of stakeholders the larger number of viewpoints might be needed. Higher management is the main concern in finding the right set of viewpoints.

To bridge the gap in practice, as educating the whole management level will take a generation, we added a functional concept to the construction model. This is the functional value that the organisation gives to the construction model in its organisation. This one-on-one functional translation is the first step to connect the functional business and construction domains of DEMO.

These were our first steps in the XOER method. Modelling all viewpoints at the same time looks promising as it helps modelling and thinking. The upcoming iteration, which has been started as we write this paper, will help us to make this method describable and educable. It will also be subject to an expert group for validation of the metamodel and the used representations.

References

1. Dietz, J.L.G.: Enterprise Ontology: Theory and Methodology. Springer, Heidelberg (2006). https://doi.org/10.1007/3-540-33149-2
2. Dietz, J.L.G., Hoogervorst, J.A.P.: The discipline of enterprise engineering. Int. J. Organ. Des. Eng. **3**(1), 86–114 (2013)
3. van Aken, J., Andriessen, D.: Handboek ontwerpgericht wetenschappelijk onderzoek. Boom Lemma, Los Angeles (2011). [Handbook for Design Science Research]
4. Recker, J.: Scientific Research in Information Systems: A Beginner's Guide. Springer, Heidelberg (2012). https://doi.org/10.1007/978-3-642-30048-6
5. Nelson, R.R.: It project management: Infamous failures, classic mistakes, and best practices. MIS Q. Exec. **6**(2) (2007)
6. Guerreiro, S., van Kervel, S.J.H., Vasconcelos, A., Tribolet, J.: Executing enterprise dynamic systems control with the demo processor: the business transactions transition space validation. In: Rahman, H., Mesquita, A., Ramos, I., Pernici, B. (eds.) MCIS 2012. LNBIP, vol. 129, pp. 97–112. Springer, Heidelberg (2012). https://doi.org/10.1007/978-3-642-33244-9_7

7. Kervel, S.J.H.V.: Ontology driven Enterprise Information Systems Engineering. Ph.D. thesis (2012); ID: urn:NBN:nl:ui:24-uuid:8c42378a-8769-4a48-a7fb-f5457ede0759; ths:Dietz, J.L.G. - org:TU Delft - dgg:TU Delft, Delft University of Technology
8. Dietz, J.L.G., Barjis, J.: Supporting the demo methodology with a business oriented petri net. In: Fourth CAiSE/ IFIP8.1 International Workshop on Evaluation of Modeling Methods in Systems Analysis and Design (EMMSAD 1999) (1999)
9. Gupta, A., Poels, G., Bera, P.: A proposal of using conceptual models for user story development and maintenance. In: 17th AIS SIGSAND Symposium (2018)
10. Janssen, T.: Enterprise Engineering: Sustained Improvement of Organizations. Springer, Heidelberg (2015)
11. Op't Land, M., Dietz, J.L.G.: Benefits of enterprise ontology in governing complex enterprise transformations. In: Albani, A., Aveiro, D., Barjis, J. (eds.) EEWC 2012. LNBIP, vol. 110, pp. 77–92. Springer, Heidelberg (2012). https://doi.org/10.1007/978-3-642-29903-2_6

Bridging Ontology and Implementation with a New DEMO Action Meta-model and Engine

Magno Andrade[1(✉)], David Aveiro[1,2(✉)], and Duarte Pinto[1(✉)]

[1] Madeira Interactive Technologies Institute, Caminho da Penteada,
9020-105 Funchal, Portugal
magnoandrade43@gmail.com, duartenfpinto@gmail.com
[2] Faculty of Exact Sciences and Engineering, University of Madeira,
Caminho da Penteada, 9020-105 Funchal, Portugal
daveiro@uma.pt

Abstract. We consider current Design and Engineering Methodology for Organizations (DEMO) Action Rules Specification to be unnecessarily complex and ambiguous. Even while using a "structured English" syntax similar to the one used in SBVR, such specifications are: incomplete while not containing enough ontological information to derive a functional implementation; and complex by containing mostly unneeded specifications. We propose a new meta-model for DEMO's Action Model in the form of an EBNF syntax which is being implemented in a prototype that directly executes DEMO models as an Information and Workflow System. This prototype includes an action engine that runs DEMO transactions and the enclosed actions specified in our approach. We are currently integrating Blockly in our solution to allow syntactically correct visual programming of our proposed new Action Rule language that includes constructs to evaluate logical conditions, update the state of internal or external information systems, obtain input and provide output (formatted with WYSIWYG template editor) to users, among others.

Keywords: Enterprise engineering · DEMO · Meta model · Action model · Action rules · Syntax · Workflow · Information systems · Requirements

1 Introduction

Many studies claim that information technology projects fail to meet initial expectations of end users. From [1], where some case studies were developed, a survey with 800 IT managers [2, 3], found that 63% of software development projects failed, 49% suffered budget overruns, 47% had higher than expected maintenance costs and 41% failed to deliver the expected business value and user's expectations.

In [4] from 2019, authors analyse many of the published papers regarding project failure and compile a list of failure factors contributing for this high failure rate. Some of the common causes were unrealistic project objectives, incomplete requirements, lack of stakeholder's and users engagement/involvement, problems in project management and control, insufficient budget, unrealistic expectations, changing

© Springer Nature Switzerland AG 2020
D. Aveiro et al. (Eds.): EEWC 2019, LNBIP 374, pp. 66–82, 2020.
https://doi.org/10.1007/978-3-030-37933-9_5

requirements, requirements and specifications inconsistency, lack of planning, lack of communication, use of new technologies that software developers didn't have adequate experience and expertise, amongst others.

DEMO [5] is a well-established enterprise engineering method associated with a solid collection of theories that aim to contribute to solving the before mentioned problems. However, regardless of how sound DEMO is in theory many open ends remain. One of the clearer examples is the models that are produced and used for isolated efforts for analysing the organization and providing support for discussing changes initiatives. Current practice very commonly leaves out one of the key pillars in the theory and one of the main components – the Action Model (AM) – which indeed is barely used in practice [6]. This happens even though the founder of the methodology himself has considered, in [5] and [7], the AM as the most important model and where all essential model information can be found. It is considered to be the differentiator model of the organization – what makes it unique – and, alone, can be used to derive the remaining three aspect models.

This paper is integrated in a broader research initiative that aims at the development of a software platform having the DEMO methodology as a solid foundation for the production of collaborative-based organizational models and diagrams for the specification of its processes, information flow, responsibilities of both human and software, procedures and other kind of organizational artefacts.

Those models and diagrams should provide an up to date "picture" of the "organizational self" at any given time and in a collaborative fashion, guiding its participants in, (1) supporting the perception of the global reality of the organization [8], (2) supporting the definition and execution of their operational work and (3) supporting the creative process for organizational change [9].

Like our initiative, other widely used approaches such as ArchiMate [10] and BPMN [11] try to tackle most of these goals but suffer from the lack of a solid formal theory behind them and from ambiguous semantics [12, 13].

Our DEMO-based approach, based on sound theory drew some inspiration from the Universal Enterprise Adaptive Object Model (UEAOM) [14], and aims at the generation and execution of DEMO models that capture crucial information of organizational responsibilities and the flows of information, often overlooked in other approaches. Using these easy to share and understand models, with a high level of abstraction, we systematically seek to derive increasingly detailed models for executable workflows and manual work instructions.

In this paper we propose Bridging Ontology and Implementation with a new DEMO Action Meta-Model and Engine by revising the DEMO Action Model and proposing a new meta-model in the form of a EBNF syntax which is currently being implemented in our prototype called DISME (Direct Information Systems Modeller and Executer).

We claim that the current way of specifying Action Rules in DEMO leads to incomplete specifications that, on one hand, do not contain enough ontological information and, on another hand, keep a reasonable amount of ambiguity. With our proposal, we can specify – still on an ontological level – a broader variety of essential details and information to allow an almost direct execution of models. Thus, we contribute to bridge the huge gap between DEMO models and the important implementation problems that arise at project time and which must be specified immediately in conjunction with ontological elements. By combining our approach with a low code platform prototype that we are developing, we aim to contribute to bridge and solve the gaps mentioned in the first paragraphs of this introduction. By having a direct execution of models we highly reduce the time to production of information systems and by using DEMO as a base we have as a starting point a more complete elicitation of requirements, one of the main points of failure in IS projects. We use the EU-rent case presented in [15] to exemplify and validate our contribution.

2 Research Method

The Information Systems Research paradigm adopted in this paper should be considered as a group of three closely related cycles of activities according to Design Science Research by Hevner [16, 17].

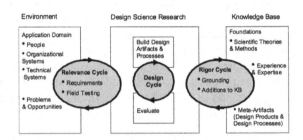

Fig. 1. Design science research cycles [17]

These activities are represented on Fig. 1. Hevner claims that only together these three activities constitute a good design science research and could render a valid output and therefore should not be applied isolated. In our research, and in relation to the first cycle, Relevance, represented in Fig. 1, we identified a clear problem of ambiguity and lack of concise and essential information about the current syntax of the DEMO Action Rules and therefore an opportunity to design a more comprehensive syntax was at hand. In regards of the second cycle of design, we propose a new grammar for DEMO's Action Rules. These rules were obtained after several iterations of exhaustive and comprehensive, design, implementation and evaluation of different grammar and language elements, as well as testing in the action executer engine in our prototype, both with the EU-Rent case and a practical project being developed in a local private company. We propose a new Action Meta Model for DEMO that we claim to allow a more concise, comprehensive and complete way for devising Action Rule Specifications. Finally, concerning the last third cycle, Rigor, the research is supported by the theoretical grounding foundations of DEMO itself.

3 Background and Theoretical Foundations

3.1 DEMO's Operation, Transaction and Distinction Axioms

In the Ψ-theory [18] – on which DEMO is based – the operation axiom [5] states that, in organizations, subjects perform two kinds of acts: production acts that have an effect in the production world or P-world and coordination acts that have an effect on the coordination world or C-world. Subjects are actors performing an actor role responsible for the execution of these acts. At any moment, these worlds are in a particular state specified by the C-facts and P-facts respectively occurred until that moment in time. When active, actors take the current state of the P-world and the C-world into account. C-facts serve as agenda for actors, which they constantly try to deal with. In other words, actors interact by means of creating and dealing with C-facts. This interaction between the actors and the worlds is illustrated in Fig. 3. It depicts the operational principle of organizations where actors are committed to deal adequately with their agenda. The production acts contribute towards the organization's objectives by bringing about or delivering products and/or services to the organization's environment and coordination acts are the way actors enter into and comply with commitments towards achieving a certain production fact [19].

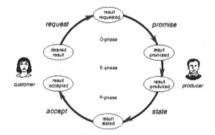

Fig. 2. Basic transaction pattern [5]

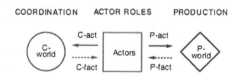

Fig. 3. Actor's Interaction with production and coordination worlds [5]

According to the Ψ-theory's transaction axiom, the coordination acts follow a certain path along a generic universal pattern called transaction [5].

The transaction pattern has three phases: (1) the order phase, were the initiating actor role of the transaction expresses his wishes in the shape of a request, and the executing actor role promises to produce the desired result; (2) the execution phase where the executing actor role produces in fact the desired result; and (3) the result phase, where the executing actor role states the produced result and the initiating actor role accepts that result, thus effectively concluding the transaction.

This sequence is known as the basic transaction pattern, illustrated in Fig. 2, and only considers the "happy case" where everything happens according to the expected outcomes. All these five mandatory steps must happen so that a new production fact is realized. In [19] we find the universal transaction pattern that also considers many other coordination acts, including cancellations and rejections that may happen at every step of the "happy path".

Even though all transactions go through the four – social commitment – coordination acts of request, promise, state and accept, these may be performed tacitly, i.e. without any kind of explicit communication happening. This may happen due to the traditional "no news is good news" rule or pure forgetfulness, which can lead to severe business breakdown. Thus the importance of always considering the full transaction pattern when designing organizations. Transaction steps are the responsibility of two specific actor roles. The initiating actor role is responsible for the request and accept steps and the executing actor role is responsible for the promise, execution and state steps. These steps may not be performed by the responsible actor as the respective subjects, may delegate on another subject one or more of the transaction steps under their responsibility, although they remain ultimately responsible for such actions [19].

The distinction axiom from the Ψ-theory states that three human abilities play a significant role in an organization's operation: (1) the *forma* ability that concerns datalogical actions; (2) the *informa* that concerns infological actions; and (3) the *performa* that concerns ontological actions [5]. Regarding coordination acts, the performa ability may be considered the essential human ability for doing any kind of business as it concerns being able to engage into commitments either as a performer or as an addressee of a coordination act [19]. When it comes to production, the performa ability concerns the business actors. Those are the actors who perform production acts like deciding or judging or producing new and original (non derivable) things, thus realizing the organization's production facts. The informa ability on the other hand concerns the intellectual actors, the ones who perform infological acts like deriving or computing already existing facts. Finally, the forma ability concerns the datalogical actors, the ones who perform datalogical acts like gathering, distributing or storing documents and or data. The organization theorem states that actors in each of these abilities form three kinds of systems whereas the D-organization supports the I-organization with datalogical services and the I-organization supports the B-organization (from Business=Ontological) with informational services [20].

3.2   DISME (Direct Information Systems Modeller and Executer)

DISME [21] is mainly comprised by three modules: (1) a Diagram Editor to create and view DEMO models as well as import and export them to the System Modeller (2) the

System Modeller to adapt and parametrize in detail the information system to the needs of the organization; and (3) the System Executer that runs in production mode the modelled information system.

In the System Modeller, one or more users take upon their selves the administrator role, and are able to shape each process of an organization creating and editing transactions, their relations as well as associating input forms to these transactions, or in specific transactions steps, together with the specification of entity and property types, that is, the main business objects and their attributes or, in other words the database of the system. Forms are dynamically generated by the System Executer component taking in account all specifications and when users are fulfilling their organizational tasks. The users that model the system, have no need for any specific programming skill only some basic knowledge of enterprise engineering modelling which is close to the "language /representation" used within organizations.

In the System Executer, users that have acquired permissions to take part in the transactions do so according to their roles following DEMO's transaction pattern.

The System Executer can be divided itself into two main components, (1) the Dashboard that provides the user interface with which the users interact with on their organizational tasks and (2) the Action Engine, that controls the flow of information according with the transactions and causal links defined in the Action Rules and Transactions and their relations (the equivalent to the Process Step Diagram).

The development of the database behind the prototype solution was heavily influenced by the DEMO way of thinking, trying to capture the essence of an organization's workflow, but without abstracting from their infological and datalogical implementations. One of the goals was to keep the platform as flexible as possible in terms of the editing possibilities available.

3.3 DEMO Action Rules

DEMO Action Rules are the specifications for handling events that actors have to respond to, business rules. The Action Model of DEMO is not comprised by this set of rules alone, but also contains work instructions regarding the execution of production acts both represented in the Action Rules Specification (ARS) [7].

The general form to represent an action rule is <event part> <assess part> <response part>. The event part specifies what event (or set of concurrent events) is responded to. The assess part in an action rule is divided in three sections, corresponding with the three validity claims: the claim to justice, the claim to sincerity, and the claim to truth. And the final part, the response, is divided in an if clause that specifies what action has to be taken if the actor considers complying with the event to be justifiable, and possibly what action must be taken if this is not the case. This way of formulating action rules allows the performer to deviate from the 'rule', if he/she thinks this is justifiable (and for which he/she will be held accountable) [7].

We consider this set of Action Rules Specification to be ambiguous because, although it uses a structured English syntax similar to the one used in Semantics of

Business Vocabulary and Rules [15] it does so in an incomplete way that does not contain all the needed ontological information to derive the implementation from it. For example, it lacks a way do deal with sets of actions or operators as we will approach in further detail on Sect. 3 New Action Rule Syntax – Specification and Implementation. And this set of rules is also complex by containing mostly unneeded specifications of three types of assessment, the justice, sincerity and truth. These claims are developed on the next section where we elaborate on our proposal. This is why we propose a new set of rules Bridging Ontology and Implementation with a new DEMO Action Meta-Model and Engine.

4   New Action Rule Syntax

In the following tables, we present, in EBNF, the current result of our iterations of development of a syntax and constructs for a runnable specification of DEMO Action Rules (Tables 1 and 2).

Table 1. EBNF specification for Action Model (the column separation means the "=") (Part 1)

when	"WHEN" transaction_type "IS" (c-fact | p-fact) action
transaction_type	string (NOTE: has to be a transaction specified in the system)
c-fact	"requested" | "promised" | "stated" | "accepted" | "revoke_request_requested" | "revoke_request_allowed" | "revoke_request_refused" | "revoke_promise_requested" | "revoke_promise_allowed" | "revoke_promise_refused" | "revoke_statement_requested" | "revoke_statement_allowed" | "revoke_statement_refused" | "revoke_acceptance_requested" | "revoke_acceptance_allowed" | "revoke_acceptance_refused" | "rejected" | "declined"
p-fact	"executed"
action	action_type [(assign_expression | causal_link)] {action }
action_type	specify_data | if | while | foreach | "C-ACT" | "WRITE_VALUE" | "READ_VALUE" | "PRODUCE_DOCUMENT" | "CLIENT_OUTPUT" | "EXTERNAL_CALL"
assign_expression	property "=" (constant_value | property_value | math_expression)
math_expression	string (NOTE: a mathematical expression evaluated by the dashboard, in principle produced by blockly mathblocks)
property	string (NOTE: has to be an existent property specified in the internal information system)
constant_value	String

Table 2. EBNF specification for Action Model (the column separation means the "=") (Part 2)

causal_link	transaction_type "[must be]" c-fact min max
min	Integer
max	Integer | *
specify_data	{property [cur_form_compute_code]} - {condition CLIENT_OUTPUT} (NOTE: for each pair (validation) condition+output if condition is true engine goes ahead if not shows CLIENT_OUTPUT)
cur_form_compute_code	ENABLE condition | math_expression
if	"IF" condition "THEN" action ["ELSE" action]
condition	["NOT"] evaluated_expression {("AND" | "OR") condition}
evaluated_expression	comp_evaluated_expression | user_evaluated_expression
comp_evaluated_expression	property operator (property_value | property)
user_evaluated_expression	String (NOTE: dashboard shows this "textual informal expression" that has to be evaluated by the user who will decide on a result of true or false)
property operator	"<" | ">" | "==" | "!=" | "~"
property_value	string (NOTE: can be a numerical value or a possible ENUM value associated to a property)
while	"WHILE" condition action
foreach	"FOREACH" set action
set	set of elements

As we can see in the previous EBNF specification, an action rule occurs in the context of a transaction type in the activation of a particular transaction state. An action rule can lead to the execution of one or more actions of a specific type. Namely, an action might imply a causal link or simply assigning some value to some property in the system. We can have a sequence of one or more actions. For each action, one needs to specify the action type that will imply what concrete operations/instructions will be executed by the action engine. We can also express logical conditions that allow us to design expressions that are evaluated by the engine and determine the path that a certain process instance must take. We can specify an action that will automatically generate a form for user input, that is, for the use to specify some data for a certain process instance. This form will be automatically generated by the dashboard according to the properties associated to the respective action. It's possible to specify, for each property in the form a condition that has to be satisfied/validated so that the process can advance. If the condition is not satisfied it's possible to define a particular output to the user. It's also possible to define simple computations regarding data in the current form. One can also specify traditional "if then else" flows and logical conditions that are evaluated automatically by the engine to control the flow. It's possible also the formulation of "informal expressions" that have to be evaluated by the user as true or false in order for the flow to continue in a certain way or another. While and for each kinds of flows are still not implemented but are planned to be included in our prototype.

The terminal symbols presented as string and set of elements are automatically parsed and interpreted by the action engine of DISME. The set of elements can be a group/array of elements that can be obtained from a customized query that returns a set of elements from the internal and/or external information system.

```
WHEN 'Car drop-off' IS stated
IF ['car is damaged']
THEN
        WRITE_VALUE 'car damage' = true
        C-ACT 'Damage handling' [must be] requested
ELSE
        WRITE_VALUE 'car damage' = false
IF ('current_date' == 'contracted drop-off date')
THEN
        WRITE_VALUE 'late return penalty' = false
ELSE
        WRITE_VALUE 'late return penalty' = true
        WRITE_VALUE 'late return penalty charge' = EXPRESSION
IF ('Actual drop-off branch' == 'Contracted drop-off branch')
THEN
        WRITE_VALUE 'location penalty' = false
ELSE
        WRITE_VALUE 'location penalty' = true
        WRITE_VALUE 'location penalty charge' = EXPRESSION
IF ('late return penalty' = true OR 'location penalty' == true
THEN C-ACT 'Penalty payment' [must be] requested
IF [car drop-off is considered justifiable]
THEN C-ACT 'Car drop-off' [must be] accepted
ELSE C-ACT 'car drop-off' [must be] rejected
```

Fig. 4. Action Rule to handle the state step of transaction Car drop-off

In Fig. 4 we can see an example of an action rule using our newly proposed syntax. After the IF we can find an expression that has to be evaluated by a human user looking physically at the car and comparing to the damage sheet signed at pickup. In case new damage is present a transaction is initiated to handle the issue, but before that, a property in the rental instance of boolean type has the value true written to it. This property works as a flag in the rental entity which is needed for general queries on rentals. We then have a couple of IF instructions where conditions can be automatically evaluated and enacted upon. Different other flags associated to the rental can be updated accordingly and the value of penalty charges can be calculated by mathematical expressions. The rule finishes with a couple more IF instructions, the first to determine if the penalty payment transaction must be requested and the final which provides another expression for the user to decide on the evaluation and eventually accept the transaction even if normally that would not be the case.

To enable the implementation of our new format for action rules in DISME, three components were implemented; (1) the Action Rules Manager, (2) the Action Manager, and (3) the Action Template manager. The above example applying our syntax can be specified in these components as to allow the engine to later interpret the rule. Action Rules Manager and Action manager – these are the components responsible for creating, editing and deleting the action rules for each transaction type and transaction state. As mentioned above one action rule has one or more actions associated. On this component there are multiple functionalities available. We can create new actions associated to that action rule or view actions that were previously created. We next present in Fig. 5 a different and older version of the action rule above, equivalent to the version of the DISME's screen shot provided also ahead as the prototype is currently being adapted to the last version of our syntax presented in this paper.

```
WHEN 'Car drop-off' IS Stated
IF 'Contracted drop-off branch' != 'Actual drop-off branch' THEN
    ATOMIC c-act
        'Penalty payment' [must be] Requested
```

Fig. 5. Example of actions for the action rule handling the state of car drop-off

The above example works as follows, when the "Car drop-off" transaction is in the Stated transaction state, the action type IF is evaluated. If the condition (automatically evaluated by the engine) evaluates to true, the ATOMIC action type c-act is performed.

When using the component Action manager, actions that belong to the action rule selected by the user are displayed. Figure 6 shows the same action rule presented in Fig. 5, but according to the DISME interface. This is the main component where we can add different actions, logical conditions, templates, etc. While on execution mode of DISME, these actions will be interpreted by the engine developed together with the dashboard interface.

Fig. 6. List of actions that belongs to a specific action rule

Action Template Manager – this component is only used together with an action. The purpose of this functionality is to have custom templates for certain actions. Note that each action can have multiple templates but a template can only belong to an action. The engine in DISME uses the specifications inserted into these three components to apply, enforce and control the flow of the transaction and subsequently perform the specified actions. This means that when a user initiates or wants to continue a transaction inside the dashboard, if the transaction has actions associated, the engine analyzes, verifies and interprets the actions associated to an action rule and carries out the respective operations in the context of that particular transaction instance. Some of these actions can be automatically performed by the engine without the need to wait for user input. Actions of type PRODUCE_DOCUMENT and CLIENT_OUTPUT use the templates specified in the Action Template Manager with a WYSIWYG editor that can use properties and values of the underlying information system to either automatically produce a PDF document or output formatted content to the client interface.

DISME allows the specification of entity types and properties in a database like fashion, allowing business users to, in a graphical user interface, specify their business objects and fields. In actions of type specify_data we can select a set of one or more existing properties that need to be specified by user input. The DISME dashboard will automatically render a form based on the input types defined previously in a form editor. After, for example, a successful reservation of a rental, the dashboard can output to the client some formatted text defined in a template and using elements of the filled form and/or other elements from the database.

We now illustrate and present an example of the dashboard interface using the action engine module that interprets our action rule specifications to control the flow.

In this example, we are using the action rule exhibited on Fig. 5, but first we need to explain the flow intended in this process. For this particular example, we will consider that we have only two transactions: T01 – Rental Contracting and T02 – Car drop-off. T02 has an action rule defined that is the same as on Fig. 6.

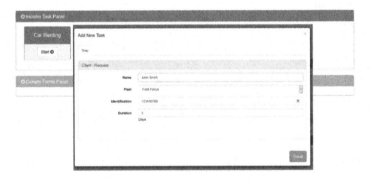

Fig. 7. Car Rental Request

In this process, the first transaction step to be performed is T01 – Request (Fig. 7). After that, transaction T02 is the next to be performed (state Request) and a field is filled by the user. When the state for the transaction T02 is "Stated" the engine module is going to retrieve previously inserted data that has been filled in T01 – Request. This data retrieved by the engine module is the data inserted previously on the field Contracted pick-up branch (T01 – Request) and evaluated with inputted data from another field. This field was filled by the user on the current transaction T02 but on another state (T02 – Request). Thereafter, the engine module decides what path to proceed always having as a base the actions specified in the action rule.

Below we can see an example of the dashboard using these action rules:

Fig. 8. T01 - Rental Contracting and the property field Contracted drop-off branch

One user initiates the transaction T01 and selects the option Lisbon Airport for the field Contracted drop-off branch as shown in Fig. 8.

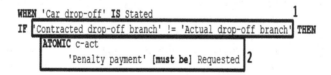

Fig. 9. T01 - Rental Contracting and the property field Contracted drop-off branch

After the initialization of T01, another user initiates the transaction T02 and selects the option Berlin Airport for the field Actual drop-off branch as show in Fig. 9 and presses the green button Continue. When the transaction state "Stated" for the transaction T02 is a fact, the engine will evaluate the expression that is inside rectangle 1 in the following Fig. 10:

```
WHEN 'Car drop-off' IS Stated                                    1
 IF 'Contracted drop-off branch' != 'Actual drop-off branch' THEN
    ATOMIC c-act
           'Penalty payment' [must be] Requested 2
```

Fig. 10. Action Rule used by the engine module after the button Continue is pressed.

Given the example case, the expression will be evaluated as true because the chosen Contracted drop-off branch in T01 and Actual drop-off branch in T02 are different ('Lisbon Airport' ! = 'Berlin Airport') and so the path chosen by the engine module will be the instructions/operations/actions within the THEN block. The instructions within the THEN block are inside rectangle 2 in Fig. 10. With theses instructions/operations/actions, a new instance/transaction of transaction type "Penalty payment" on the state "Request" is created automatically by the engine.

5 Discussion

In the current official standard, the specification of Action Rules is devised with the following structure (see example in Fig. 11): <event part> <assess part> <response part>. Although in [7] it is claimed that action rules specified with the grammar of 'structured English' are very simple, it is also stated that when presenting this grammar to members of the board, some of them appeared to be confused with the explanation of this first action rule.

when	membership start for new Membership is requested	(T1/rq)
	with the member of Membership is some PERSON	
	the starting day of Membership is some DAY	

assess	justice:	the performer of the request is the member of Membership	
	sincerity:	< no specific condition >	
	truth:	the starting day of Membership is the first day of some MONTH;	
		the age of the member of Membership on the starting day of Membership is equal	
		to or greater than the minimal age in the year of the starting day of Membership;	
		the number of members on the starting day of Membership	
		is less than the max members in the year of the starting day of Membership	

if	complying with request is considered justifiable	
then	promise membership start for Membership	[T1/pm]
else	decline membership start for Membership	[T1/dc]

Fig. 11. Action Rule in 'structured English"

One of the problems of this grammar lies at the root of its specification. The author also states that the action rule should be written so we can understand them as formal, this arises that the formulation of these action rules is apparently too formal and difficult to read for people outside the scope of DEMO theory and even to new and inexperienced people using DEMO.

Comparing it to our approach, we can specify a set of actions for an action rule, each with a specific type which denotes what the system should execute/perform in a more simple, literal, structured and systematic way, already oriented to implementation. We argue that the notions of claims to justice, sincerity and truth specified in the <assess part> bring unnecessary complexity and ambiguity. With our approach, actions inside an action rule can be specified as a group of structured acts, some with direct effect on the information system with eventual associated expressions (logical and/or arithmetical) that control the flow of actions. This allows collaborators like system analysts, who are not aware of the social side of DEMO theory expressed in the truth, justice and sincerity claims, to understand and write action rules in a simpler and more powerful way. There is no need to complicate the action rules with the language action paradigm claims as, even with our structure, rules can become somewhat complex in some cases as the example we presented previously in Fig. 4.

Our grammar is more flexible and has many other options and functionalities as compared to the current standard. For example, we can perform inputs and outputs to the client, such as producing documents or showing information which is necessary for the proper and informed functioning of the organization's process. Collaborators acting as analysts can specify actions with the simple constructs of our language which, in their essence and syntax, specify clearly what is intended with them and without the need of knowledge of technical programming languages. DISME's action engine automatically interprets the specified rules and we are currently adapting Google' Blockly platform to our prototype so it's even easier for business analysts to design action rules.

We will now discuss in a more specific and detailed way some aspects of the two grammars of action rules. On Fig. 12, another action rule in the format of the structured English grammar is displayed. The <assess part> doesn't specify causal links in the multiple conditions specified in this part, this does not happen in our grammar because we evaluate and verify in a simple way properties that belong to a certain entity type related to the current action being executed.

when	car drop off **for** Rental <u>is stated</u>		(T4/st)
	with	the actual drop off location of Rental **is some BRANCH**	
assess	*justice:*	the <u>performer</u> of the <u>statement</u> **is the** driver of Rental;	
		the <u>addressee</u> of the <u>statement</u> **is the** car issuer of Rental;	
	sincerity:	< no specific condition >	
	truth:	the actual drop off location of Rental **is the** drop off location of Rental;	
		Today **is less than or equal to the** ending day of Rental	
if	*complying with statement is considered justifiable*		
then	<u>accept</u>	drop off **for** Rental	[T4/ac]
	with	the <u>addressee</u> of the <u>acceptance</u> **is the** driver of Rental;	
else	<u>reject</u>	drop off **for** Rental	[T4/rj]
	with	the <u>addressee</u> of the <u>rejecti</u> **is the** driver of Rental;	
	<u>request</u>	penalty payment **for** Rental	[T5/rq]
	with	the <u>addressee</u> of the <u>request</u> **is the** driver of Rental;	
		the <u>requested production time</u> of penalty payment **for** Rental **is Now**	
		the <u>requested</u> penalty amount of Rental **is equal to**	
		the location penalty charge of Rental **plus the** late return penalty charge of Rental	

Fig. 12. EU-Rent Rule TEOO [7]

Regarding the <truth> claim there is no way of specifying the consequences that can occur if conditions present here are not individually fulfilled; different actions might need to be executed due to different conditions and different values might need to be updated like shown in our example in Fig. 4. If we compare Figs. 12 and 4, we can immediately conclude that syntax and simplicity are not the strength of the current grammar of Action Rules for DEMO and that it is not specified anywhere in the action rule what consequences can arise if the 'Actual drop-off branch' is not the same as the 'Contracted pick-up branch'. The same does not happen in the action rule defined in our grammar, as specified in Fig. 4. We can specify consequences for different conditions depending if they are either true or false. In our example we can call 3 different transactions in a way that would not be possible with current standard syntax.

As mentioned above, each action rule is a set of actions, so for each action inside the action rule, we also define what kind of action (action type) will happen at a certain point in the action rule, for this particular case the consequences that can happen are of the action type WRITE_VALUE as shown on Fig. 4. In this case, if we are within the ELSE block, the 'location penalty' property of the rental will have its value assign automatically to 'true', and on the other hand, the 'location penalty charge' property will have its value obtained from an 'expression', for example this 'expression' can be a mathematical operation between two values, or even two distinct properties.

In the <response part>, that is displayed on the Fig. 13, when an action rule calls for other or multiple transactions, it is not immediately apparent not only which particular condition originates a call to other transactions nor how to handle information, inputs and outputs. It is not clear at all how to do something of this kind in the TEOO [7] grammar. Several parts of the action rule, especially the ones starting with the *with* clause or the justice claim lines are redundant or ambiguous. There should be no need to specify elements such as the addressees or requested production time of a transaction as those elements are automatically part of the context of an instance of a process performing these actions. These add unneeded complexity to the action rule.

if	complying with statement is considered justifiable		
then	accept	drop off for Rental	[T4/ac]
	with	the addressee of the acceptance is the driver of Rental;	
else	reject	drop off for Rental	[T4/rj]
	with	the addressee of the rejecti is the driver of Rental;	
	request	penalty payment for Rental	[T5/rq]
	with	the addressee of the request is the driver of Rental;	
		the requested production time of penalty payment for Rental is Now	
		the requested penalty amount of Rental is equal to	
		the location penalty charge of Rental plus the late return penalty charge of Rental	

Fig. 13. <response part> of the EU-Rent Rule of TEOO. [7]

```
IF ('late return penalty' = true OR 'location penalty' == true
THEN C-ACT 'Penalty payment' [must be] requested
IF [car drop-off is considered justifiable]
THEN C-ACT 'Car drop-off' [must be] accepted
ELSE C-ACT 'car drop-off' [must be] rejected
```

Fig. 14. Excerpt from the action rule in our format

As shown on Fig. 14, our grammar allows a much easier way to understand which actions/conditions lead to calls of other transactions, such as C-ACT 'Penalty payment [must be] requested', and that same transaction type can also have an action rule with its set of actions to be carried out, which will take in account the values written/evaluated as specified. We find the current standard brings also ambiguity with the use of the *some* clause. In the example being analysed, the drop-off branch should be clearly defined by the context/instance at run time and a different specification should be done or not needed at all. It is claimed that DEMO models are supposed to be independent of implementation and/or infological/datalogical aspects. In other works we have been defending that DEMO models allow us an abstraction from reality and a reduction of complexity, but they cannot be separated from reality/implementation and action rules are the perfect spot to realize this connection. DEMO's Construction Model which has the higher level and complete view of a process as a tree of transactions and actor roles indeed is quite abstracted from implementation. But delving onto the domain of business rules and execution, which is addressed on DEMO's Action Rules, there is a dire need for a more systematic and simple connection to reality/implementation. Current use of *with* clauses are in fact connecting to reality/implementation with clauses such as: the requested production time of penalty payment is Now and also dealing with infological/datalogical issues with clauses like the one calculating the penalty amount, so it's only natural that we "walk the last mile" and allow the specification of implementation details in the action rule specifications, to the point of client output, database updates, external calls to other systems, etc. and still in a way that is independent of specific technology. We are in fact allowing a very detailed specification of the implementation model, as per the GSDP [5] philosophy associated with DEMO theories. This model can then be directly run (with no compilation steps) in a live system like our DISME prototype.

6   Conclusions and Future Work

As can be seen from the above discussion, the Action Rule Syntax we propose in this paper is more complete, flexible and easier to read/understand/implement/run.

Our approach is better because we clearly specify what types of action will be undertaken and what inputs or outputs will be made by the system/user, what asynchronous calls to other transactions or IS will be performed. The Action Model is the perfect place to bridge the higher level models (Construction Model and State Model) to the implementation model. As it can be seen by the Action Rules examples in TEOO, specifying action rules in an abstracted way from the implementation leads to complex and impractical rules, especially difficult to interpret due to the orientation to the claims on justice, sincerity and truth. Business analysts should be able to design action rules already thinking and designing implementation issues such as logical rules that control the flow and assigning system properties to forms for input, to logical and arithmetical expressions for evaluation and output. The practical engineering approach we are following allows that, with minimal training on certain language constructs, specialized business analysts are able to "program" the flow of their enterprise in a way that directly connects strategic high level models with low level details of implementation. There are many open ends in our current prototype like how to handle external calls to other systems in the IT environment, either for input our output and we foresee the number and complexity of our action types will for sure increase. However, the philosophy that we follow and was presented in this paper seems to be a promising approach.

References

1. Dalal, S., Chhillar, R.S.: Case studies of most common and severe types of software system failure. Int. J. Adv. Res. Comput. Sci. Softw. Eng. **2**, 341–347 (2012)
2. Shull, F., et al.: What we have learned about fighting defects. In: Proceedings of 8th International Software Metrics Symposium, pp. 249–258 (2002)

3. Zeller, A., Hildebrandt, R.: Simplifying and isolating failure–inducing input. IEEE Trans. Softw. Eng. **28**(2), 183–200 (2002). https://doi.org/10.1109/32.988498
4. Ibraigheeth, M., Fadzli, S.A.: Core factors for software projects success. JOIV: Int. J. Inform. Vis. **3**, 69–74 (2019)
5. Dietz, J.L.G.: Enterprise Ontology: Theory and Methodology. Springer, Heidelberg (2006). https://doi.org/10.1007/3-540-33149-2
6. Dumay, M., Dietz, J.L.G., Mulder, H.: Evaluation of DEMO and the language/action perspective after 10 years of experience. In: Proceedings of LAP 2005 (2005)
7. Perinforma, A.P.C.: The Essence of Organisation: An Introduction to Enterprise Engineering. Sapio Enterprise Engineering, Leidschendam (2015)
8. Aveiro, D., Silva, A.R., Tribolet, J.: Towards a G.O.D. organization for organizational self-awareness. In: Albani, A., Dietz, Jan L.G. (eds.) CIAO! 2010. LNBIP, vol. 49, pp. 16–30. Springer, Heidelberg (2010). https://doi.org/10.1007/978-3-642-13048-9_2
9. Aveiro, D., Silva, A.R., Tribolet, J.: Extending the design and engineering methodology for organizations with the generation operationalization and discontinuation organization. In: Winter, R., Zhao, J.Leon, Aier, S. (eds.) DESRIST 2010. LNCS, vol. 6105, pp. 226–241. Springer, Heidelberg (2010). https://doi.org/10.1007/978-3-642-13335-0_16
10. The Open Group: ArchiMate® 2.1. http://pubs.opengroup.org/architecture/archimate2-doc/
11. Object Management Group: BPMN 2.0. http://www.omg.org/spec/BPMN/2.0/
12. Dijkman, R.M., Dumas, M., Ouyang, C.: Semantics and analysis of business process models in BPMN. Inf. Softw. Technol. **50**, 1281–1294 (2008)
13. Ettema, R., Dietz, J.L.G.: ArchiMate and DEMO – mates to date? In: Albani, A., Barjis, J., Dietz, J.L.G. (eds.) CIAO!/EOMAS -2009. LNBIP, vol. 34, pp. 172–186. Springer, Heidelberg (2009). https://doi.org/10.1007/978-3-642-01915-9_13
14. Aveiro, D., Pinto, D.: Universal enterprise adaptive object model. In: Presented at the 5th International Conference on Knowledge Engineering and Ontology Development (KEOD), Vilamoura, Portugal, September 2013
15. Bollen, P.: SBVR: a fact-oriented OMG standard. In: Meersman, R., Tari, Z., Herrero, P. (eds.) OTM 2008. LNCS, vol. 5333, pp. 718–727. Springer, Heidelberg (2008). https://doi.org/10.1007/978-3-540-88875-8_96
16. Hevner, A.R., March, S.T., Park, J., Ram, S.: Design science in information systems research. Manag. Inf. Syst. Q. **28**, 75–106 (2004)
17. Hevner, A.R.: A three cycle view of design science research. Scand. J. Inf. Syst. **19**, 4 (2007)
18. Dietz, J.L.G.: Is it PHI TAO PSI or Bullshit? Presented at the Methodologies for Enterprise Engineering Symposium, Delft (2009)
19. Dietz, J.L.G.: On the nature of business rules. In: Dietz, J.L.G., Albani, A., Barjis, J. (eds.) CIAO!/EOMAS -2008. LNBIP, vol. 10, pp. 1–15. Springer, Heidelberg (2008). https://doi.org/10.1007/978-3-540-68644-6_1
20. Dietz, J.L.G., Albani, A.: Basic notions regarding business processes and supporting information systems. Requir. Eng. **10**, 175–183 (2005). https://doi.org/10.1007/s00766-005-0002-9
21. Andrade, M., Aveiro, D., Pinto, D.: DEMO based dynamic information system modeller and executer. In: IC3K 2018 (2018)

On Models and Enterprise Architecture

Engineering the Black-Box Meta Model
of Data Exploration

Robert Winter[1]($^{(\boxtimes)}$) and Li Yang[2]

[1] University of St. Gallen, 9000 St. Gallen, Switzerland
robert.winter@unisg.ch
[2] Southwest Petroleum University, Chengdu 610500, China
yangli0027@163.com

Abstract. With an increasing amount and diversity of available data, data exploration is becoming critical for many businesses to create insights for business innovation. From an analysis and design perspective, however, data exploration is still dominated by IT-oriented modeling concepts that make it difficult to engage business users because they are not used to think in terms of (even conceptual) data structures, but rather in terms of business questions, intended insights, decision context, information quality, etc. This study elaborates requirements for conceptualizing data exploration from a business perspective, discusses to what extent existing business-oriented conceptualizations fulfil such requirements, and consolidates promising modeling concepts into a meta model proposal that links purpose, context, domain knowledge, exploration history, business question, available data, user, decision, business insight, presentation and non-user stakeholder as key concepts. The meta model is demonstrated by instantiating it to conceptualize five exemplary data exploration use cases, and first evaluative evidence is presented. The paper closes with a discussion how to transform the proposed meta model into an innovative data exploration analysis and design tool.

Keywords: Data exploration · Meta model · Data blackboxing · User-oriented data modelling · Data use canvas

1 Introduction

In order to leverage the potentials of data for business innovation, three stakeholder groups need to cooperate: business domain experts, data engineers and data scientists. Business experts bring in their domain knowledge and innovation ideas, data engineers bring in their ability to handle complex data models and management systems, and data scientists bring in their business analytics methodological competence. While their educational and disciplinary background usually allows data engineers and data scientists to create "common ground" quite easily, it is much harder to incorporate business domain experts into data exploration analysis and design discussions. It is however business domain experts who usually own budgets, who should drive business innovation and who thus need to understand and design appropriate data exploration options.

© Springer Nature Switzerland AG 2020
D. Aveiro et al. (Eds.): EEWC 2019, LNBIP 374, pp. 85–101, 2020.
https://doi.org/10.1007/978-3-030-37933-9_6

Data exploration is all about developing and testing hypotheses using rich data [1]. Before venturing into any advanced analysis of data, it is essential to study the main features of the data [2, 3]. For an insightful and timely interpretation of data by business domain experts, it appears not to be sufficient to present available data in "conceptual" data models. Data dependencies/references or technical metadata are not only irrelevant to business domain experts, but even obstruct how data could be purposefully identified, combined, analyzed and interpreted.

The business domain expert mindsets focus on how using data to support business goals, usually by decision/objective oriented "local" integration across data from different sources. In contrast, the data engineering and data science mindsets focus mainly on (1) how to analyze and design information systems to manage data and facilitate leveraging data, usually by a holistic representation of dependencies and technical metadata, and (2) how to apply analysis methods and tools to create desired insights. While data engineers and data scientists have their focused modeling approaches for data and analytics, their traditional interface to business domain experts are "conceptual data models". While such models abstract both from technical implementation and analysis details, they focus on "conceptual" data items and their relations/dependencies. Important business aspects such as analysis purpose, underlying business question, decision context, or combination potentials (resulting from compatible data dimensions) are however not covered in most conceptual data models. It is therefore not surprising that many businesses are struggling to create valuable insights from data [3–5]. Our hypothesis is that one of the reasons is a lacking business-oriented conceptual basis that is capable to align analysis potentials with analysis requirements.

While "conceptual" (yet data management and not data use oriented) data models have a long history and are widely used in IS analysis and development, truly business-oriented (i.e. data use oriented) conceptualizations are rare and often not very mature. Therefore, our aim is to advance business-oriented conceptual data modelling by proposing a "black-box" meta model aimed at closing the gap between existing, data management and data use oriented data models on the one side, and business innovation requirements on the other (business domain expert) side. The proposed "black-box" meta model is supposed to

(1) be sufficiently descriptive by allowing discourse not only among business users (such as domain experts, business analysts, decision makers, business management, etc.), but also between business users and implementers [6];

(2) be "data agnostic" by hiding ("black-boxing") not only traditional implementation aspects (logical data design, data types, references, etc.), but also "conceptual" data modeling aspects (associations, dependencies, etc.);

(3) comprehensively cover all important business concerns by supporting different use perspectives such as local business view, business coordination view, legal & compliance, controlling (KPIs), senior management (strategy implementation), etc.

For that purpose, in Sect. 2, a proposal for the "black-box" meta model is introduced and the components are elaborated. In Sect. 3, the proposed meta model is demonstrated by instantiating it to five exemplary data exploration use cases. First evaluative evidence is presented in Sect. 4. Section 5 proposes the "data use canvas", a concrete usage concept for the "black-box" data model in the context of business domain expert interaction with data managers and data scientists. The paper is concluded by a discussion of implications and an outlook on future research in Sect. 6.

2 Developing the "Black-Box" Meta Model for Conceptualizing Data Exploration

2.1 Related Work

We classify related work into approaches for conceptual modeling of (data-driven) decision-making and business-driven conceptual data models. Conceptual decision-making models appear to be too general for data exploration as they try to cover decision-making in a highly generalized form without considering the specifics of data exploration. Conceptual data models which claim to be business-driven, on the other hand, often focus too much on the way data is represented and/or processed in information systems. Although these models do not meet our objectives sufficiently, they are inspiring us and the most suitable ones will be discussed in what follows.

Our overall approach is to integrate the candidate elements from the relevant related work and demonstrate the proposed "black-box" meta model's usefulness by instantiating it to several real-world data exploration use cases. Since they are (a) focusing on business aspects, (b) are not too general for data exploration, (c) are not focusing on a sub-aspect such as decision-making and (d) try to abstract from "technical" conceptualization approaches, the following four proposals are selected:

- CMCD (from Contextual Model to Conceptual Design) Framework [7]
- Goal-Oriented Business Intelligence Decision-Making Framework [8]
- BIM (Business Intelligence Model) [9], and
- Conceptual Modeling Framework for business-driven data analytics [10].

The CMCD framework [7] was proposed for the conceptual modeling of data warehouse systems based on goal models and business process diagrams. It aims to reduce the risk of inaccuracies between business requirement analysis and data warehouse modeling design by building up the formal relationship between contextual requirements analysis and data warehouse conceptual modeling phase. Figure 1 shows our reconstruction of the CMCD Framework's meta model from a data blackboxing perspective.

The Goal-Oriented Business Intelligence Decision-Making framework [8] aims to bridge the gap between the technical data model and decision model. It aggregates goal models and KPIs. Its elements include goals, soft goals, tasks, actors, key performance indicators, and dimensions. Starting from an initial model, iterative refinement helps to develop the conceptualization by expanding data sources and building historical decision trails that informs future models. Figure 2 shows our reconstruction of the meta model of the Goal-Oriented Business Intelligence Decision-Making Framework from a data blackboxing perspective.

BIM [9] aims at bridging the gap between the business and the data used by Business Intelligence technology and helping business users to understand enterprise data. BIM includes concepts such as goals, situations, influences, and indicators which decision-makers are familiar with, and focuses on reasoning about these concepts. BIM reveals the detailed relationship between each component and the reasoning process. Figure 3 shows our reconstruction of its meta model from a data blackboxing perspective.

The Conceptual Modeling Framework for Business-driven Data Analytics [10] is proposed for requirements analysis and design of data analytics systems. It is comprised of three modeling views: business view, analytics design view, and data preparation view. The "Business View" represents an enterprise in terms of strategies, actors, decisions, analytics questions, and required insights. It aims to bridge enterprise strategy and business analytics requirements. Figure 4 shows our reconstruction of its meta model from a data blackboxing perspective.

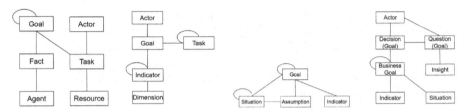

Fig. 1. Meta model of CMCD framework

Fig. 2. Meta model of goal-oriented business intelligence decision-making framework

Fig. 3. Meta model of business intelligence model

Fig. 4. Meta model of the conceptual modeling framework for business-driven data analytic

From a data blackboxing perspective, several elements can be extracted from the four reconstructed meta models. Table 1 summarizes all these concepts. Candidate elements are the ones that we can adopt directly. Referential elements are the ones that we refer to indirectly.

Table 1. Candidate elements for the black-box meta model.

Source model	Candidate elements	Referential elements
CMCD Framework	Goal, Task, Actor, Fact	Resource
Goal-Oriented Business Intelligence Decision-Making Framework	Goal, Task, Indicator, Dimension	Decision Trail
Business Intelligence Model	Goal, Indicator, Situation	
The conceptual modeling framework for business-driven data analytics	Goal, Actor, Question, Insight, Indicator, Situation	Differentiation of Business Goal, Decision Goal and Question Goal

By consolidating all candidate elements, resolving synonyms, and renaming where appropriate, we yield the following set of concepts: Goal, Insight, Indicator, Actor, Fact, Question (merged from Question and Task), Context (substitution for Situation) and Dimension. "Resource" is a general element, motivating the idea of "domain knowledge". "Decision Trail" represents historical decisions, motivating the idea of "exploration history". The differentiation of different goals motivates the idea of hierarchically structuring business purpose.

2.2 Proposed Meta Model

The proposed "black-box" meta model is created by linking all identified concepts to the focal concept Data Exploration (see Fig. 5). The components of the proposed meta model are characterized in the following.

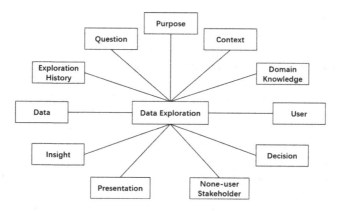

Fig. 5. Black-box meta model of data exploration

Purpose

Every data exploration is motivated by a specific purpose. It is not only important for decision-makers to maintain the fit between purpose data, insights, and actions [11]. Even more importantly, legal requirements such as the GDPR (for protecting personal data in the European Union) require that data can only be analysed for purposes for which they have been collected and which are approved by the data providers [12].

We differentiate between purpose, goal, strategy, and objective. The purpose is the high-level direction of the goals. The goal is what specifically is to be achieved by a data exploration, derived from the purpose. The strategy represents the way by which goals are going to be achieved. The objective relates to the steps and actions being taken to achieve the strategy. Purposes, goals, strategies and objectives correspond to indicators for measuring the achievement. As the business strategies and objectives are usually transformed into a set of indicators (e.g. KPIs, balanced scorecards), we can define the need to be considered and supported in data exploration [5, 13].

Context

Context refers to the information used to characterize the situation of circumstances and facts that are considered relevant to the centre of interest [14, 15]. Generally, context is a prerequisite for interpreting data in a meaningful way [3, 12, 13, 16–21].

The IS discipline needs to develop context-dependent methodologies that strengthen prediction, such as modelling based on the understanding of the business context, identifying variables relevant to analysis context and exploring data in semantical structures, evaluating solutions for questions in the specific business environment, etc. [17–20]. However, the understanding of "context" is often ambiguous and/or generic because "the term has an intuitive meaning for humans" [15, 22]. Thus, an ontological analysis is needed to define a common vocabulary to understand context and to model context elements and their relationships on that foundation [14, 22, 23]. Based on the ontology, we can develop a "context meta-model", which is a "schema for defining the concrete representations of the elements in the ontology" [22].

Domain Knowledge

Domain knowledge is fundamental in decision-making [18, 24] as it is essential to allow understanding a business situation or a problem.

Domain knowledge can be classified into background knowledge and subject knowledge. The background knowledge is general and gained from the experiences. Subject knowledge is specific knowledge of a specialized field. It is valuable within specific situations, but relatively useless outside of its domain. Compared to subject knowledge, background knowledge may or may not be limited to a specific subject, but it contributes to the cognition and understanding of the topic. The combination of background knowledge and subject knowledge help business people to explore data intensively (subject knowledge) with extensive basis (background knowledge). Domain knowledge becomes more important toward the higher layers [19]. Experience, intuition and subject knowledge can help in generating actionable insights substantially [13].

Exploration History

Exploration history refers to relevant past explorations which may have an impact on a current exploration. It is not about using historical data to run analyses, but the exploration behaviour itself. Data exploration is "not characterized by monotonic progress towards a goal, but rather involves much backtracking and opportunistic goal revision" [25]. From data to information to knowledge and then to wisdom, "insights are possible at every step. Looking back and ahead at every phase can make the entire process more effective and meaningful" [26:12]. We need to scrutinize data with fresh and multiple perspectives. Then we evaluate the discovery and receive feedback from others or from ourselves. Not only can we reduce the duplication of work, but the exploration history, along with the continual reassessment, might form a new understanding of the area you explore. Innovation might be generated through accumulated similar projects exploration history. Furthermore, the common data exploration path or norm would be formed in the long run.

Business Question

In data exploration, users are normally fixated on one or more questions. Each analytic insight is a relevant observation derived directly from one or more enquiries [19]. To provide useful insights to support decision-making, formulating key business questions is the first step [27, 28]. Starting from formulating the business questions at hand, not starting from data, is a good and practical approach to data exploration [21, 29].

Business questions can be classified into three subclasses: highly-structured, unstructured, and semi-structured. Highly-structured questions (e.g., How many new customers do we have in the last quarter?) request the least interaction with decision-makers. In contrast, unstructured questions (e.g., Should we seek growth by creating new markets in other countries?) need decision-makers to define the key variable [30]. The questions need to align to the business objectives, then strategies, goals, and purposes. Thus, formulating appropriate business questions is critical for performing analytics, making an informed decision, and eventually creating business value [10].

Data

Data is the object we explore. We consider three facets of data when modelling: dimension, fact and data lifecycle.

Each dataset has dimensions, e.g., sales usually reference a product, a sales channel, a transaction time, etc. Dimensions guide how to drill up, drill down or link facts [21, 31]. Dimension coverage information can help business users to identify questions or data relations, in turn, that have not yet been asked [32].

Facts are often the core of what data exploration is about. We collect, analyse and use the fact and prepare it in a way into actionable information from hindsight and foresight perspectives [16], and then for informed decision-making. If different facts are to be combined, their dimensions and lifecycles need to be aligned.

Data lifecycle defines a set of time-ordered stages of data from "birth to death" [33]. Generally, most business domains are not interested in the entire lifecycle of data [34]. They may only use part of the dataset which is in a specific phase of the entire lifecycle. As the foundation of data exploration, data management based on data lifecycle [2, 25, 33] is essential, because we need to choose "the adequate lifecycle" [2] that matches the business purpose.

User

The term "user" is a generic concept. It is critical to describe the type of users in a specific way [26:192]. In this study, business users can be the ones who analyse the data as a service for other business users ("data scientists"), the ones who explore the data for their own insights ("explorers"), or the ones who use insights to make decisions ("decision-makers"). Data scientists bridge the gap between business domain and IT domain. Explorers bridge the gap between data scientists and decision-makers.

Regardless of their specific role, business users fall into two categories: actors and beneficiaries. Actors actively explore data. They need to understand the data to solve the problems based on actionable insight and informed decision-making. They need to have a good perception of the context and dig the relationship behind the data semantically. Beneficiaries hold specific stakes (often benefits) from data exploration, but not necessarily actively explore data.

(Business) Decision

In data exploration, decision-makers make critical decisions to achieve the objectives and strategies [10]. Guided by the specific business goals, decision-makers make decisions on condition of experience and skills, a particular culture and enterprise background, data capabilities for specific questions [30].

Representing decisions appropriately contributes to managing decisions and exploring decisions. Business Logic can be a good reference: "Business logic is the means by which the business derives conclusions from facts" [35]. The atomic business logic statements consists of three elements: Fact Type, Operator and Operand [35]. For example, Person Employment History (a Fact Type) is (an Operator) Poor (an operand) [35]. The representation deliver accurate and clear business logic. This method can be adopted to structure and represent decisions.

Insight

The insight is discontinuous discovery and understanding about the problem situation, resulting in a new set of beliefs to solve a problem in the user domain [13, 19, 36]. Insight is one of the results which is facilitated from IS, but not created by IS. It is the understanding and interpretation of the IS output made by humans. Getting insight "typically begins by posing questions of the data, often to uncover the 'unknown unknowns'" [4].

Insights are expected through data exploration and can be gained through several methods such as data visualization, statistical analysis, process simulation, building models, generation and testing hypothesis, descriptive, diagnostic, predictive and prescriptive techniques or analytics [16, 29, 30]. There are two models which can contribute to represent insights in the meta model: Anchor model of insight [36] and HIVE framework [19]. The Anchor model reflects that insights are not just about the understanding of situation, but also about how to act differently [36]. The HIVE framework suggests that insight components are hierarchical, from the lower-level Analytic Insight, over the middle-level Synergic Insight, up to the upper-level Prognostic Insight [19].

Presentation

The most common presentations are data visualization and descriptive statistics [37]. Visualization of data help decision-making, not only because represent models visually can inspire better insights, but because visual format are much better understood [29]. The information presented by statistics influence data exploration as well, mainly in whether the key characteristics of the dataset are present entirely.

A taxonomy representing the visualization serves two functions: (1) helping users to comprehensively understand visualization; (2) helping users to adopt the right steps and methods for exploring data. Several efforts to develop data and information visualization taxonomy have been made, including the data type taxonomy for information visualization [38], the taxonomy of visualization techniques [39], and the visual analytic taxonomy for insight provenance [40].

Non-user Stakeholder

Stakeholders can influence decision-making, even if they do not do actively explore data or use the insights directly. Stakeholders like, e.g., customers, may be indirectly involved in all stages of decision-making [41]. However, customers' values are a critical part of business decision landscape. The fact that business intelligence and analytics research leads to unprecedented intelligence on consumer opinion, customer needs, and recognizing new business opportunities is a good demonstration [28]. In addition, customers or auditing bodies may be affected by data exploration based on legal requirements (e.g., GDPR in the European Union) or business governance practice.

3 Demonstration

In the following, we selected five documented data exploration cases to instantiate the proposed meta model for demonstration purposes: corporate banking data exploration [16], hospital data exploration [42], Sydney Olympic Park data exploration [43], patent data exploration [44, 45], and air pollution data exploration [46].

3.1 Case Summaries

The Corporate Banking Data Exploration [16] is based on the Triple A model (Availability, Accessibility and Analytics). In Open Banking, banks perform data exploration on internal and external data. Descriptive exploration provide insights; diagnostic analytics identify the cause of outcomes of past events; predictive analytics predict future events based on historical patterns; prescriptive analytics identify optimal decisions. The elements mapping to the proposed meta model are purpose, question, data, user, insight, and non-user stakeholder. Context and domain knowledge are elements implied in this use case. Exploration history, decision and presentation are not used.

The Hospital Data Exploration [42] explores intensive care unit (ICU) patients including demographics, physical information, disease codes and blood test results for insights. The explorer first proposes questions (e.g. what were age distributions of different diseases?). By interacting with the visualization tool, the explorer analyzes data by different combination of dimensions (e.g. disease, age, BMI) and creates insights. The elements mapping to the proposed meta model are question, data, insight, presentation, and user. Context, exploration history and domain knowledge are elements implied. Purpose, presentation and non-user stakeholder are not used.

The Sydney Olympic Park Data Exploration [43] aims at identifying monitoring gaps and helping to improve monitoring. First, users develop critical questions, e.g. "What are the spatial and temporal patterns of indicators?" They use visual tools to analyze data spatially and temporally. They consider the time factor, which could be seen as relevant to the data lifecycle and compare the results with indicators to make decisions. The elements mapping to the proposed meta model are purpose, question, data, user, insight and presentation. Context, exploration history, domain knowledge and decision are elements implied. Non-user stakeholder is not used.

The goal of Patent Data Exploration [44, 45] is to discover technological trends through patent information in order to gain competitive advantage. The exploration starts by guiding questions, e.g., "Which industry fields have increased the level of attention throughout given periods?" Goals of different steps are differentiated. The formed exploration pattern are used in different domains. As an indicator of patent, patent age is relevant to data lifecycle. Additionally, during the exploration, patent trends of different time periods are compared. Thus, we conclude that data lifecycle is relevant here. The elements mapping to the proposed meta model are purpose, domain knowledge, question, data, user, insight and presentation. Context, exploration history and decision are elements implied. Non-user stakeholder is not used.

The Air Pollution Data Exploration [46] aims to discover the spatio-temporal air pollution information quickly and represent it directly and clearly. Preliminary analysis leads to hypotheses such as relationships between variables or time-related fluctuation of pollutant concentrations. The users verify these hypotheses based on visualization methods. Multi-perspective analyses are performed mainly regarding temporal and spatial. "The time series data" and "separating data according to seasons or year" make data lifecycle a reasonable element. The elements mapping to the proposed meta model are purpose, question, data, user, insight, presentation and non-user stakeholder. Context, domain knowledge, exploration history and decision are elements implied.

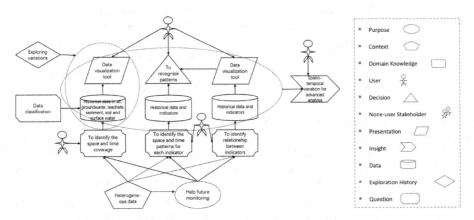

Fig. 6. Meta model instantiation for Sydney olympic park data exploration

3.2 Meta Model Instantiations

We used the above mentioned five data exploration cases to demonstrate the ability of the proposed meta model to capture the essence of data exploration. Due to space restrictions, only two of the instantiations are illustrated here: Sydney Olympic Park Data Exploration (see Fig. 6) and the Patent Data Exploration (see Fig. 7). Three steps were taken: Firstly, appropriate elements of the meta model were selected according to each of the data exploration processes; Secondly, eleven elements of the meta model were notated for the instantiation; Lastly, the data exploration use cases were instantiated by the notations and the exploration processes.

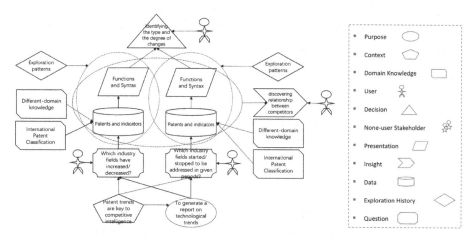

Fig. 7. Meta model instantiation for patent data exploration

Nearly all the proposed meta model components are already covered by these two instantiations. Table 2 comprehensively exhibits how all proposed meta model components have been used in all five data exploration conceptualizations.

We find that: (1) All meta model components have been used; (2) Multiple aspects of data exploration are represented in a comprehensive yet business user-oriented way; (3) Resulting black-box models have a good potential to serve as a boundary object between different business users, and as well between business and IT.

We are also aware of some challenges. Firstly, of particular concern is that "Hypothesis" is a critical element in the Sydney Olympic Park data exploring process, but is not included in the meta model proposal. However, the concept of hypothesis is closely related to questions and insights. Secondly, we have proposed a "Purpose" meta model component which is not used in any data exploration use case. While purpose-related concepts were mentioned in some use cases, it was not differentiated between purpose, goal, strategy and objective – and data privacy considerations were also not considered in these documented cases.

Table 2. Elements of the five data exploration cases mapping to the black-boxing meta model

Use cases	Purpose	Context	Domain know-ledge	Explora-tion history	Question	Data	User	Decision	Insight	Pre-sentation	Non-user stake-holder
Corporate Banking	✓	●	●	✗	✓	✓	✓	✗	✓	✗	✓
Hospital	✗	●	●	●	✓	✓	✓	✗	✓	✓	✗
Sydney Olympic Park	✓	●	●	●	✓	✓	✓	●	✓	✓	✗
Patent	✓	●	✓	●	✓	✓	✓	●	✓	✓	✗
Air Pollution	✓	●	●	●	✓	✓	✓	●	✓	✓	✓

Legend: ✓ represents the elements mentioned explicitly in the use case.

● represents the elements not mentioned explicitly but implicitly in the use case.

✗ represents the elements neither mentioned explicitly nor implicitly in the use case.

4   Evaluation

The discussion of related work, the proposed "black-box" meta model and its five instantiations were presented and discussed in a focus group comprising data management and analysis executives of six large European banks in December 2018. The focus group exists since six years; Its purpose is to discuss and exchange innovative data management and business analytics practices in particular from the perspective of very large organizations on a regular basis. Most participants have the roles of heads of analytics, senior analytics manager, or senior data architects in their organizations – mostly as a part of the bank's IT function.

Table 3. Quantitative evaluation of the meta model proposal

Aspect	++	+	O	–	––
Significance of data blackboxing	6	3	3	0	0
Completeness of objectives	2	8	2	0	0
Appropriateness of proposed meta model components	3	8	0	1	0
Comprehensiveness of proposed meta model	3	7	2	0	0
Simplicity of proposed meta model	0	5	5	1	1
Usefulness of proposal as a "common language"	3	4	5	0	0
Usefulness of proposal as a "checklist"	4	4	3	1	0
Usefulness of proposal to facilitate discussions	3	3	5	2	0

The quantitative evaluation by the twelve bank representatives is summarized in Table 3 (numbers indicate number of votes). Based on this very supportive overall assessment, the focus group suggested for future meta model design iterations to (1) develop a data exploration design method based on the proposal which is centered around the benefits for different involved stakeholder groups, (2) to revisit the differentiation between purpose and question and reconsider simplifications (e.g., for objectives), (3) to elaborate how the additional analysis/design effort is useful for implementing business innovations more efficiently, (4) to consider including (data/information) quality into the meta model, (5) to provide simplified model versions for certain stakeholder groups and (6) to consider developing canvas-like collaboration tools based on the meta model proposal in order to facilitate the notoriously difficult business-IT alignment discussions in large organizations.

5   Using the "Black-Box" Meta Model for Designing Data Exploration

This study aims at facilitating the collaboration of business domain experts, data management experts and data scientists in the context of analyzing and designing data exploration in complex organizations. The involved stakeholder groups have different disciplinary backgrounds and different work practices, but yet need to integrate their expertise to analyze and design data exploration for business innovation. This problem is a nice example for "joint inquiry", i.e. the way how diverse teams try to solve a "wicked" problem [47]. For problems of this type, Avdiji et al. [48] proposed design principles for what they call "visual inquiry tools", i.e. tools that facilitate collaboration among different stakeholder groups and help to find solutions even for complex, "wicked" problems. A very successful example for such a visual inquiry tool is Osterwalder/Pigneurs Business Model Canvas (BMC) [49]. Its ability to facilitate joint inquiry among different stakeholder groups (e.g. production, sales, finance) in the context of business model analysis and design has made it widely adapted and a quasi-standard for business modelling.

In the light of this discussion and the practitioner evaluation finding 6 (canvas-like collaboration tools based on the meta model proposal), the clear consequence is that the proposed "black-box" meta model for data exploration should be implemented as a visual inquiry tool, the "data use canvas" (DUC). Like the BMC was derived from Osterwalder's business model ontology [50], we can use the "black-box" meta model proposed in this study to derive the DUC.

Since, however, canvas-like tools are collaboration tools (that facilitate problem-solving processes) rather than modeling tools (that focus on representation aspects), the canvas derivation is not just a translation of identified concepts into canvas fields. The arrangement of the fields on the canvas, the "use instructions" (for guiding the joint inquiry process) and the "translation rules" (from DUC to data exploration requirements) are much more important for this class of visual tools than for traditional modelling tools. Many "data canvas" proposals appear to be visualized meta models of some aspect of data exploration, but obviously lack the proper design and testing behind successful visual tools for joint inquiry. Many further evaluation rounds and maybe also A/B testing will be needed to develop an effective and efficient visual collaboration support tool from the concepts identified in this study.

6   Conclusions and Outlook

Aimed at facilitating the collaboration of business domain experts, data management experts and data scientists, this paper proposed a meta model for conceptualizing data exploration from a business domain expert perspective. The proposed meta model consists of eleven components: purpose, context, domain knowledge, exploration history, business question, data, user, business decision, insight, presentation, and non-user stakeholder. It captures important "functional", business-oriented aspects of data exploration, thus providing a "black-box" perspective that significantly differs from the more or less data modeling perspective that dominates most existing conceptual models in the field. The meta model has been demonstrated by applying it in five documented real-word data exploration cases - one limitation being that some of the use cases are not business related in a traditional sense. First evaluative feedback is encouraging and, in addition to certain amendments, suggests to propose concrete application practices for the "black-box" model in order to prove its usefulness. Drawing on the rich academic discourse on joint inquiry and visual inquiry tools, we propose to apply existing visual tool design principles to create the "data use canvas", a visual tool that supports business domain experts, data management experts and data scientists to find "common ground" when analyzing and designing data exploration in complex organizations.

Early evaluative evidence supports the claimed innovativeness and usefulness of a business-oriented conceptualization for data exploration, but also points to many extensions and improvements. A second round of instantiations of a next meta model iteration as well as extensive tests of derived "data use canvases" will show whether the presented approach can achieve better collaboration between business domain experts, data management experts and data scientists in large organizations in which data exploration practices and data science competence centers are already established, but which still struggle to integrate the business into analyzing and designing data exploration.

References

1. Winter, R.: Blackboxing data-conceptualizing data-driven exploration from a business perspective. In: Bergener, K., Räckers, M., Stein, A. (eds.) The Art of Structuring, pp. 153–163. Springer, Cham (2019). https://doi.org/10.1007/978-3-030-06234-7_15
2. El Arass, M., Tikito, I., Souissi, N.: Data lifecycles analysis: towards intelligent cycle. In: IEEE ISCV, vol. 1, pp. 1–8. Fez Morocco (2017). https://doi.org/10.1109/isacv.2017.8054938
3. Bumblauskas, D., Nold, H., Bumblauskas, P., Igou, A.: Big data analytics: transforming data to action. Bus. Process Manag. J. **23**(3), 703–720 (2017). https://doi.org/10.1108/BPMJ-03-2016-0056
4. From insight to impact: unlocking opportunities in big data, 18 October 2018. https://www.cgma.org/resources/reports/insight-to-impact-big-data.html
5. Elbashir, M.Z., Collier, P.A., Sutton, S.G., Davern, M.J., Leech, S.A.: Enhancing the business value of business intelligence: the role of shared knowledge and assimilation. J. Inf. Syst. **27**(2), 87–105 (2013). https://doi.org/10.2308/isys-50563

6. Robinson, S., Arbez, G., Birta, L.G., Tolk, A., Wagner, G.: Conceptual modeling: definition, purpose and benefits. In: Yilmaz, L., et al. (ed.) Proceedings of the 2015 Winter Simulation Conference, pp. 2812–2826. IEEE Press, Piscataway (2015). https://doi.org/10.1109/wsc.2015.7408386

7. Chakiri, H., El Mohajir, M., Assem, N.: CMCD: A data warehouse modeling framework based on goals and business process models. In: 2017 IEEE AFRICON, Cape Town, pp. 923–928 (2017). https://doi.org/10.1109/afrcon.2017.8095605

8. Pourshahid, A., Richards, G., Amyot, D.: Toward a goal-oriented, business intelligence decision-making framework. In: Babin, G., Stanoevska-Slabeva, K., Kropf, P. (eds.) MCETECH 2011. LNBIP, vol. 78, pp. 100–115. Springer, Heidelberg (2011). https://doi.org/10.1007/978-3-642-20862-1_7

9. Horkoff, J., et al.: Strategic business modeling: representation and reasoning. Softw. Syst. Model. 13(3), 1015–1041 (2014). https://doi.org/10.1007/s10270-012-0290-8

10. Nalchigar, S., Yu, E.: Business-driven data analytics: a conceptual modeling framework. Data Knowl. Eng. 117, 359–372 (2018). https://doi.org/10.1016/j.datak.2018.04.006

11. LaValle, S., Hopkins, M., Lesser, E., Shockley, R., Kruschwitz, N.: Analytics: the new path to value (2010). https://sloanreview.mit.edu/projects/analytics-the-new-path-to-value/

12. Forgó, N., Hänold, S., Schütze, B.: The principle of purpose limitation and big data. In: Corrales, M., Fenwick, M., Forgo, N. (eds.) New Technology, Big Data and the Law. PLBI, pp. 17–42. Springer, Singapore (2017). https://doi.org/10.1007/978-981-10-5038-1_2

13. Christoffersson, A., Karlsson, C.H.: Developing a framework for business analytics: a structure for turning data into actionable insights. Master's thesis of Chalmers University of Technology, Göteborg, Sweden, Report No. E2015:092 (2015)

14. Sotsenko, A.: A Rich Context Model Design and Implementation. Faculty of Technology, Linnaeus University, Växjö (2017)

15. Antunes, B., Correia, F., Gomes, P.: Towards a software developer context model. In: CEUR Workshop Proceedings, p. 618 (2010)

16. Open Banking Working Group: Data exploration opportunities in corporate banking (2017). https://www.abe-eba.eu/epaper/epaper-data_exploration_opportunities_in_corporate_banking/epaper/ausgabe.pdf

17. Zhao, D.: Frontiers of big data business analytics: patterns and cases in online marketing. In: Liebowitz, J. (ed.) Big Data and Business Analytics, pp. 43–67. Auerbach Publications, New York (2013)

18. Goes, P. Big data and IS research. MIS Q. 38(3), III–VIII (2014)

19. Tan, S., Chan, T.: Defining and conceptualizing actionable insight: a conceptual framework for decision-centric analytics. Presented at the Australasian Conference on Information Systems (2015). arXiv:1605.01032

20. Bohanec, M., Robnik-Šikonja, M., Borštnar, M.K.: Decision-making framework with double-loop learning through interpretable black-box machine learning models. Ind. Manag. Data Syst. 117(7), 1389–1406 (2017)

21. Kohavi, R., Rothleder, N.J., Simoudis, E.: Emerging trends in business analytics. Commun. ACM 45(8), 45–48 (2002)

22. Reichle, R., et al.: A comprehensive context modeling framework for pervasive computing systems. In: Meier, R., Terzis, S. (eds.) DAIS 2008. LNCS, vol. 5053, pp. 281–295. Springer, Heidelberg (2008). https://doi.org/10.1007/978-3-540-68642-2_23

23. Kotte, O., Elorriaga, A., Stokić, D., Scholze, S.: Context sensitive solution for collaborative decision making on quality assurance in software development processes. Front. Artif. Intell. Appl. 255, 130–139 (2013). https://doi.org/10.3233/978-1-61499-264-6-130

24. Hoerl, R.W., Snee, R.D., De Veaux, R.D.: Applying statistical thinking to 'Big Data' problems. WIREs Comput. Stat. 6(4), 222–232 (2014)

25. Derthick, M., Roth, S.F.: Enhancing data exploration with a branching history of user operations. Knowl.-Based Syst. **14**(1–2), 65–74 (2001). https://doi.org/10.1016/S0950-7051(00)00101-5

26. Whitney, H.: Data Insights: New Ways to Visualize and Make Sense of Data. Elsevier/Morgan Kaufmann, Amsterdam (2012)

27. James Bell Associates: Guide to data-driven decision making: using data to inform practice and policy decisions in child welfare organizations. Children's Bureau, Administration for Children and Families, U.S. Department of Health and Human Services, Washington, DC (2018)

28. Chen, H., Roger, H.L.C., Storey, V.C.: Business intelligence and analytics: from big data to big impact. MIS Q. **36**(4), 1165–1188 (2012). https://doi.org/10.2307/41703503

29. Frank, U.: Multi-perspective enterprise modeling: foundational concepts, prospects and future research challenges. Softw. Syst. Model. **13**(3), 941–962 (2014). https://doi.org/10.1007/s10270-012-0273-9

30. Davenport, T.H., Harris, J.G., Delong, D.W., Jacobson, A.L.: Data to knowledge to results: building an analytic capability. Calif. Manag. Rev. **43**(2), 117–138 (2001)

31. Law, P., Basole, R.C.: Designing breadth-oriented data exploration for mitigating cognitive biases, 15 November 2018. http://decisive-workshop.dbvis.de/wp-content/uploads/2017/09/0107-paper.pdf

32. Sarvghad, A., Tory, M., Mahyar, N.: Visualizing dimension coverage to support exploratory analysis. IEEE Trans. Visual Comput. Graph. **23**(1), 21–30 (2017)

33. Plale, B., Kouper, I.: Chapter 4 - The centrality of data: data lifecycle and data pipelines. In: Chowdhury, M., Apon, A., Dey, K. (eds.) Data Analytics for Intelligent Transportation Systems, pp. 91–111. Elsevier (2017). https://doi.org/10.1016/b978-0-12-809715-1.00004-3

34. Hubert Ofner, M., Straub, K., Otto, B., Oesterle, H.: Management of the master data lifecycle: a framework for analysis. J. Enterp. Inf. Manag. **26**(4), 472–491 (2013). https://doi.org/10.1108/JEIM-05-2013-0026

35. A primer on the decision model. https://www.sapiensdecision.com/wp-content/uploads/2016/09/A-Primer-on-The-Decision-Model-1.pdf

36. Klein, G., Jarosz, A.: A naturalistic study of insight. J. Cogn. Eng. Decis. Making **5**(4), 335–351 (2011). https://doi.org/10.1177/1555343411427013

37. El Arass, M., Tikito, I., Souissi, N.: Data lifecycles analysis: towards intelligent cycle. In: Proceeding of The Second International Conference on Intelligent Systems and Computer Vision, ISCV 2017, pp. 1–8 (2017). https://doi.org/10.1109/isacv.2017.8054938

38. Shneiderman, B.: The eyes have it: a task by data type taxonomy for information visualizations. In: Proceedings 1996 IEEE Symposium on Visual Languages, pp. 336–343 (1996). https://doi.org/10.1109/vl.1996.545307

39. Chi, E.H.: A taxonomy of visualization techniques using the data state reference model. In: Proceedings of IEEE Symposium on Information Visualization, pp. 69–75 (2000). https://doi.org/10.1109/infvis.2000.885092

40. Gotz, D., Zhou, M.X.: Characterizing users' visual analytic activity for insight provenance. Inf. Vis. **8**(1), 42–55 (2008)

41. Wee, B., et al.: Data-driven decision-management: a values-focused approach to enable traceable decision analytics for adaptive climate resilience. Paper presented at the ESIP Winter Meeting, Bethesda, MD (2017). https://doi.org/10.6084/m9.figshare.4515722

42. Eichmann, P., Zgraggen, E., Zhao, Z., Binnig, C., Kraska, T.: Towards a benchmark for interactive data exploration. Bull. Tech. Comm. Data Eng. **39**(4), 50–61 (2016)

43. Shao, Q., Li, Y., Campbell, E., De Boer, E.S., Laginestra, E., Statzenko, A.: Statistical visualization for data exploration: a case study on Sydney Olympic Park. Chemosphere **52**(9), 1601–1614 (2003). https://doi.org/10.1016/S0045-6535(03)00500-9

44. Nunes, T., Schwabe, D.: Frameworks for information exploration-a case study. In: Proceedings of the 5th International Workshop on Intelligent Exploration of Semantic Data-IESD, IESD@ISWC, p. 16 (2015)
45. Shih, M., Liu, D., Hsu, M.: Discovering competitive intelligence by mining changes in patent trends. Expert Syst. Appl. **37**(4), 2882–2890 (2010). https://doi.org/10.1016/j.eswa.2009.09.001
46. Li, H., Fan, H., Mao, F.: A visualization approach to air pollution data exploration-a case study of Air Quality Index (PM2.5) in Beijing, China. Atmosphere **7**(3), 35 (2016). https://doi.org/10.3390/atmos7030035
47. Edmondson, A.C., Harvey, J.-F.: Cross-boundary teaming for innovation: integrating research on teams and knowledge in organizations. Hum. Resour. Manag. Rev. **28**(4), 347–360 (2017)
48. Avdiji, H., Elikan, D., Missonier, S., Pigneur, Y.: Designing tools for collectively solving ill-structured problems. In: 51st Hawai'i International Conference on System Sciences (HICSS 51), pp. 400–409. IEEE (2018)
49. Osterwalder, A., Pigneur, Y.: Business Model Generation: A Handbook for Visionaries, Game Changers, and Challengers. Wiley, Hoboken (2010)
50. Osterwalder, A.: The business model ontology-a proposition in a design science approach. Ph.D. thesis, University of Lausanne (2004)

Enterprise Architecture as a Public Goods Dilemma

An Experimental Approach

Jannis Beese, Kazem Haki, Stephan Aier[(✉)], and Robert Winter

University of St. Gallen, 9000 St. Gallen, Switzerland
{jannis.beese,kazem.haki,stephan.aier,
robert.winter}@unisg.ch

Abstract. Enterprise architecture management (EAM) in organizations often requires coping with conflicts between long-term enterprise-wide goals and short-term goals of local decision-makers. We argue that these goal conflicts are similar to the goal conflicts that occur in public goods dilemmas: people are faced with a choice between an option (a) with a high collective benefit for a group of people and a low individual benefit, and another option (b) with a low collective benefit and a high individual benefit. Building on institutional theory, we hypothesize how different combinations of institutional pressures (coercive, normative, and mimetic) affect decision makers' behavior in such conflictive situations. We conduct a set of experiments for testing our hypotheses on cooperative behavior in a delayed-reward public goods dilemma. As preliminary results, we find that normative and mimetic pressures enhance cooperative behavior. Coercive pressure, however, may have detrimental effects in settings that normative and mimetic pressures are disregarded. In future work, we plan to transfer the abstract experimental design of an online-lab experiment into a field experiment setting and thus into the real-world context of EAM.

Keywords: Enterprise architecture · Experiment · Institutional theory · Public goods dilemma

1 Introduction

Organizations are considered as complex sociotechnical systems, in which humans interact with one another and with IT resources to achieve both personal and collective benefits [1]. In large organizations, guiding people and IT resources in the pursuit of multiple, often conflicting goals is a multifaceted endeavor that bears the potential of coordination failures such as free-riding or a lack of trust [2]. Consequently, large organizations require norms, rules, and conventions that enable to resolve goal conflicts between individual, group, and organizational interests, thereby promoting collective welfare [3]. Institutional theory postulates how such norms, rules, and conventions arise and consequently shape organizations [4]. Institutional theory explains how formal and informal institutions define the "rules of the game" [5] that guide the behavior

© Springer Nature Switzerland AG 2020
D. Aveiro et al. (Eds.): EEWC 2019, LNBIP 374, pp. 102–114, 2020.
https://doi.org/10.1007/978-3-030-37933-9_7

of actors in organizations. In particular, institutional theory allows explaining human behavior in complex and conflicting situations [2, 6].

Within the information systems (IS) discipline, Enterprise Architecture Management (EAM) is a prevalent approach to create collective benefits in organizations through architectural coordination i.e., through creating short-term, local benefits in line with long-term, enterprise-wide goals [7]. To this end, EAM needs to not only consider both IT- and business-related components [8], but also the values, norms, and culture that promote cooperative behavior and thus leverage collective benefits [9, 10]. Consequently, there have been several efforts to investigate the institutionalization of EAM in different organizational contexts [11–16]. In general, these studies conclude that the presence of adequate institutional pressures is a prerequisite for achieving desirable EAM outcomes [12, 14, 15, 17]. Considering that real-world institutional environments are highly diverse and conflicted [18, 19], we propose a lab experiment to directly observe how institutional pressures impact cooperative behavior and the achievement of collective benefits in typical EAM scenarios.

In the experiment we thereby focus on goal conflicts between long-term, shared organizational goals and short-term goals of local decision-makers, which is a common issue in institutionalizing EAM [20]. We argue that these EAM-related goal conflicts are similar to abstract public goods dilemmas, in which participants are faced with a choice between two options: (a) a high collective benefit and a low personal benefit, and (b) a low collective benefit and a high personal benefit [2]. As a first step, this paper proposes a specific public goods dilemma, termed delayed-reward public goods dilemma that reflects the challenges observed in the institutionalization of EAM in organizations (i.e., shared long-term benefits vs. local short-term benefits). We then present the results of a pilot experiment, relying on Amazon MTurk [21] to recruit participants. This pilot experiment investigates how different institutional pressures impact cooperative behavior in the abstract delayed-reward public goods dilemma. Thus, we seek to answer the following research question:

RQ: What is the relative effect of different combinations of institutional pressures on cooperative behavior in a delayed-reward public goods dilemma?

In future work, we plan to transfer this public goods dilemma from its artificial lab experiment setting to a more specific EAM context in the field in order to test the applicability of our results to real-world EAM settings. However, we already obtain interesting results from the pilot lab experiment. In particular, we confirm that institutional pressures do not act in isolation, rather there is an interplay among them in affecting human behavior [4]. Specifically, our results show that normative and mimetic pressures generally enhance cooperation. Coercive pressure, however, needs to be employed with care, as it may have devastating effects in settings without adequate normative and mimetic pressures. In such settings, people tend to spend significant resources to sanction the behavior of others without observable benefits, even at the cost of decreasing their own welfare, in addition to decreasing overall group welfare.

2   Theoretical Background and Research Model

In this section, we introduce the theoretical foundation of our research. First, we briefly discuss institutional theory. Then, we argue that many issues in EAM and architectural coordination in organizations may be conceptualized as public goods dilemmas. Finally, we describe the conceptual model that is the basis for our experimental design.

2.1   Institutional Theory

Institutional theory is one of the dominantly used theoretical lenses in examining various IS phenomena [22]. Institutional theory assumes that organizations are social constructions that constantly seek to gain legitimacy in their social context i.e., in order to survive, organizations must adhere to the rules and belief systems prevailing in their environment [5, 23–25].

Institutional theory distinguishes coercive, normative, and mimetic pressures as the central elements that shape behavior in institutions [5]. Each of these pressures delineate distinct mechanisms that, in turn, define the processes by which specific rules, norms, and beliefs gain legitimacy in organizations [18]. Coercive pressure represents a set of mechanisms through which organizations constrain and regularize behavior. It encompasses formally enforced rules and corresponding enforcement mechanisms, such as sanctions for not following the rules. Normative pressure represents social norms, values, and beliefs [26]. The presence of social structure in organizations may range from closely-knit social frameworks that prioritize group welfare, to individualistic environments that emphasize personal interests and achievements [27]. Finally, mimetic pressure reflects the shared conceptions that an organization's actors have about their social reality [26]. Once such shared conceptions have formed in an organization, they determine the frame of reference through which things are perceived [5]. That is, once people have accepted a certain type of behavior to be the default, all other options are compared to this "taken-for-granted" behavior [26]. Therefore, mimetic pressure is evident when actors encounter uncertain situations, in which they unconsciously model themselves on the other actors [18].

In a nutshell, institutional theory posits that coercive, normative, and mimetic pressures constitute the fundamental elements that shape and constrain behavior in organizations [5].

Institutional theory literature, however, often focuses an inter-organizational level of analysis. That is, it aims to explain, why organizations that face the same set of environmental conditions become similar (institutional isomorphism) [28]. Recently, there has been a shift of focus to the individual decision makers in organizations [29–33]. Understanding how individuals interpret and respond to institutional pressures in their organizational context [32], provides an opportunity to better understand institutional processes. In line with these advancements, we take an intra-organizational perspective and examine institutional pressures' effects on individuals' decision making.

2.2 Architectural Coordination as a Delayed Public Goods Dilemma

EAM is concerned with organizing a company's business processes and corresponding technology infrastructure [9, 34]. Common activities include, for example, standardization activities that aim at the enterprise-wide reuse of applications for given business tasks, rather than allowing custom developments within single local units (e.g., departments), which incur unnecessary overhead costs and compatibility issues [34]. The problem in such cases is that, there is often an immediate and direct benefit for an individual local unit to disregard architectural coordination and to make a unilateral IT decision. In contrast, the benefits of EAM are only apparent in the long-term (*delayed*) and shared throughout the organization (*public good*). As an illustration, consider the following excerpt from an EAM case study conducted by Cram et al. [34]:

> *"Interviewees indicated that some business and project leaders were fundamentally at odds with the objectives of the EA process and were unwilling to make financial sacrifices on individual initiatives in order to reap longer-term architectural benefits."*

Thus, major issues in EAM institutionalization may be considered as goal conflicts between long-term, enterprise-wide goals and short-term goals of local units [20].

Behavioral scientists studied similar goal conflicts in abstract public goods dilemmas [2, 6]. In a public goods dilemma, a group of participants is faced with the following scenario: each individual may either contribute to a public good with a high payoff that is shared between group members (receiving less personally but increasing group welfare) or contribute to a private good with a lower payoff (receiving more personally but decreasing group welfare). In the context of EAM and architectural coordination, the benefit from contributing to the public good is not only shared, but also *delayed* (as it takes time to manifest). Consequently, we first test this specific delayed-rewards public goods dilemma in a lab experiment before attempting to transfer extant theoretical knowledge to the EAM context in the field.

For this purpose, we build on research that connects public goods dilemma experiments with institutional theory [e.g., 2, 6]. Regarding the basic public goods dilemma, previous research has repeatedly established that humans behave significantly more cooperative than game theory would rationally predict. Thus, there needs to be something more than pure rationality to explain human behavior. Consequently, behavioral social scientists have tested several variations of the public goods dilemma that correspond to varying institutional pressures. We build on these experiments to develop a conceptual model for our own experiments on the *delayed*-rewards public goods dilemma (see Fig. 1).

Regarding *coercive pressure*, researchers tested the effect of different sanctioning mechanisms on cooperative behavior and thus on collective benefits [35]. A common experiment design gives participants the option to use a part of their own payoff to sanction non-cooperative behavior of other players [36]. Researchers found that this option is frequently used, with the specific frequency depending on the associated costs and the fee-to-fine ratio [35]. Results regarding the collective benefits are mixed, with some studies finding increased collective group welfare [e.g., 6] whereas others find no such benefits or even worse outcomes at the group level [e.g., 37, 38]. Considering these mixed results, we hypothesize an impact, but no specific direction:

H1: *Coercive pressure impacts cooperative behavior in a delayed-rewards public goods dilemma.*

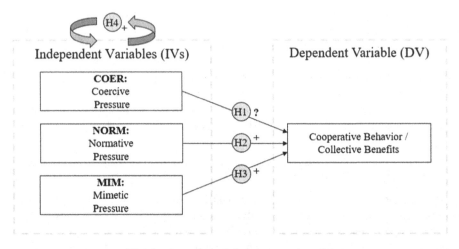

Fig. 1. Overview of the conceptual model

Concerning normative pressure, studies generally find that enhancing communication will increase cooperation [6]. In these experiments, the behavior of participants was tested in settings where people were easily enabled to communicate with one another, compared to settings where communication was difficult or impossible. Introducing normative pressure facilitates the enactment of social structure in public goods dilemmas, which dramatically improves the outcomes of the experiments [6]. Even in settings where all actual choices were completely anonymous, simply enabling people to discuss the optimal strategy, to raise expectations and to voice their frustration in the group, significantly increases cooperation [2]. Therefore, we hypothesize

H2: *Normative pressure increases cooperative behavior in a delayed-rewards public goods dilemma.*

Regarding mimetic pressure, several experiments conclude that providing transparency about the individual contributions to the public good increases observed cooperative behavior [2]. Enabling participants to observe the actions of the other members of their group was found to significantly decrease the percentage of individuals that acted completely egoistic and that never contribute to the public good [39]. Consequently, we hypothesize

H3: *Mimetic pressure increases cooperative behavior in a delayed-rewards public goods dilemma.*

Finally, we expect interaction effects in our setting. For example, existing research found that sanctioning mechanisms are more effective when participants could clearly see that these sanctions were consistently applied to those who did not cooperate or did not contribute to the public good [40, 41]. Similarly, if participants were able to develop their own sanctioning mechanisms (thereby creating a clear frame of reference for expected behavior), these mechanisms were found to be more effective [38]. Thus, we hypothesize

H4: *There are positively reinforcing interaction effects between all institutional pressures.*

3 Methodology

Our primary interest lies in understanding human behavior in a delayed-reward public goods dilemma, because it provides a promising basis for theorizing the institution-alization of architectural rules, norms, and beliefs in organizations [12, 14]. Experimental research helps to understand the theoretical foundations of such questions by enabling researchers to test different variations of variables in a controlled setting [6]. Thus, an experimental approach is suitable to test our hypothesized conceptual model, since we can control for the multitude of other potentially confounding variables that may influence behavior in real-world organizations [3].

One important design dimension for experiments is it level of abstraction from the real-world situation, i.e. its artificiality [42]. Lab experiments on the one hand show a high level of abstraction. They operationalize the precise constructs relevant to the research, and control for everything else. The advantage of such an abstract lab environment is its internal validity—causes and their effects can be clearly associated. Natural field experiments on the other side of the spectrum are more concerned with the predictive power of a theory in foreseeing real-world behavior (external validity) [42]. The differentiation between lab and field experiment, however, is not clear-cut. It is a continuum with lab experiments on the high internal and low external validity end, and natural field experiments on the low internal and high external validity end. In this specific study we chose to design an online-lab experiment with a rather high-level of abstraction. This means we do not involve employees of large organizations in a specific EAM setting in the field. Instead, and as our first step, we abstract from such field settings by purposefully designing an artificial setting for a delayed-rewards public goods dilemma that reflects the specific context of EAM while exactly focusing the constructs of interest.

In line with our theoretical discussion, we treat the three institutional pressures as independent variables and cooperative behavior, measured in terms of collective benefits, as the dependent variable. In the experiments, we thus purposefully vary the presence of the institutional pressures and then, after randomly assigning participants to such a combination of institutional pressures, observe whether participants show increasingly cooperative or non-cooperative behavior.

We employ a baseline public goods dilemma design similar to Amir [43]. Following this design, participants are split into groups of four players (labelled $i = 1...4$) and each player receives an initial endowment $e_{i,1}$ of 50 points. We then conduct an iterative game over ten rounds ($t = 1...10$). During each round t, players simultaneously choose an amount $x_{i,t}$ to invest in the public good; the remainder $y_{i,t} = e_{i,t} - x_{i,t}$ is invested in the private good. The investment in the private good $y_{i,t}$ offers an immediate return of 10%, so that player i will receive $1.1 \cdot y_{i,t}$ in the next round $t+1$. The investment in the public good, however, is paid out over six rounds (5% return each round; total return of 30%) and split evenly among all players. Furthermore, we deduct six points from each player every round to instill a sense of urgency on the players. We measure cooperation via the overall collective benefits of the group. Since more contributions to the public good will lead to a higher collective benefit, this is indicative of cooperative behavior. The presence of coercive pressure is operationalized by giving players the option to spend some of their own payoff to sanction the behavior of other players [6, 37]. We operationalize normative pressure by giving players the option to communicate with each other via a shared chat window that is displayed throughout the experiment [44]. Mimetic pressure is operationalized by making players' choices, payoffs, and punishments visible to all participants, thereby enabling mimetic behavior [2]. Table 1 provides an overview of our construct operationalization for institutional pressures.

We recruited 136 participants (40 participants for the initial baseline experiment and 96 participants to test different combinations of institutional pressures) via Amazon's Mechanical Turk (MTurk) platform, an online labor market that is often employed for behavioral research [21]. Each participant was informed beforehand that they are going to participate in a cooperative decision-making experiment and that their payoff (50¢ plus 1¢ per point above 50 at the end of the experiment) will depend on their own decisions as well as on the decisions of the other participants. Since some participants dropped out during an experiment, we needed to recollect roughly 15% of our data to reach 136 usable data sets.

Table 1. Operationalization of institutional structures

	Coercive	Normative	Mimetic
Not present	No punishment for not contributing to the public good	No communication between participants	Choices and payoffs are anonymous
Present	Participants may sanction other players for their actions	Participants may communicate by chat throughout the experiment	Choices and payoffs/punishments are visible to anyone
Reason	Forced behavior through sanctions and emphasis on direct consequences	Morally governed behavior through communicated expectations	Mimetic behavior through shared logics of action

4   Results of the Pilot Study

Theoretically, the ideal cooperative strategy in any setup is that all players invest everything into the public good from round 1 up until round 8 and invest everything into the private good in rounds 9 and 10. This will yield 90.89 points for each player in the final round. If all players always cooperate (i.e., invest everything into the public good), this will yield 86.69 points at the end, and if all players act purely egoistically (i.e., invest everything into the private good), this will yield 36.42 points. If players always split their investments evenly between the private and the public good, it will yield 61.65 points at the end. Figure 2 shows the calculated results of these strategies.

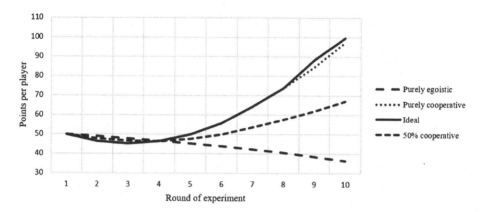

Fig. 2. Overview of calculated payoffs for different cooperative players strategies

We find that the actual behavior of participants in the experiments differs significantly from the game-theoretic prediction. To compare the observed behavior of humans to the theoretical setting, we first tested the baseline experiment (no coercive, normative, and mimetic pressures) with 10 groups (i.e., 40 people). Figure 3 shows the progress of this baseline experiment over ten rounds, displaying the average points per player, the average contribution of a player to the public good, and the standard deviation of the contributions of the players in each round and group.

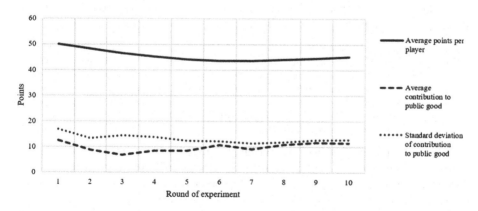

Fig. 3. Progress of the baseline experiment

At the end of the baseline experiment, players had 45.19 points on average, which is significantly less than the ideal collective benefits of 90.89 points, but also significantly more than the purely egoistic outcome of 36.42 points, predicted by game theory. This observation is in line with previous studies that find people contributing to collective benefits, even if no individual incentives are provided [6].

Table 2. Final points; no coercive pressure

	NORM = 0	NORM = 1
MIM = 0	43.96	50.18
MIM = 1	45.90	49.60

Table 3. Contribution; no coercive pressure

	NORM = 0	NORM = 1
MIM = 0	10.37	14.28
MIM = 1	11.73	12.85

Table 4. Final Points; with coercive pressure

	NORM = 0	NORM = 1
MIM = 0	26.83	23.30
MIM = 1	21.16	41.37

Table 5. Contribution; with coercive pressure

	NORM = 0	NORM = 1
MIM = 0	5.93	8.21
MIM = 1	1.27	9.63

Comparing Figs. 2 and 3, we further analyzed the dynamic effects over time in more detail by looking at (i) the average contributions to the public good (indicating cooperation between players) and the standard deviation of contributions to the public good within a group of players (indicating how "unfair" contributions and rewards are spread; see the dotted lines in Fig. 3). At first (rounds 1–3), the overall contribution to the public good decreases. This is not surprising, as early investments only pay off later and due to the 6-point deduction, there is a pressure to keep the points above 50 and the private investment brings an immediate reward. Only after a while, the cumulative benefit of investing in the public good becomes apparent (approximately round 3 to round 6 in Fig. 3), and the investment to the public good slightly increases. Furthermore, the lack of transparency and communication is hindering cooperation in this setting [2]. As one participant wrote in the experiment feedback:

> *"The workers on Amazon Mechanical Turk are mostly here to make money. In these tests of decision-making, all of us almost always choose to keep the points and to NOT share. But, you set up the test so that we lose 6 points on every round, forcing us to share or else go completely bankrupt. I cannot see what the other three are sharing. This is a drawback. I was only able to judge my contribution after the round was finished and all the points were toted up. I tried being very generous; I tried being very stingy. My total points continued dropping. I seemed to benefit the most when I shared 0 points."*

After piloting the baseline experiment, we tested what happens when we add different combinations of the three institutional pressures to the experiment, by conducting an experiment with 3 groups (12 people) per combination of institutional pressures. Tables 2, 3, 4 and 5 show the results of this experiment.

For our analysis, we distinguish the experimental data by the presence of coercive pressure (Tables 2 and 3 without coercive pressure; Tables 4 and 5 with coercive pressure) and we separately consider average final points (Tables 2 and 4, indicating how successfully participants cooperated) and average contributions to the public good (Tables 3 and 5). Within each table, we display the results for normative (NORM) and mimetic (MIM) pressures being present (=1) or not (=0).

First, we find that coercive pressure is indeed used to sanction others, leading to overall less collective benefits for groups in these settings (compare Tables 2 and 4). This is particularly true in settings without mimetic pressure (top right in Table 4), without normative pressure (bottom left in Table 5), and with neither normative nor mimetic pressures (top left in Table 4). A better result is only achieved if all three institutional pressures are present (bottom right in Table 4).

At the end of the baseline experiment, players had 45.19 points on average, which is significantly less than the ideal collective benefits of 90.89 points, but also significantly more than the purely egoistic outcome of 36.42 points, predicted by game theory. This observation is in line with previous studies that find people contributing to collective benefits, even if no individual incentives are provided [6].

On the other hand, if no coercive pressure is present, the difference between the (NORM = 0, MIM = 0)-scenario (43.96 final points, top left in Table 2) and the (NORM = 1, MIM = 1)-scenario (49.60 final points, bottom right in Table 2) is comparatively minor. In this setting (Table 2), there is a benefit both from providing normative pressure (NORM = 0 to NORM = 1) and from providing mimetic pressure (MIM = 0 to MIM = 1), but the relative effect is smaller than in Table 4 (i.e., with coercive pressure).

5 Discussion and Outlook

Using an experimental approach, we can isolate pressures, outlined by institutional theory, that affect cooperative behavior in the institutionalization of EAM in organizations [2]. In sum, we find major differences in cooperative behavior in delayed-reward public goods dilemmas for different combinations of institutional pressures. Furthermore, the received feedback from MTurk participants is similar to issues observed in EAM practice: similar to decisions in the experiment, the desirable EAM outcomes are often delayed, and local decision-makers are often under pressure to solve immediate problems for which they prioritize their own benefits over enterprise-wide benefits [11, 12, 20].

Specifically, we observe that normative and mimetic pressures enhance cooperative behavior (H2 and H3). Coercive pressure, however, needs to be employed with care (H1): emphasizing coercive control is only successful, if people can clearly communicate their actions and intentions, and if the consequences of their actions are transparent (H4). Otherwise, people spent significant resources to sanction the behavior of others without observable benefits, thereby decreasing both their own and the overall groups' welfare.

The experimental setting enables us to analyze how group interactions unfold over time and to understand how participants perceive their situation. An analysis of the chat logs clearly indicated that some experiments in settings with coercive pressure derailed: participants sanctioned other players in their group almost randomly. This happened primarily when the actions of the participants were anonymous. On the other hand, groups that could communicate showed more positive interactions, often starting with simple messages such as "Hi! We need to share to profit from this!".

While the experimental setup with MTurk enabled us to pilot test the design of our experiment and to collect initial data on our hypotheses with arguable high internal validity, its external validity has not yet been tested. This means that it is yet unclear whether our findings hold in and can directly be transferred to real-world EAM contexts. For example, in most organizations face-to-face communication is easily possible, which has been shown to have stronger effects than electronically mediated communication [6, 44]. Similarly, the intrinsic motivation of people in a typical organization differs from the average MTurker [45], which is expected to affect cooperative behavior in an experiment. Consequently, we plan to conduct a follow-up experiment that transfers the basic idea of the delayed-reward public goods dilemma to the EAM context in the field. This experiment will then be conducted with enterprise architects and IT decision-makers, so that we can employ actual EAM case descriptions [12, 46] to derive more realistic goal conflicts and scenarios.

Still, these initial experiments are a valuable contribution because they confirm the anticipated effects in an abstract setting, which is the precondition for entering much more critical experiments with rather scarce domain experts.

References

1. Pache, A.-C., Santos, F.: Inside the hybrid organization: selective coupling as a response to competing institutional logics. Acad. Manag. J. **56**(4), 972–1001 (2013)
2. Ostrom, E.: Collective action and the evolution of social norms. J. Econ. Perspect. **14**(3), 137–158 (2000)
3. Thau, S., Pitesa, M., Pillutla, M.M.: Experiments in organizational behavior. In: Webster, M., Sell, J. (eds.) Laboratory Experiments in the Social Sciences, pp. 433–447. Academic Press, London (2014)
4. Scott, W.R.: Institutional theory: contributing to a theoretical research program. In: Great Minds in Management: The Process of Theory Development, pp. 460–484. Oxford University Press, Oxford (2005)
5. Scott, W.R.: Institutions and Organizations: Ideas, Interests, and Identities, 4th edn. Sage Publications, Thousand Oaks (2014)
6. Ostrom, E.: The value-added of laboratory experiments for the study of institutions and common-pool resources. J. Econ. Behav. Organ. **61**(2), 149–163 (2006)
7. Schilling, R.D., Haki, K., Aier, S.: Dynamics of control mechanisms in enterprise architecture management: a sensemaking perspective. In: Proceedings of 39th International Conference on Information Systems (ICIS 2018), San Francisco, USA (2018)
8. Winter, R., Fischer, R.: Essential layers, artifacts, and dependencies of enterprise architecture. In: Proceedings of EDOC Workshop on Trends in Enterprise Architecture Research (TEAR 2006) within the Tenth IEEE International EDOC Conference (EDOC 2006), Hong Kong, p. 30. IEEE Computer Society (2006)
9. Ross, J.W., Weill, P., Robertson, D.: Enterprise Architecture as Strategy: Creating a Foundation for Business Execution. Harvard Business Press, Boston (2006)

10. Aier, S.: The role of organizational culture for grounding, management, guidance and effectiveness of enterprise architecture principles. Inf. Syst. E-Bus. Manag. **12**(1), 43–70 (2014)

11. Beese, J., Aier, S., Winter, R.: On the role of complexity for guiding enterprise transformations. In: Aveiro, D., Pergl, R., Valenta, M. (eds.) EEWC 2015. LNBIP, vol. 211, pp. 113–127. Springer, Cham (2015). https://doi.org/10.1007/978-3-319-19297-0_8

12. Dang, D.D.: Enterprise architecture institutionalization: a tale of two cases. In: Proceedings of 25th European Conference on Information Systems (ECIS), Guimarães, Portugal, pp. 842–857 (2017)

13. Haki, M.K., Legner, C., Ahlemann, F.: Beyond EA frameworks: towards an understanding of the adoption of enterprise architecture management. In: Proceedings of The 20th European Conference on Information Systems, Barcelona, Spain (2012)

14. Weiss, S., Aier, S., Winter, R.: Institutionalization and the effectiveness of enterprise architecture management. In: Proceedings of 34th International Conference on Information Systems (ICIS 2013), Milano, Italy (2013)

15. Brosius, M., Aier, S., Haki, K., Winter, R.: Enterprise architecture assimilation: an institutional perspective. In: Proceedings of Proceedings of the 39th International Conference on Information Systems (ICIS 2018), San Francisco, USA (2018)

16. Aier, S., Weiss, S.: An institutional framework for analyzing organizational responses to the establishment of architectural transformation. In: Proceedings of 20th European Conference on Information Systems (ECIS 2012), Barcelona, Spain (2012)

17. Winter, R.: Establishing 'Architectural Thinking' in organizations. In: Horkoff, J., Jeusfeld, M.A., Persson, A. (eds.) PoEM 2016. LNBIP, vol. 267, pp. 3–8. Springer, Cham (2016). https://doi.org/10.1007/978-3-319-48393-1_1

18. Scott, W.R.: Institutional carriers: reviewing modes of transporting ideas over time and space and considering their consequences. Ind. Corp. Change **12**(4), 879–894 (2003)

19. Greenwood, R., Raynard, M., Kodeih, F., Micelotta, E.R., Lounsbury, M.: Institutional complexity and organizational responses. Acad. Manag. Ann. **5**(1), 317–371 (2011)

20. Brosius, M., Aier, S., Haki, K.: Introducing a coordination perspective to enterprise architecture management research. In: Proceedings of Trends in Enterprise Architecture Research (TEAR), Quebec City, pp. 71–78. IEEE Computer Society (2017)

21. Mason, W., Suri, S.: Conducting behavioral research on Amazon's Mechanical Turk. Behav. Res. Methods **44**(1), 1–23 (2012)

22. Mignerat, M., Rivard, S.: Positioning the institutional perspective in information systems research. J. Inf. Technol. **24**(4), 369–391 (2009)

23. Powell, W.W., DiMaggio, P.J. (eds.): The New Institutionalism in Organizational Analysis. University of Chicago Press, Chicago (1991)

24. Meyer, J.W., Rowan, B.: Institutionalized organizations: formal structure as myth and ceremony. Am. J. Sociol. **83**(2), 340–363 (1977)

25. Zucker, L.G.: The role of institutionalization in cultural persistence. Am. Sociol. Rev. **42**(5), 726–743 (1977)

26. Kostova, T., Roth, K., Dacin, M.T.: Institutional theory in the study of multinational corporations: a critique and new directions. Acad. Manag. Rev. **33**(4), 994–1006 (2008)

27. Lee, H.S., Griffith, D.A.: Comparative insights into the governance problems of agency theory: the influence of institutional environment on the basic human tenets. AMS Rev. **2**(1), 19–33 (2012)

28. Mizruchi, M.S., Fein, L.C.: The social construction of organizational knowledge: a study of the uses of coercive, mimetic, and normative isomorphism. Adm. Sci. Q. **44**, 653–683 (1999)

29. Cardinale, I.: Beyond constraining and enabling: toward new microfoundations for institutional theory. Acad. Manag. Rev. **43**(1), 132–155 (2018)
30. Powell, W.W., Colyvas, J.A.: Microfoundations of institutional theory In: Greenwood, R., Oliver, C., Sahlin, K., Suddaby, R. (eds.) The SAGE Handbook of Organizational Institutionalism, pp. 276–298. Sage Publications, Thousand Oaks (2008)
31. Powell, W.W., Rerup, C.: Opening the black box microfoundations of institutions. In: Greenwood, R., Oliver, C., Lawrence, T.B., Meyer, R.E. (eds.) The Sage Handbook of Organizational Institutionalism, pp. 311–335. Sage Publishers (2017)
32. Schilke, O.: A micro-institutional inquiry into resistance to environmental pressures. Acad. Manag. J. **61**(4), 1431–1466 (2018)
33. Bitektine, A., Haack, P.: The "macro" and the "micro" of legitimacy: toward a multilevel theory of the legitimacy process. Acad. Manag. Rev. **40**(1), 49–75 (2015)
34. Cram, W.A., Brohman, M.K., Gallupe, B.R.: Addressing the control challenges of the enterprise architecture process. J. Inf. Syst. **29**(2), 161–182 (2015)
35. McCabe, K., Rassenti, S., Smith, V.: Game theory and reciprocity in some extensive form experimental games. Proc. Natl. Acad. Sci. U.S.A. **93**(23), 13421–13428 (1996)
36. Ostrom, E., Walker, J., Gardner, R.: Covenants with and without a sword: self-governance is possible. Am. Polit. Sci. Rev. **86**(2), 404–417 (1992)
37. Dreber, A., Rand, D.G., Fudenberg, D., Nowak, M.A.: Winners don't punish. Nature **452**, 348–351 (2008)
38. Rockenbach, B., Wolff, I.: Designing institutions for social dilemmas. German Econ. Rev. **17**(3), 316 (2016)
39. Bohnet, I., Frey, B.: Social distance and other-regarding behavior in dictator games: comment. Am. Econ. Rev. **89**(1), 335–339 (1999)
40. Cardenas, J.C., Stranlund, J., Willis, C.: Local environmental control and institutional crowding-out. World Dev. **28**(10), 1719–1733 (2000)
41. D'Exelle, B., Coleman, E., Lopez, M.C.: Community-driven reconstruction in Colombia: an experimental study of collective action beyond program beneficiaries. World Dev. **101**, 188–201 (2018)
42. Gupta, A., Kannan, K., Sanyal, P.: Economic experiments in information systems. MIS Q. **42**(2), 595–606 (2018)
43. Amir, O., Rand, D.G., Gal, Y.K.: Economic games on the internet: the effect of $1 stakes. PLoS ONE **7**(2), e31461 (2012)
44. Rocco, E., Warglien, M.: Computer Mediated Communication and the Emergence of "Electronic Opportunism", Techreport, Cognitive and Experimental Economics Laboratory, Department of Economics, University of Trento, Italia (1996)
45. Paolacci, G., Chandler, J.: Inside the turk: understanding Mechanical Turk as a participant pool. Curr. Dir. Psychol. Sci. **23**(3), 184–188 (2014)
46. Haki, M.K., Legner, C.: The dynamics of IS adaptation in multinational corporations: a new theoretical lens. In: Proceedings of 34th International Conference on Information Systems (ICIS 2013), Milano, Italy (2013)

Maturity Assessment of TOGAF ADM Using Enterprise Architecture Model Analysis and Description Logics

Diogo Proença[1]([⊠]) and José Borbinha[1,2]

[1] 1INESC-ID - Instituto de Engenharia de Sistemas e Computadores
Investigação e Desenvolvimento, Lisbon, Portugal
{diogo.proenca,jlb}@tecnico.ulisboa.pt
[2] Instituto Superior Técnico, Universidade de Lisboa, Lisbon, Portugal

Abstract. A Maturity Model represents a path towards an increasingly organized and systematic way of doing business. It is therefore a widely used technique valuable to assess certain aspects of organizations, as for example business processes. A maturity assessment can enable stakeholders to clearly identify strengths and improvement points, and prioritize actions in order to reach higher maturity levels. Doing maturity assessments can range from simple self-assessment questionnaires to full-blown assessment methods, such as those recommended by the ISO/IEC TS 33030 or the SEI SCAMPI. A main caveat of these assessments is the resources they encompass. In addition, many times the lack of automation renders benchmarks not possible. Assuming that the wide spread of Enterprise Architecture practices is making the modeling of business domains a fact, and considering the recent state of the art on the representation of those models as ontologies, this paper proposes how existing semantic technology can be used to automate TOGAF ADM maturity assessment of organizations by automating the analysis of enterprise architecture models in ArchiMate.

Keywords: TOGAF · Enterprise Architecture · Maturity Model · Ontology · Description Logics · ArchiMate · OWL

1 Introduction

A Maturity Model (MM) is a technique that, when applied to relevant aspects of the organizations, can provide: (1) A measuring for auditing and benchmarking; (2) A measuring of progress assessment against objectives; (3) An understanding of strengths, weaknesses and opportunities (which can support decision making concerning strategy and project portfolio management).

Usually a MM consists of a number of "maturity levels", from the lowest to the highest, often five (for example Initial, Managed, Defined, Quantitatively Managed and Optimizing. However, the number of levels can vary, depending on the domain and the concerns motivating the model).

This technique goes back to [1], having great visibility with the Software Engineering Institute Capability Maturity Model Integration (CMMI) [2, 11] and the

D. Aveiro et al. (Eds.): EEWC 2019, LNBIP 374, pp. 115–134, 2020.
https://doi.org/10.1007/978-3-030-37933-9_8

ISO/IEC 15504 [3]. Both these key references were born in the Software Engineering domain, culminating decades of development and refinement of the corresponding models. Moreover, there is certification for these two references, as they are the de facto assessment techniques used when benchmarking organizations for their software engineering process implementation and maturity. As such, in order for the results to be comparable, there is a detailed maturity assessment method behind each of these MMs. These methods detail how to plan and conduct an assessment, how the maturity levels are calculated and how to present the results to the organization. These methods make each assessment repeatable and comparable with results from other organizations, allowing for benchmarking.

In the computer science domain, we can find several definitions for ontologies. One of the most widely used definitions describes ontologies as a "formal, explicit specification of a shared conceptualization" [4]. Conceptualization refers to an "abstract, simplified view of the world" [5], containing "the objects, concepts, and other entities that are assumed to exist in some area of interest and the relationships that hold among them" [6]. The Web Ontology Language (OWL) is a "semantic web language designed to represent rich and complex knowledge about things, groups of things, and relations between things" [7]. Moreover, the use of ontologies and computational inference mechanisms for representing and analyzing Enterprise Architecture (EA) models has already be proven in [8], and the use of such mechanisms for the purpose of supporting maturity assessment methods has been demonstrated in [10].

This paper discusses how to use Description Logics (DL) and EA models expressed as ontologies for the automation of the assessment of a maturity model for TOGAF ADM already proposed in [9]. For that purpose, it introduces the related work on ontologies and DL. Then, based on the findings provided by such analysis, it proposes an architecture template for TOGAF ADM including the ArchiMate models and DL queries necessary to perform the assessment. It then demonstrates the use of such constructs, following the application methods proposed in [10], in real scenarios by performing a maturity assessment to five organizations and detailing the results, which takes advantage of the expressive power of DL for enterprise architecture model analysis and maturity level determination.

The structure of paper is as follows. Section 2 presents related work in the domain of Ontologies and DL. Then, Sect. 3 describes a proposal in terms of how to use EA models analysis and DL to automate MM assessments. A demonstration of the proposal in compliance analysis of specific TOGAF ADM implementations using five organizational scenarios is in Sect. 4. Finally, Sect. 5 presents conclusions on this work.

2 Background

In this section, we describe relevant related work in Ontologies and DL.

2.1 Ontologies

The term ontology originates on the Greek language, being a combination of "ontos" (being) and "logos" (word) [12]. From the perspective of philosophy, ontology is the "systematic explanation of existence" [13]. In the computer science domain, there are several definitions for the term. One of the most widely used definitions is in [4], building upon earlier definitions provided in [14] and [15]. Such definition describes ontologies as a "formal, explicit specification of a shared conceptualization" [4]. According to [5], "conceptualization" refers to an "abstract, simplified view of the world", containing "the objects, concepts, and other entities that are assumed to exist in some area of interest and the relationships that hold among them" [6]. "Explicit" refers to the explicit definition of the "type of concepts used, and the constraints on their use" [4]. "Formal" refers to the fact that the conceptualization "should be machine readable" [4]. "Shared", reflects that the ontology "captures consensual knowledge" shared between several parties [4].

We can classify the uses of ontologies into three categories [16]: human communication, interoperability, and systems engineering. In human communication, ontologies reduce conceptual and terminological confusion and enable shared understandings between "people with different needs and viewpoints arising from their particular contexts" [16]. When used for interoperability ends, it can support the exchange of data with success among heterogeneous sources. When engineering systems, informal (simple) ontologies can be the basis for manual checking of designs against specifications, to improve systems reliability; ontologies can also foster reusability, enabling the reuse of knowledge models in new applications (in this case, ontologies are used to make the underlying assumptions of software component design explicit [12, 16]). An overview of research domains making use of ontologies is in [17], listing for example: "knowledge engineering, knowledge representation, qualitative modelling, language engineering, database design, information modelling, information integration, object-oriented analysis, information retrieval and extraction, knowledge management and organization, and agent-based systems design".

2.2   Description Logics

Description Logics is "a family if knowledge representation formalisms that represent the knowledge of an application domain (the "world") by first defining the relevant concepts of the domain (its terminology), and then using these concepts to specify properties of objects and individuals occurring in the domain (the world description)" [18] and can be seen as a "decidable fragment of first-order logic" [19]. Using this technique, the description of a domain consists of concepts, roles and individuals. Logical statements named axioms make possible to declare relations between roles and concepts. There are several types of DL, which differ on their expressivity. The DL language is $\mathcal{AL}$ which stands for attributive language. $\mathcal{AL}$ is a minimal language which can be seen as a family of languages which are deemed extensions of $\mathcal{AL}$. One example is $\mathcal{ALC}$ which stands for attributive language with complements. $\mathcal{ALC}$ is the most widely used DL in reasoners and is obtained by adding a negation complement operator $(\neg)$ to $\mathcal{AL}$.

Axioms in DL can be of two kinds, terminological or assertional. Terminological axioms describe concepts and properties for the concepts, while assertional axioms are statements compatible with the terminological axioms about individuals belonging to the concepts. A TBox is any finite set of terminological axioms, while an ABox is a finite set of assertional axioms. The TBox and ABox statements make up a knowledge base (KB) and has semantics that make it equivalent to a set of axioms in first-order predicate logic. The most used form of TBox axioms are called general concept inclusions [20]. ABox can contain two kinds of axioms, "one for asserting that an individual is an instance of a given concept, and the other for asserting that a pair of individuals is an instance of a given role" [20].

3   Automated Maturity Model Assessment

Current maturity assessment methods focus on highly complex and specialized tasks performed by competent assessors in an organizational context. These tasks mainly focus on manually collecting evidence to substantiate the maturity level calculation. Because of the complexity of these methods, maturity assessment becomes an expensive and burdensome activity for organizations.

These methods usually start by creating an assessment plan, which describes how to conduct the assessment, as well as, the schedule, people involved, necessary documents and how to collect evidence. Then a group of assessors, denominated assessment team follows the assessment plan, they collect all the necessary evidence, calculate the maturity levels and assemble the assessment report, which details the findings and maturity levels of the assessment. Then, based on the assessment results, the organization can plan for improvement by following an improvement plan.

As such, the objective is to develop methods and techniques to automate maturity assessment. There are several examples of models used to represent an organization architecture, such as, ArchiMate, BPMN or UML. These models are descriptive and can be detailed enough to allow to perform, to some extent, maturity assessment. For example, the collected evidence from an organization can be synthetized into a set of model representations that to use when analyzing and calculating the maturity levels.

However, in order for these models to become relevant for maturity assessment there should be a formal representation for both MMs and model representations.

One hypothesis is that it is possible to represent them as ontologies. Then, by representing MMs and EA models of real organizational scenarios using ontologies we can verify if the organizational models, as represented, match the requirements to reach a certain maturity level using ontology query and reasoning techniques, such as SPARQL and DL inference.

The final objective is thus to identify how these methods and techniques can be used in existing maturity assessment methods, so that they can be relevant to enable the automation of certain aspects of maturity assessment, such as, the maturity level determination. In order to do this, there should be an exploration of what types of analysis can be performed using the information on model representations that is relevant in a maturity assessment effort.

However, in the scope of this paper we focus on the analysis of EA models, modelled in ArchiMate [23], using DL inference. In order to use these techniques there are two perspectives to take into consideration. The MM developer and assessor perspective.

Regarding the developer perspective, we can find several development methods, procedures and design principles, some quite popular among scholars based on their respective citation counts. For example, the general design principles from Roglinger et al. [24], the Design Science Research (DSR) perspective on MMs by Mettler [25], the development guidelines from Maier et al. [26], and the procedure model based on DSR from Becker et al. [27]. For the purpose of this paper, we decided to focus on the development procedure of Becker et al. [27], based on DSR, which, as result, offers a sound methodological foundation, suitable for application in the research approach. This development procedure gives a stringent and consistent approach to the DSR guidelines of Hevner et al. [28].

As depicted in the procedure model in Fig. 1 the first steps focus on the problem identification. First, is the identification and detailing of the research problem, with the specification of the practical relevance of the problem and the justification the value of the artifact. Then follows the comparison with existing MMs. This must use the problem identification of the first step and analysis of existing MM in the domain, which leads to the identification of weaknesses in these models

The next step deals with the determination of the research strategy outlined in this section of the paper. Then follows the iterative MM development. The following steps (5 and 6) is where MM developers can incorporate the type of analysis detailed in this paper. Step 5, conception of transfer and evaluation is where developers develop the assessment criteria to use for the assessment of the MM. During this step, and in order to be able to use these techniques, developers should identify all the criteria possible to assess through EA model analysis. Then, in step 6, implementation of transfer media, developers can develop software tools that will incorporate the criteria identified in step 5 as suitable for assessment using DL inference to automate, in part or fully, the assessment. The last step evaluates the MM against the requirements.

Finally, regarding the MM assessor perspective, we can find two main assessment methods in literature. The first is the Software Engineering Institute Standard CMMI Appraisal Method for Process Improvement (SEI SCAMPI [29]) and the ISO/IEC TS 33030 Assessment Method [30]. SCAMPI as the name suggests is the appraisal method used by CMMI to perform assessments and is depicted in the top half of Fig. 2. It contains three main tasks (1) Plan and Prepare for Assessment, (2) Conduct Appraisal, and (3) Report Results. It is possible to decompose these steps into several sub-steps not relevant for the purpose of this paper. The ISO/IEC TS 33030 assessment method is composed of seven main steps as depicted in the bottom half of Fig. 2. As can be seen in Fig. 2 there is a correlation between the steps of both assessment methods as these have a common background behind their development [2].

From an assessor perspective and regarding these two assessment methods, the technique proposed by this paper regarding the use of EA models analysis and DL inference can be useful while conducting the appraisal (in SCAMPI) and while performing the Data Validation and Process Attributes Rating (in ISO/IEC TS 33030). In the Data Validation step assessors can benefit from this technique to validate if a certain EA model developed during the data collection is sound and complete to calculate the maturity levels. Finally, in the Process Attributes Rating assessors can benefit from these techniques as a way to automate the determination of the maturity levels and as way to substantiate the maturity levels determination.

One aspect to take into consideration is that the best scenario is that MM developers begin planning to use this technique right when the MM is in the development stage. In this way, MM developers can guarantee that the assessment criteria are verifiable by analyzing EA models and using DL inference.

In order to use the techniques proposed in this paper we created two possible methods for governing the instantiation of the artefacts presented in this paper. From a MM developer viewpoint, these methods have the purpose of translating existing maturity assessment questionnaires into an ontology and then translating the assessment questions into DL queries which answers will be provided by reasoning engines over the ontology. From a MM assessor viewpoint, these methods enable them to instantiate a specific MM ontology and collect the assessment results for a given MM.

The roles associated with these methods activities are the following: (1) *Maturity Model Developer* is responsible for developing the MM and creating the assessment questionnaire that will be used by the architect to develop a template architecture model; (2) *Architect* is responsible for formalizing the assessment questionnaire into a template architecture model, to make sure that the template faithfully represents the assessment questionnaire and to verify the ontology converted from the architecture models is complete and correct; (3) *Ontology Engineer* is responsible for converting the architecture models into an ontology and translating the assessment questions into DL Queries over the ontology; and (4) *Assessor* is responsible for performing a maturity assessment, instantiate the architecture model template, executing the DL queries over the instantiated architecture models, execute reasoners over populated ontologies of specific MMs, analyze and collecting the assessment results.

The first method (Method 1), depicted in Fig. 3, goal is to develop the Architecture Model Template and DL Queries for a specific MM for use when assessing real organizational scenarios. This method can either be used when developing a new MM or by using an existing MM. It starts with Identification of the Assessment Questions by the MM Developer. An Architect can then use these questions to develop the Architecture Model Template, which must be fully aligned with the language used in the Assessment Questions and must be enough to satisfy all the assessment criteria. The Architecture Model Template is then converted to an ontology by an Ontology Engineer. Finally, follows the development of the DL Queries to assess a given scenario according to the assessment questions and the Architecture Model Template.

The second method (Method 2) goal is to support the assessment of specific organizational scenarios using the Architecture Model Template and DL Queries developed with the specific purpose of supporting the assessment of a MM. This method starts with assessor instantiating the Architecture Model Template. Then follows the conversion of the Instantiated Architecture Models into an ontology. Then, using the DL Queries already developed for this MM and the Architecture Model Template, the Assessor performs an analysis of the results and determines the one or more maturity levels according to the MM definition.

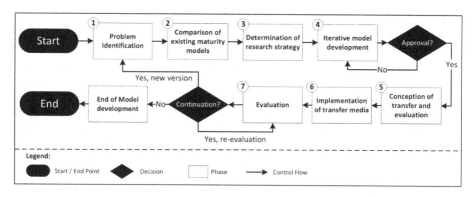

Fig. 1. Procedure model of the research approach (adopted from Becker et al. [27])

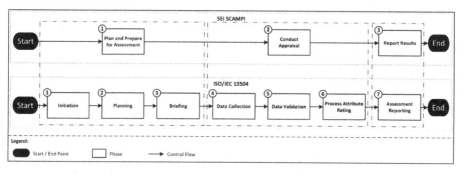

Fig. 2. Maturity Models Assessment Methods (SEI SCAMPI [29] and ISO/IEC TS 33030 [30])

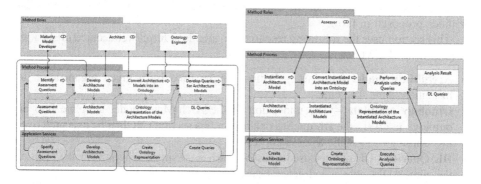

Fig. 3. Instantiation Methods (Method 1 on the left and Method 2 on the right)

4 Demonstration Using the TOGAF ADM

TOGAF [21] is a high-profile EA, providing methods and tools to support architecture development. It comprises seven modules that can be partly used independently of each other. The core of TOGAF is the Architecture Development Method (ADM) and the Architecture Content Framework.

The ADM is a cyclical process structured in nine phases, as shown in Fig. 4. After a preliminary phase in which the context, relevant guidelines, standards and the architecture process goal are identified, the main process begins with the elaboration of an architecture vision and the principles that should guide the architecture. This provides the basis for developing the business architecture, information systems architecture, and technology architecture.

On this basis, solutions are developed, and migration and implementation are planned and governed. Finally, Architecture Change Management ensures that the architecture continues to be fit for purpose. The ADM can be adapted for various purposes, and in more complex situations, the architecture can be scoped and partitioned so that several architectures can be developed and later integrated using an instance of the ADM to develop each one of them.

This section demonstrates the use of the computational inference mechanisms that can be used together with ontologies for assessing the TOGAF ADM maturity in organizations according to the assessment criteria defined by the maturity model proposed in [9]. In order to demonstrate the utility of this proposal, first we applied the instantiation method 1 previously described in Sect. 3. This means that we developed the ArchiMate template (examples of the template are provided in Figs. 6, 7, 8, 9, 10, 11, 12, 13 and 14) used for the assessment of a given organizational scenario, as well as, the translation of the assessment questions into DL queries to use to gather the final assessment results. Examples of the DL Queries are depicted in Table 2.

It presents the ArchiMate template used for the assessment of a given organizational scenario, as well as, the translation of the assessment questions into DL queries that can then be used to gather the final assessment results, following the instantiation methods proposed in [10].

This section uses the following resources (available at http://web.tecnico.ulisboa.pt/diogo.proenca/EEWC.rar):

- **ArchiMate model template** – Which can be used by a given organization to instantiate their scenario;
- **Ontology template** – The translation of the ArchiMate model template into an ontology in OWL, the DL queries detailed in this section can then be executed over this ontology to get the assessment results;
- **DL Queries** - DL queries used to assess each assessment criterion for the each of the eight ADM phases and general questions.

Table 1 details the DL queries used to verify which ADM phases to assess. In case any of these queries cannot be executed this means that specific business function is not available in the organization and in turn results in that ADM phase not being assessed for that organization.

Figure 5 details the business process overview of all the maturity dimensions. In the middle is the enterprise architecture development business function which contains the business functions for all the maturity dimensions according to the phases of TOGAF ADM. The enterprise architecture development business function is associated with the four business functions that are used to assess maturity levels 4 and 5 according to the general assessment questions.

Figures 6, 7, 8, 9, 10, 11, 12, 13 and 14 detail the business process view for the preliminary and architecture vision phases of the ADM. The other each of the six ADM phases and the general questions used to assess maturity levels 4 and 5 for all dimensions of the maturity model can be found in the ArchiMate model template available at the URL provided earlier. It contains all the business processes, business objects and relations deemed necessary to assess that specific ADM phase according to the assessment questionnaire detailed by the TOGAF ADM maturity model [9].

Table 2 details examples of the DL queries used to assess each assessment criterion for the each of the eight ADM phases and general questions. In case any of these queries cannot be executed this means that specific assessment criterion is not achieved. For a complete collection of the DL Queries please check the PDF file available at the URL detailed previously.

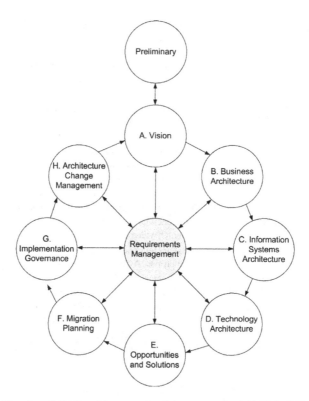

Fig. 4. TOGAF architecture development method (ADM) [21].

For each assessment criterion there is an identifier that is defined as "ADM Phase (First Letter)" "Maturity Level". "Criterion ID", as an example the second criterion for maturity level 3 of the preliminary phase would be "P3.2". In this sense, "P" stands for the preliminary phase, then "A" to "H" stands for each of the ADM phases according to Fig. 4. Then, "R" stands for the requirements management phase. "RA" is used for the assessment criteria of the requirements management dimension that applies to all ADM phases. On the other hand, "RM" is used for the assessment criteria specific to the requirements management ADM phase. Finally, "GL" is used for each criterion belonging to the general questions.

This means, that for a given phase, if all the DL queries for a given maturity level and the levels below return a result, the organization achieves that maturity level in that phase. For example, if an organization is compliant with all the criteria for maturity levels 2 and 3 in the preliminary phase it will achieve maturity level 3 for the preliminary phase. This also means that the DL queries for maturity levels 2 and 3 for the preliminary phase were correctly executed over the ontology representation of the enterprise architecture models of the organization.

Table 1. DL queries to check which ADM phases to assess.

Dimension	DL query
Preliminary Phase	BusinessFunction and {Preliminary_Phase} and componentOf value Enterprise_Architecture_Development
Architecture Vision	BusinessFunction and {Architecture_Vision} and componentOf value Enterprise_Architecture_Development
Business Architecture	BusinessFunction and {Business_Architecture} and componentOf value Enterprise_Architecture_Development
Information Systems Architecture - Data Architecture	BusinessFunction and {Information_Systems_Architecture_-_Data_Architecture} and componentOf value Enterprise_Architecture_Development
Information Systems Architecture - Application Architecture	BusinessFunction and {Information_Systems_Architecture_-_Application_Architecture} and componentOf value Enterprise_Architecture_Development
Technology Architecture	BusinessFunction and {Technology_Architecture} and componentOf value Enterprise_Architecture_Development
Opportunities and Solutions	BusinessFunction and {Opportunities_and_Solutions} and componentOf value Enterprise_Architecture_Development
Migration Planning	BusinessFunction and {Migration_Planning} and componentOf value Enterprise_Architecture_Development
Implementation Governance	BusinessFunction and {Implementation_Governance} and componentOf value Enterprise_Architecture_Development
Architecture Change Management	BusinessFunction and {Architecture_Change_Management} and componentOf value Enterprise_Architecture_Development
Requirements Management	BusinessFunction and {Requirements_Management} and componentOf value Enterprise_Architecture_Development

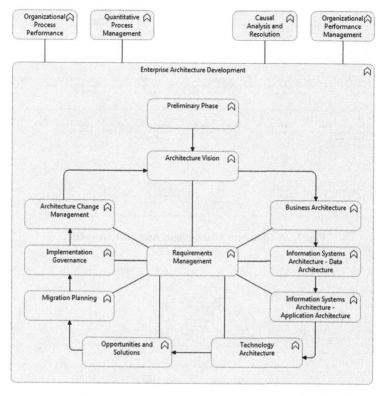

Fig. 5. TOGAF ADM Overview ArchiMate template.

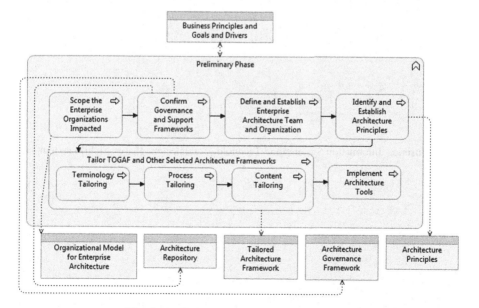

Fig. 6. Preliminary phase ArchiMate template.

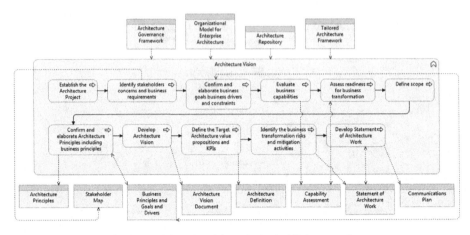

Fig. 7. Architecture vision phase ArchiMate template.

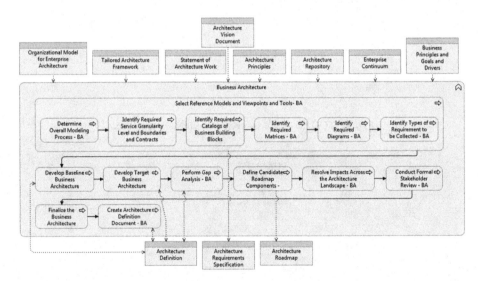

Fig. 8. Business, Information Systems and Technology architecture phases ArchiMate template.

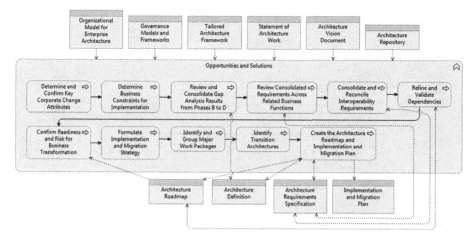

Fig. 9. Opportunities and solutions phase ArchiMate template.

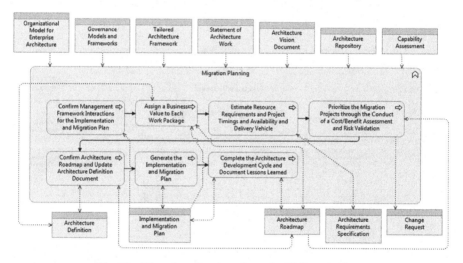

Fig. 10. Migration planning phase ArchiMate template.

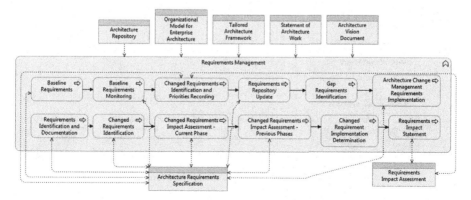

Fig. 11. Requirements management phase ArchiMate template.

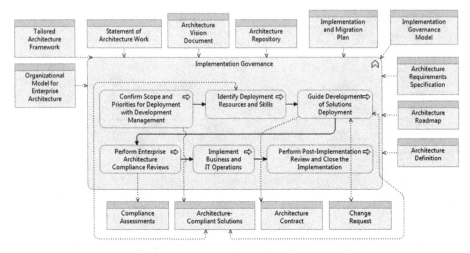

Fig. 12. Implementation governance phase ArchiMate template.

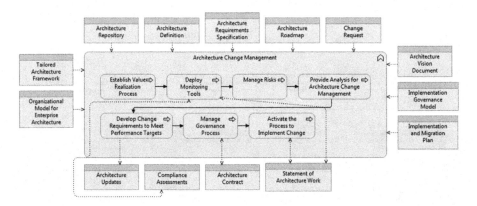

Fig. 13. Architecture change management phase ArchiMate template.

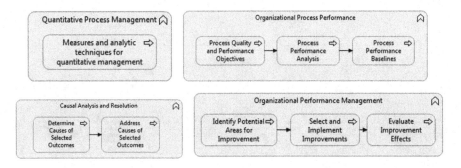

Fig. 14. General questions ArchiMate template.

Following this first step, we created five real organizational scenarios by following the instantiation method 2. Each organizational scenario was instantiated in ArchiMate using this maturity model's architecture model template, which was then converted into an ontology in OWL that resulted in one ArchiMate model and one OWL ontology for each scenario which are available at http://web.tecnico.ulisboa.pt/diogo.proenca/EEWC.rar.

Next is an overview of each of the five organizational scenarios:

- **Organization Alpha (α)** as the public institute responsible for promoting and developing administrative modernization. Its operation is structured into three axes: customer service, digital transformation and simplification.
- **Organization Beta (β)** as part of the business sector that produces and supplies goods and services that require high security standards, namely: coins, banknotes, and documents, such as, citizen's card and passports.
- **Organization Gamma (γ)** as a public higher education institution.
- **Organization Delta (δ)** as a public institution for scientific and technological research and development whose purpose is to contribute to the creation, development and diffusion of research in fields related to civil engineering.
- **Organization Omega (ω)** as a private organization which focus on software development and maintenance providing services all over the globe.

For each of these five organizations we took the role of assessors, instantiated the Architecture Model template to its organizational scenario, then used a converter to create the ontology representation of that architecture model, which resulted in an OWL file for each organization. Then, in each ontology representation of the organizations, the DL queries were executed, and the results analyzed which resulted in the assessment results depicted in Table 2.

In order to achieve a certain maturity level, the organization must comply with all the criteria for that specific level and the levels below, which means that an organization at maturity level 3 complies with all the criteria for maturity levels 2 and 3.

Table 3 details the final enterprise architecture maturity levels determined through the analysis of the results of DL queries and the maturity level determination rules defined by the maturity model. "OS" means that TOGAF ADM phase is out of the scope of the assessment.

These scenarios showed the utility of the constructs proposed by this work as a technique that can be used to assess TOGAF ADM maturity in organizational scenarios. The assessment criteria defined in the maturity model were translated to DL queries that can then be used over architecture models of specific scenarios, with the use of computational inference, to gather the assessment results for that scenario.

These results are useful to identify weak points and strengths for each scenario. Using the assessment results, it is then possible for organizations to identify points of improvement which can then lead to the creation of an improvement plan.

Table 2. Examples of DL Queries for Maturity Assessment of the TOGAF ADM.

Criterion	DL query
Dimension: Architecture Capability	
ADM Phase: P - Preliminary	
P2.1	BusinessProcess and {Scope_the_Enterprise_Organizations_Impacted} and hasAccessTypeWrite value Organizational_Model_for_Enterprise_Architecture and componentOf value Preliminary_Phase
P2.2	BusinessProcess and {Implement_Architecture_Tools} and componentOf value Preliminary_Phase
P3.1	BusinessProcess and {Confirm_Governance_and_Support_Frameworks} and hasAccessTypeWrite value Architecture_Governance_Framework and hasAccessTypeWrite value Architecture_Repository and componentOf value Preliminary_Phase
P3.3	BusinessProcess and {Identify_and_Establish_Architecture_Principles} and hasAccessTypeWrite value Architecture_Principles and componentOf value Preliminary_Phase
ADM Phase: A - Architecture Vision	
A2.1	BusinessProcess and {Identify_stakeholders_concerns_and_business_requirements} and hasAccessTypeWrite value Stakeholder_Map and componentOf value Architecture_Vision
A2.2	BusinessProcess and {Evaluate_business_capabilities} and hasAccessTypeWrite value Capability_Assessment and componentOf value Architecture_Vision
A2.3	BusinessProcess and {Assess_readiness_for_business_transformation} and hasAccessTypeRead_Write value Capability_Assessment and componentOf value Architecture_Vision
Dimension: Architecture Development	
ADM Phase: B, C, D – Business, Information Systems and Technology Architecture	
B/C/D 2.1	BusinessProcess and {Identify_Required_Catalogs_of_Data_Building_Blocks} and componentOf some (BusinessProcess and {Select_Reference_Models_and_Viewpoints_and_Tools_-_DA} and hasAccessTypeRead_Write value Architecture_Requirements_Specification and componentOf value Information_Systems_Architecture_-_Data_Architecture)
B/C/D 2.2	BusinessProcess and {Identify_Required_Matrices_-_DA} and componentOf some (BusinessProcess and {Select_Reference_Models_and_Viewpoints_and_Tools_-_DA} and hasAccessTypeRead_Write value Architecture_Requirements_Specification and componentOf value Information_Systems_Architecture_-_Data_Architecture)
Dimension: Transition Planning	
ADM Phase: E – Opportunities & Solutions	
E2.1	BusinessProcess and {Determine_Business_Constraints_for_Implementation} and componentOf value Opportunities_and_Solutions
E2.2	BusinessProcess and {Consolidate_and_Reconcile_Interoperability_Requirements} and hasAccessTypeRead_Write value Architecture_Requirements_Specification and componentOf value Opportunities_and_Solutions
E2.3	BusinessProcess and {Refine_and_Validate_Dependencies} and hasAccessTypeRead_Write value Architecture_Roadmap and componentOf value Opportunities_and_Solutions
ADM Phase: F – Migration Planning	
F2.1	BusinessProcess and {Assign_a_Business_Value_to_Each_Work_Package} and hasAccessTypeRead value Implementation_and_Migration_Plan and hasAccessTypeRead_Write value Architecture_Roadmap and componentOf value Migration_Planning
F2.2	BusinessProcess and {Estimate_Resource_Requirements_and_Project_Timings_and_Availability_and_Delivery_Vehicle} and hasAccessTypeRead_Write value Architecture_Requirements_Specification and componentOf value Migration_Planning
F3.1	BusinessProcess and {Confirm_Management_Framework_Interactions_for_the_Implementation_and_Migration_Plan} and hasAccessTypeRead value Implementation_and_Migration_Plan and componentOf value Migration_Planning

(continued)

Table 2. (*continued*)

Criterion	DL query
Dimension: Architecture Governance	
ADM Phase: G – Implementation Governance	
G2.1	BusinessProcess and {Identify_Deployment_Resources_and_Skills} and hasAccessTypeRead_Write value Architecture-Compliant_Solutions and componentOf value Implementation_Governance
G2.2	BusinessProcess and {Implement_Business_and_IT_Operations} and componentOf value Implementation_Governance
G3.1	BusinessProcess and {Confirm_Scope_and_Priorities_for_Deployment_with_Development_Management} and hasAccessTypeWrite value Architecture-Compliant_Solutions and componentOf value Implementation_Governance
ADM Phase: H – Architecture Change Management	
H2.1	BusinessProcess and {Manage_Governance_Process} and hasAccessTypeRead_Write value Architecture_Contract and componentOf value Architecture_Change_Management
H2.2	BusinessProcess and {Activate_the_Process_to_Implement_Change} and hasAccessTypeRead_Write value Statement_of_Architecture_Work and componentOf value Architecture_Change_Management
H3.1	BusinessProcess and {Establish_Value_Realization_Process} and componentOf value Architecture_Change_Management
H4.1	BusinessProcess and {Deploy_Monitoring_Tools} and hasAccessTypeRead_Write some (BusinessObject and {Architecture_Updates, Statement_of_Architecture_Work}) and componentOf value Architecture_Change_Management
Dimension: Architecture Requirements Management	
ADM Phase: R – Requirements Management; A – ADM steps	
RA2.1	BusinessProcess and {Requirements_Identification_and_Documentation} and hasAccessTypeRead_Write value Architecture_Requirements_Specification and componentOf value Requirements_Management
RA2.2	BusinessProcess and {Changed_Requirements_Identification} and hasAccessTypeRead_Write value Architecture_Requirements_Specification and componentOf value Requirements_Management
RA2.3	BusinessProcess and {Changed_Requirement_Implementation_Determination} and componentOf value Requirements_Management
RA3.1	BusinessProcess and {Changed_Requirements_Impact_Assessment_-_Current_Phase} and hasAccessTypeRead_Write value Architecture_Requirements_Specification and componentOf value Requirements_Management
ADM Phase: R – Requirements Management; M – Requirements management steps	
RM2.1	BusinessProcess and {Changed_Requirements_Identification_and_Priorities_Recording} and hasAccessTypeRead_Write some (BusinessObject and {Architecture_Requirements_Specification, Requirements_Impact_Assessment}) and componentOf value Requirements_Management
RM2.2	BusinessProcess and {Requirements_Repository_Update} and hasAccessTypeRead_Write value Architecture_Requirements_Specification and componentOf value Requirements_Management
RM3.1	BusinessProcess and {Baseline_Requirements} and hasAccessTypeRead_Write value Architecture_Requirements_Specification and componentOf value Requirements_Management
Dimension: General	
GL4.1	BusinessProcess and {Process_Quality_and_Performance_Objectives} and componentOf some (BusinessFunction and {Organizational_Process_Performance} and association value Enterprise_Architecture_Development)
GL4.2	BusinessProcess and {Measures_and_analytic_techniques_for_quantitative_management} and componentOf some (BusinessFunction and {Quantitative_Process_Management} and association value Enterprise_Architecture_Development)
GL5.1	BusinessProcess and {Identify_Potential_Areas_for_Improvement} and componentOf some (BusinessFunction and {Organizational_Performance_Management} and association value Enterprise_Architecture_Development)
GL5.2	BusinessProcess and {Select_and_Implement_Improvements} and componentOf some (BusinessFunction and {Organizational_Performance_Management} and association value Enterprise_Architecture_Development)

Table 3. Maturity assessment results - Final maturity levels.

TOGAF ADM phase	α	β	γ	δ	ω
Dimension: Architecture Capability					
Preliminary Phase	ML5	ML2	ML3	ML3	ML4
Architecture Vision	ML5	ML2	ML3	ML2	ML4
Dimension: Architecture Development					
Business Architecture	ML5	ML4	ML2	ML3	ML4
Information Systems Architecture - Data Architecture	ML5	OS	OS	ML3	ML4
Information Systems Architecture - Application Architecture	ML5	OS	OS	ML3	ML4
Technology Architecture	ML5	OS	OS	ML3	ML4
Dimension: Transition Planning					
Opportunities and Solutions	ML5	ML2	ML2	ML3	ML4
Migration Planning	ML5	ML2	ML2	ML3	ML4
Dimension: Architecture Governance					
Implementation Governance	ML5	ML4	ML3	OS	ML2
Architecture Change Management	ML5	ML4	ML3	OS	ML2
Dimension: Architecture Requirements Management					
Requirements Management	ML5	ML4	OS	ML3	OS

5 Conclusion

This paper presented an approach for maturity assessment of the TOGAF ADM using EA model analysis and DL. For that purpose, we present an analysis of the related work in ontologies and DL reasoning, concluding that such techniques are in fact relevant for our purpose.

Based on those findings, a proposal is presented for taking advantage of ontologies in the representation, extension, and analysis of EA models for the purpose of supporting the assessment of TOGAF ADM maturity based on an existing maturity model for this purpose. An EA model template, expressed in ArchiMate, with the purpose of assessing the TOGAF ADM maturity in organizations is presented, as well as, the set of DL queries used to assess a given organizational scenario that must be executed over an ontology representation of that EA model template. This demonstrates the proposal of how to formalize the assessment criteria in an existing maturity model and how to verify the compliance to those assessment criteria. Next, we detailed how to use this template and DL queries, by assessing five synthetic scenarios and detailing the assessment criteria that was satisfied and the final maturity levels for each scenario.

Despite the capabilities brought to table by ontologies, we must acknowledge limitations. There are different types of analysis that rely on different types of techniques that offer features not always possible with ontologies. One example of such limitation is that the quality of the analysis is dependent on the quality of the information captured in the EA model. By quality of the information we refer to the detail, amount, accuracy, or others, depending on the objective and scope of the MM assessment, this provides an insight on the effectiveness of the approach.

Future work will focus on developing a system that allows MM developers to upload their MMs as well as, the assessment criteria, expressed in DL queries to verify the compliance of an organizational scenario against the MM assessment criteria. Users can then log into this system select the MM which they which to assess their organization against and provide the EA models deemed necessary by the MM developer to get an assessment report that can then be used as an input for an improvement plan.

Work is already ongoing and a first version of this system, named Maturity Model Architect (MMArch) [22] is available at http://web.tecnico.ulisboa.pt/diogo.proenca/MMArch/ (Username: "TestUser"/Password: "TestUser_pwd!").

This first version was developed using the Microsoft .NET framework, and SQL Server and supports the instantiation methods proposed in [10].

The developed solution is a web application that provides a maturity assessment repository that allows users to create and manage maturity models. After creating a maturity model, users can assign maturity dimensions, maturity levels, capabilities and assessment criteria to the maturity model. Users can also export the maturity model definition to OWL. This feature is useful for maturity model developers to develop DL queries used to assess the assessment criteria and also as way to execute reasoners over the ontology.

The maturity assessment center allows user to assess their organization against the maturity models in the repository. Users can create a new maturity assessment against any of the public maturity models in the repository. After finishing the assessment, users can get the results of the assessment and export the maturity assessment to OWL.

The OWL export feature allows users to export the maturity model definition or a maturity assessment according to a maturity model definition to OWL, by means of an automatic mechanism.

References

1. Nolan, R.L.: Managing the computer resource: a stage hypothesis. Commun. ACM **16**, 399–405 (1973)
2. Ahern, D.M., Clouse, A., Turner, R.: CMMI Destilled: A Pratical Introduction to Integrated Process Improvement, 3rd edn. Addison Wesley Professional, Boston (2008)
3. ISO/IEC 15504:2004: Information technology - Process assessment. International Organization for Standardization and International Electrotechnical Commission Std. (2004)
4. Studer, R., Benjamins, R., Fensel, D.: Knowledge engineering: principles and methods. Data Knowl. Eng. **25**, 161–198 (1998)
5. Guarino, N., Oberle, D., Staab, S.: What is an ontology? In: Staab, S., Studer, R. (eds.) Handbook on Ontologies. IHIS, pp. 1–17. Springer, Heidelberg (2009). https://doi.org/10.1007/978-3-540-92673-3_0
6. Genesereth, M.R., Nilsson, N.J.: Logical Foundations of Artificial Intelligence. Morgan Kaufmann, Los Altos (1987)
7. W3C: OWL 2 Web Ontology Language Structural Specification and Functional-Style Syntax, 2nd edn. World Wide Web Consortium Recommendation (2012). http://www.w3.org/TR/owl2-syntax/. Accessed Jan 2015
8. Antunes, G.: Analysis of enterprise architecture models: an application of ontologies to the enterprise architecture domain. Ph.D. thesis, University of Lisbon (2015)

9. Proença, D., Borbinha, J.: Enterprise architecture: a maturity model based on TOGAF ADM. In: 19th IEEE Conference on Business Informatics, Thessaloniki, Greece (2017)

10. Proença, D., Borbinha, J.: Using enterprise architecture model analysis and description logics for maturity assessment. In: The 33rd ACM/SIGAPP Symposium on Applied Computing (SAC 2018), Pau, France (2018)

11. CMMI Product Team: CMMI for development, version 1.3. Software Engineering Institute - Carnegie Mellon University, Technical report, CMU/SEI-2010-TR-033 (2010)

12. Breitman, K., Casanova, M.A., Truszkowski, W.: Semantic Web: Concepts, Technologies and Applications. Springer, Heidelberg (2007). https://doi.org/10.1007/978-1-84628-710-7

13. Gomez-Perez, A., Benjamins, R.: Overview of knowledge sharing and reuse components: ontologies and problem-solving methods. In: Proceedings of IJCAI-99 Workshop on Ontologies and Problem Solving Methods (KRR5), Stockholm, Sweden (1999)

14. Gruber, T.R.: A translation approach to portable ontology specifications. Knowl. Acquisition 5, 199–220 (1993)

15. Borst, W.N.: Construction of engineering ontologies. Ph.D. thesis, University of Twenty, Enschede (1997)

16. Uschold, M., Gruninger, M.: Ontologies: principles, methods and applications. Knowl. Eng. Rev. 11, 93–136 (1996)

17. Guarino, N.: Formal onthology in information systems. In: Proceedings of the First International Conference (FIOS 1998), Trento, Italy, 6–8 June 1998

18. Baader, F., Calvanese, D., McGuiness, D., Nardi, D., Patel-Schneider, P.: The Description Logic Handbook: Theory, Implementation, and Applications, 1st edn. Cambridge University Press, New York (2003)

19. Vaculin, R.: Process mediation framework for semantic web services. Ph.D. thesis, Department of Theoretical Computer Science and Mathematical Logic, Faculty of Mathematics and Physics, Charles University (2009)

20. Baader, F., Horrocks, I., Sattler, U.: Description Logics (2007). http://www.cs.ox.ac.uk/ian.horrocks/Publications/download/2007/BaHS07a.pdf

21. The Open Group: TOGAF Version 9.2. Van Haren Publishing (2018)

22. Proença, D., Borbinha, J.: Maturity model architect - a tool for maturity assessment support. In: 20th IEEE Conference on Business Informatics (CBI 2018), Vienna, Austria (2018)

23. The Open Group: Archimate 3.0.1 Specification (2017). http://pubs.opengroup.org/architecture/archimate3-doc/

24. Röglinger, M., Pöppelbuß, J.: What makes a useful maturity model? A framework for general design principles for maturity models and its demonstration in business process management. In: Proceedings of the 19th European Conference on Information Systems, Helsinki, Finland, June 2011

25. Mettler, T.: A design science research perspective on maturity models in information systems. St. Gallen: Institute of Information Management, University of St. Gallen (2009)

26. Maier, A., Moultrie, J., Clarkson, P.: Assessing organizational capabilities: reviewing and guiding the development of maturity grids. IEEE Trans. Eng. Manag. 59(1), 138–159 (2012)

27. Becker, J., Knackstedt, R., Pöppelbuß, J.: Developing maturity models for IT management: a procedure model and its application. Bus. Inf. Syst. Eng. 3, 213–222 (2009)

28. Hevner, A., Ram, S., March, S., Park, J.: Design science in information systems research. MISQ 28, 75–105 (2004)

29. CMMI Product Team: Standard CMMI Appraisal Method for Process Improvement (SCAMPI) A, Version 1.3: Method Definition Document. Software Engineering Institute - Carnegie Mellon University, Technical report, CMU/SEI-2011-HB-001 (2011)

30. ISO/IEC TS 33030:2017: Information technology—Process assessment—An exemplar documented assessment process. International Organization for Standardization and International Electrotechnical Commission Std. (2017)

Analysing Strategic Alignment Problems Using Inter-domain Matches of Enterprise Architecture Models

Dóra Őri and Zoltán Szabó[✉]

Department of Information Systems, Corvinus University of Budapest,
Budapest, Hungary
{DOri,Szabo}@informatika.uni-corvinus.hu

Abstract. The goal of this paper is to discuss and analyse enterprise architecture management (EAM)-based opportunities for supporting strategic alignment, focusing on inter-domain relationships of enterprise architecture models. Recently EAM is a major facilitator of IT-related planning and development efforts. Strategic alignment is a management approach to harmonize organization and technology in several dimensions, and EAM can be a useful facilitating tool. The paper drafts how EAM-based analysis methods can be used to explore misalignment problems. Alignment-related problems and symptoms are categorized and discussed using the concepts of EAM. The paper focuses on inter-domain matching between business, application, data and technology domains, and provides a systematic review of the relevant analysis perspectives and available EAM artefacts appropriate for discovering misalignment symptoms.

Keywords: Enterprise architecture management · Modelling · Strategic alignment · Misalignment

1 Introduction

In recent years when information systems facilitate the success of business strategies, and digitalization is a major trend that makes IT induced organizational reconfiguration a central topic, the importance of business - IT harmonization (alignment) is unquestionable. Strategic alignment is based on the concept that strategic choices related to internal and external domains must be consistent. Organizational structure and competencies must be suited to implement strategy and to enable efficient and effective operations. IT has become a major enabler of organizational change and business innovations, it is a key factor in organizational reconfiguration. A crucial issue for many organizations is to find the right mix of digitalization and the organizational renewal.

Strategic alignment is a classic issue in management, and there are many attempts to design a framework that describes harmonization. One of the most influential approach was the strategic alignment model of Henderson and Venkatraman [10]. The model has four key domains of strategic choice: (1) Business Strategy, (2) Organisational Infrastructure and Processes, (3) IT Strategy and (4) IT Infrastructure and Processes. The model is a complex co-alignment of strategy, organization and management processes.

© Springer Nature Switzerland AG 2020
D. Aveiro et al. (Eds.): EEWC 2019, LNBIP 374, pp. 135–146, 2020.
https://doi.org/10.1007/978-3-030-37933-9_9

The overall process involves a series of process stages, each concerned with one potential triangle. Many aspects of strategic alignment (maturity, implementation, culture, etc.) are extensively discussed in the literature, this paper focuses on the "hard" organizational dimensions (goals, structure, processes, infrastructure).

Frequent changes in business environment and emerging new technologies enforce organizations to innovate and reconfigure many aspects of organization (structure, process, management, motivation, knowledge, culture, etc.). There is no trivial way of achieving optimal alignment in companies, and as a result of organic, fast changes, we can expect more chance for sub-optimized solutions, unrecognized opportunities, even faults – alignment problems. As the result of organisational and IT complexity, neither the exploration of alignment related problems, nor the evaluation of the effectiveness of alignment process is self-evident. Alignment can be measured by different approaches, including e.g. typologies and taxonomies, fit models, mathematical calculations, survey items, qualitative assessments and psychological measures [4]. Recent studies show that strategic alignment is still among the top issues of CIOs [9, 11]. In complex companies operating hundreds of business processes and IT applications the exploration and analysis can be a cumbersome activity that can be efficiently supported by Enterprise Architecture Management (EAM) related methods.

This paper focuses on EAM-based analysis of Strategic Alignment by assessing inter-domain relationships of enterprise architecture (EA) models. The paper addresses how EAM-based analysis methods can be utilized to reveal misalignment problems, by categorizing and assessing alignment-related malfunctions with the help of EAM-based concepts. The study presents inter-domain matches between business, application, data and technology architecture domains, and shows a systematic review of the relevant analysis perspectives and available EA models appropriate for discovering misalignment symptoms.

The rest of the paper is organized as follows: Sect. 2 introduces misalignment problems and EAM concept. Section 3 presents EAM-based opportunities for alignment and misalignment assessment by depicting the main characteristics of the four EAM domains and providing typical misalignment symptoms using inter-domain EAM matches. Section 3 also contains a systematic analysis of misalignment symptoms focusing on inter-domain matches of EA models. At the end of the paper conclusions are drawn and future research directions are determined.

2   Misalignment Problems and EAM

Organizations are growingly technology-dependent, utilizing IT-based innovative models. Technology complexity is not the only challenge: human resource (knowledge and skills), processes, structure and even culture should be harmonized, but legal constraints, compliance requirements and ethical issues must also be considered. Alignment can be defined [10] as a degree of fit between business and IT strategy, as well as business and IT infrastructure, while misalignment is a misfit situation that negatively influences organizational performance. We can illustrate typical misfit problems like business processes, that are not optimized to utilize underpinning technology [22], solutions that do not perfectly support business needs [24], partially successful IT applications and the related work-arounds [18], the collection of data that are not used for business purposes. While organisations struggle to achieve alignment, problems, malfunctions can occur, which can be described as misalignment indicators. Several approaches can be taken to classify these indicators (for classification schemes see e.g. [3]). One of them is the symptom-based approach, which considers misalignment symptoms as the evidences of malfunctions, inefficiencies in business-IT alignment.

From another perspective, misalignment symptoms can be classified by the structure of the potential evaluation one wants to apply. In this sense, misalignment symptoms can refer (1) to the presence or even the lack of something (e.g. lack of business owners, lack of application interfaces), (2) to the complexity and cardinality of a network (e.g. application functionality does not support at least one business process activity, technological heterogeneity), or (3) to different comparisons (e.g. out of date technological infrastructure, under capacity infrastructure). Misalignment symptoms can be detected with several methods, one of them is an enterprise architecture-based analysis, in which EA models are assessed and the signs of the symptoms are revealed from the models, using different detection techniques.

Enterprise architecture (EA) can be characterized as the fundamental construction of an organization, describing the constituent parts, the relationships as well as the main principles and guidelines that support the construction and maintenance of the enterprise [25]. EA is regarded as an organising logic and an integrating force from business processes into IT infrastructure in order to manage and control the whole operation of the enterprise [25]. EA integrates the whole enterprise into a coherent map and helps to capture a detailed vision about the entire system considering its dimensions and complexity [21]. Several frameworks, methods, and tools have been developed to cope with architecture complexity [19]. TOGAF (The Open Group Architecture Framework) is a commonly-used, holistic architecture framework, that divides an enterprise architecture into 4 domains. EAM improves IT efficiency (by reducing redundancy, ensuring homogeneity, integration, consistency, reusability); enables IT effectiveness (by ensuring goals, results and schedule orientation); improves IT reliability (reducing risk) [14]. Strategic EAM [1, 12, 19] facilitates agile, flexible adaptation to the ever-changing environment, improved coordination of changes, and the management of costs and risks.

EAM can be a significant facilitator of strategic alignment by detecting, analysing and preventing misalignment problems. EA displays the fundamental structure of the different architecture layers and attaches all dimensions from business strategy to IT infrastructure, and therefore, provides a helpful opportunity to business-IT alignment assessment. EA-based analysis can both cover sole architecture layer assessment and fit analysis between the different EA layers. Enterprise architecture-based alignment assessment can result in re-alignment or re-architecture, using re-alignment techniques [8]. Several EA-based strategic alignment methods have been proposed in the last few years (e.g. [2, 6, 23]). There are also studies specifically in the field of EA-based misalignment assessment (e.g. [3, 5, 7, 17]). In a previous achievement [16], an EAM based method was introduced and tested to detect the symptoms of misalignment in EA models. The analysis method utilized the strategic alignment perspectives and detected misalignment symptoms with rule assessment techniques. The analysis method used three main steps to detect misalignment symptoms [15]:

- Strategic alignment perspectives served as a classification aspect. Perspectives were provided with typical misalignment symptoms.
- Relevant EA models (artefacts) were displayed, which potentially contain the symptoms.
- EA analysis types were recommended to the misalignment symptoms, which were able to explore the symptoms in the artefacts.

On implementation level, the analysis method used rule construction and rule testing techniques and examined the XML export of the EA models with XML validation techniques, using the Schematron assertion query language. Further details on the method can be found in [15].

3 Analysing Misalignment Symptoms Using EAM Concepts

3.1 Characteristics of EAM Domains

An enterprise architecture is commonly regarded as a pile of architecture domains. In the perception of TOGAF [21], an EA consists of business, data, application and technology layers. Each domain contains sole, basic architecture contents (within-domain) as well as inter-domain architecture building blocks to implement cross-domain relations between the primal architecture domains. *Business Architecture* describes organisation, processes, roles, products and services of an enterprise. This domain presents how business is supported with lower-layer architecture content. *Data Architecture* displays the data components and the data flows, covers the organising logic of enterprise data and the inter-relatedness with other domains. *Application Architecture* presents the design and operation of enterprise applications, the interaction between applications and how the application portfolio connects to business, data and technology levels. *Technology Architecture* depicts the technical infrastructure of an enterprise. Beyond logical and physical technological components, the domain also describes how these hardware and software components support the application architecture level.

This differentiation appears on EA model-level as well. Within-domain EA models describe the basic logic and the fundamental building blocks of the architecture domain in question, while inter-domain EA models present the inter-relatedness of the different architecture domain contents.

3.2 EAM Domains and Misalignment Symptoms

The following section presents an analysis of typical misalignment symptoms to inter-domain matches of a complex enterprise architecture. Misalignment symptoms related to architecture domain matches stem from malfunctions in terms of inter-domain matches. The following typical symptoms provide examples on the perceptions of business-IT malfunctions in EA context. These exemplary symptoms introduce the affected EA layers and point out the typical problems that EA-based assessments can reveal. The following symptoms originally stem from recent literature on EA-based misalignment symptom collections [3, 13, 20]. Symptoms describing the mismatches between Business Architecture and other architecture domains cover specific inter-domain deficiencies regarding e.g. how enterprise data is used by business processes, how business operation is supported by enterprise applications, how applications contribute to achieving business mission and goals. Indicators of the mismatch of Business and Data Architecture include the following examples [20]:

- Not all information entity attributes are read by at least one business process activity;
- Not all information entities derive from known sources and have business people responsible for its coherence, accuracy, relevance and quality control.

Typical symptoms describing the mismatches of Business and Application Architecture include [20]:

- Not each business process is supported by the minimum number of applications;
- Critical business processes are not supported by scalable and highly available applications;
- The sign that recovering from a failed operation across multiple systems requires careful human analyses to roll back to a coherent state.

Furthermore, there are some typical symptoms that reveal the mismatches between Business and Technology Architecture [3, 13], e.g.:

- Competencies need to be kept on several different technologies, operating systems, and DBMS;
- Lack or poor systems performance monitoring;
- Only Technical IT Metrics are used, which are not related to business;
- Sporadically existing or Technical Service Level Agreements.

Typical symptoms related to the matches of Data Architecture with Application and Technology Architecture cover the way how enterprise data is stored in enterprise applications building on technology components, and mainly, how enterprise data flows between application interfaces. Symptoms typically present related to these matches include [3, 20]:

- Multiple replicas keep the same data coherent, because data are updated by multiple applications;
- Data structure transformation is needed when data migrates between applications;
- Unprotected confidential information.

Finally, the mismatch between Application and Technology Architecture stem from the difficulties of the application implementation and how they build on technology components. Typical misalignment symptoms include e.g. [3]:

- Frequent periods when applications are unavailable;
- Under capacity infrastructure.

3.3   EA Layers and Discovering Misalignment Symptoms

This section introduces inter-domain EA models related to every domain matching opportunity and provides typical signs of malfunctions on different levels. First, Fig. 1 presents inter-domain EA models for the possible business, data, application and technology architecture comparisons. The figure represents a chain from business strategy and goals to underlying technological infrastructure through enterprise data and applications. In the following parts of the section, typical misalignment symptoms will be attached to the possible domain matches of the four basic architecture domains.

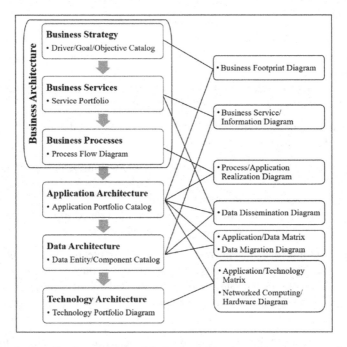

Fig. 1. A collection of EA models for inter-domain architecture comparison

Table 1 introduces inter-domain EA models for Business Architecture-related matches. The analysis contains typical misalignment symptoms that might be present in the corresponding EA domain matches. Typical symptoms can be detected via assessing the conforming inter-domain EA models. This view is appropriate to analyse the strategy execution (Business Strategy and Business Structure matching), or even competitive potential aspects of the SAM model can be assessed. Underutilized data assets, unsupported business processes, service level problems can be discovered using the inter-domain matches.

Table 1. Business-related inter-domain EA models with typical misalignment symptoms (based on [21])

Domain matching	Inter-domain EA models	Typical misalignment symptoms
Business Arch. & Data Arch. Matching	Data Entity/Business Function Matrix Data Security Diagram Data Lifecycle Diagram Data Dissemination Diagram	Not all information entity attributes are read by at least one business process activity Not all information entities derive from known sources and have business people responsible for its coherence, accuracy, relevance, quality For each information entity, there are no responsible person for assessing the usefulness and cost/benefits of information and sustain its continued use
Business Arch. & Application Arch. Matching	Application/Organisation Matrix Role/Application Matrix Application/Function Matrix Application and User Location Diagram Process/Application Realisation Diagram Data Dissemination Diagram	Not each business process is supported by the minimum number of applications Critical business processes are not supported by scalable and highly available applications Recovery from a failed operation across multiple systems requires careful human analysis to roll back to a coherent state
Business Arch. & Technology Arch. Matching	Environments and Locations Diagram Processing Diagram Software Distribution Diagram	Competencies need to be kept on several different technologies, operating systems, DBMS Lack or poor systems performance monitoring Only Technical IT Metrics are used, which are not related to business Sporadically existing or Technical SLAs

Table 2 presents Data Architecture-related inter-domain EA models and typical misalignment symptoms that can be explored with analysing these models.

Table 2. Data-related Inter-domain EA models with misalignment symptoms (based on [21])

Domain matching	Inter-domain EA models	Typical misalignment symptoms
Data Arch. & Business Arch. Matching	Data Entity/Business Function Matrix Data Security Diagram Data Lifecycle Diagram Data Dissemination Diagram	Not all information entity attributes are read by at least one business process activity Not all information entities derive from known sources and have business people responsible for its coherence, accuracy, relevance, quality For each information entity, there are no business people who are responsible for assessing the usefulness and cost/benefits of information and sustain its continued use
Data Arch. & Application Arch. Matching	Application/Data Matrix Data Migration Diagram Data Dissemination Diagram Data Security Diagram	Multiple replicas keep the same data coherent, because data are updated by multiple applications Data structure transformation is needed when data migrates between applications
Data Arch. & Technology Arch. Matching	Data Security Diagram	Unprotected confidential information

Mostly procedural, business related problems, poor management of the valuable data assets, unnecessary collection of data, poor allocation of responsibilities and other process related problems can be explored using this view, the matching of IT and business structure (Service level in the SAM model) can be evaluated.

Table 3. Application-related inter-domain EA models with typical misalignment symptoms (based on [21])

Domain matching	Inter-domain EA models	Typical misalignment symptoms
Application Arch. & Business Arch. Matching	Application/Organisation Matrix Role/Application Matrix Application/Function Matrix Application and User Location Diagram Process/Application Realisation Diagram Data Dissemination Diagram	Not each business process is supported by the minimum number of applications Critical business processes are not supported by scalable and highly available applications Recovery from a failed operation across multiple systems requires careful human analysis to roll back to a coherent state
Application Arch. & Data Arch. Matching	Application/Data Matrix Data Migration Diagram Data Dissemination Diagram Data Security Diagram	Multiple replicas keep the same data coherent, because data are updated by multiple applications Data structure transformation is needed when data migrates between applications
Application Arch. & Technology Arch. Matching	Software Distribution Diagram Application/Technology Matrix Environments and Locations Diagram Processing Diagram	Frequent periods when applications are unavailable Under capacity infrastructure

Table 4. Technology-related inter-domain EA models with typical misalignment symptoms (based on [21])

Domain matching	Inter-domain EA models	Typical misalignment symptoms
Technology Arch. & Business Arch. Matching	Environments and Locations Diagram Processing Diagram Software Distribution Diagram	Competencies need to be kept on several different technologies, operating systems, DBMS Lack or poor systems performance monitoring Only Technical IT Metrics are used, which are not related to business Sporadically existing or Technical SLAs
Technology Arch. & Data Arch. Matching	Data Security Diagram	Unprotected confidential information
Technology Arch. & Application Arch. Matching	Software Distribution Diagram Application/Technology Matrix Environments and Locations Diagram Processing Diagram	Frequent periods when applications are unavailable Under capacity infrastructure

Table 3 contains typical misalignment symptoms and containing inter-domain EA models for Application Architecture-related domain matches. Matching can be useful to assess Technology Transformation (IT Strategy and IT Structure matching) related problems of the SAM model. Business process related issues, poor performance of IT services and IT domain related weaknesses can be investigated in this view.

Table 4 introduces inter-domain EA models for Technology Architecture-related domain matches. The analysis also reveals typical misalignment symptoms that can be present in the corresponding domain matches. This view again helps us to explore business strategy and IT strategy, or business structure and IT structure related problems, and identify technology transformation, strategy execution related issues.

The analysis focused on the inter-domain matches between business, application, data and technology domains, and provided a systematic approach for EA-based misalignment symptom detection. The analysis method introduced several typical alignment problems along the possible architecture domain matches and listed the corresponding inter-domain EA models to detect the symptoms. The next table (Table 5) provides general examples of queries that can be used to evaluate certain types of the misalignment symptoms described earlier.

Table 5. Misalignment symptom detection from EA models – query types with sample query skeletons

Query type	Query skeleton and example
Symptoms in which the presence or lack of certain type of attributes has to be investigated	Pattern: Presence or lack of attributes Rule context: Node type Necessary objects: Object definition, attribute definition, attribute type
	Example: <pattern name="Lack of data ownership"> <rule context="Object Definition[@Node Type='{data entity}']"> <assert test="Attribute Definition[@Attribute Type= '{responsible person}']"> Alert: Lack of data ownership </assert></rule></pattern>
Symptoms in which the cardinality of certain connection types has to be analysed	Pattern: Cardinality of connection types Rule context: Node type Necessary objects: Object definition, connection definition, connection type, count function, parent, following or preceding sibling, node type
	Example: <pattern name="Business process task supported by more than one application"> <rule context="Object Definition[@Node Type='{business process task}']"> <report test="count(Connection Definition [@ToObjectDefinition.IdRef=parent::Object Definition/following or preceding-sibling:: Object Definition[@Node Type='{application function}']/ @ObjectDefinition.ID])>1"> Alert: Business process task supported by more than one application </report></rule></pattern>

4   Conclusion and Further Research

In the era of digitalization, strategic alignment is a prevalent challenge in organisations. Alignment can be considered as the harmonization between the building blocks of the organization – IT and business domains, structure, procedures and applications, etc. To assess this harmonization, an analysis based on the evidences of EA models and available metrics can be a useful method. This paper contributed to bridge the gap between strategic alignment assessment methods and enterprise architecture-based concepts and proposed an EA-based analysis for strategic (mis)alignment assessment by evaluating the inter-domain relationships of enterprise architecture models and detecting symptoms of business-IT mismatches. The novelty of the systematic, EAM-based analysis of misalignment symptoms lied in: (1) approaching the phenomenon of strategic alignment from misalignment perspective, (2) utilizing a symptom-based approach to detect the state of misalignment in a complex EA model structure, (3) using the concept of EAM to address misalignment symptom detection and (4) using formal, XML-based rule testing techniques for alignment assessment in EAM environment.

With the categorization of typical inter-domain misalignment symptoms considerable insight has been gained to the applicability of the proposed EAM-based misalignment symptom detection framework. The systematic approach provided us with the relevant analysis perspectives, and the prospective EA artifacts which are appropriate to detect the symptoms of misalignment. Directions for future research include (1) collecting empirical evidences on the applicability, correctness and usefulness of the proposed analysis method, (2) proposing additional queries that can explore further misalignment symptoms, (3) the analysis of alignment initiatives as a process, where changes in EAM objects can be considered covering a longer time-period.

Acknowledgement. The publication was prepared within the Széchenyi 2020 program framework (EFOP-3.6.1-16-2016-00013) under the European Union project titled: „Institutional developments for intelligent specialization at the Székesfehérvár Campus of Corvinus University of Budapest.

References

1. Ahlemann, F., Stettiner, E., Messerschmidt, M., Legner, C.: Strategic Enterprise Architecture Management: Challenges, Best Practices, and Future Developments. Springer, Heidelberg (2012). https://doi.org/10.1007/978-3-642-24223-6
2. Bounabat, B.: Enterprise architecture based metrics for assessing IT strategic alignment. In: The European Conference on Information Technology Evaluation, vol. 13, pp. 83–90 (2006)
3. Carvalho, G., Sousa, P.: Business and information systems misalignment model (BISMAM): an holistic model leveraged on misalignment and medical sciences approaches. In: Proceedings of the Third International Workshop on Business/IT Alignment and Interoperability (BUSITAL 2008). CEUR, vol. 336, pp. 104–119. CEUR-WS, Aachen (2008)
4. Chan, Y.E., Reich, B.H.: State of the art. IT alignment: what have we learned? J. Inf. Technol. **22**(4), 297–315 (2007)
5. Chen, H.M., Kazman, R., Garg, A.: BITAM: an engineering-principled method for managing misalignments between business and IT architectures. Sci. Compu. Program. **57**(1), 5–26 (2005). https://doi.org/10.1016/j.scico.2004.10.002
6. Dahalin, Z.M., Razak, R.A., Ibrahim, H., Yusop, N.I., Kasiran, M.K.: An enterprise architecture methodology for business-IT alignment: adopter and developer perspectives. In: Communications of the IBIMA, pp. 1–15 (2011). https://doi.org/10.5171/2011.222028
7. Elhari, K., Bounabat, B.: Platform for assessing strategic alignment using enterprise architecture: Application to e-government process assessment. IJCSI Int. J. Comput. Sci. Issues **8**(1), 257–264 (2011)

8. Enagi, M.A., Ochoche, A.: The role of enterprise architecture in aligning business and information technology in organisations: Nigerian government investment on information technology. Int. J. Eng. Technol. **3**(1), 59–65 (2013)

9. Gerow, J., Thatcher, J., Grover, V.: Six types of IT-business strategic alignment: an investigation of the constructs and their measurement. Eur. J. Inf. Syst. **24**(5), 465–491 (2014). https://doi.org/10.1057/ejis.2014.6

10. Henderson, J.C., Venkatraman, N.: Strategic alignment: leveraging information technology for transforming organisations. IBM Syst. J. **32**(1), 4–16 (1993)

11. Kappelman, L., et al.: The 2017 SIM IT issues and trends study. MIS Q. Exec. **17**, 53–88 (2018)

12. Lankhorst, M.: Enterprise Architecture at Work. Modelling, Communication and Analysis. Springer, Heidelberg (2013). https://doi.org/10.1007/978-3-642-29651-2

13. Luftman, J.: Assessing business-IT alignment maturity. Commun. Assoc. Inf. Syst. **4**(14), 1–50 (2000)

14. Niemann, K.D.: From Enterprise Architecture to IT Governance, vol. 1. Springer Fachmedien, Heiddelberg (2006). https://doi.org/10.1007/978-3-8348-9011-5

15. Őri, D.: On exposing strategic and structural mismatches between business and information systems: Misalignment symptom detection based on enterprise architecture model analysis, Ph.D. Thesis, Corvinus University of Budapest, May 2017

16. Őri, D., Szabó, Z.: Pattern-based analysis of business-IT mismatches in EA models: insights from a case study. In: Hallé, S., Dijkman, R., Lapalme, J. (eds.) Proceedings of the 2017 IEEE 21st International Enterprise Distributed Object Computing Conference Workshops and Demonstrations (EDOCW 2017), pp. 92–99 (2017)

17. Pereira, C.M., Sousa, P.: Business and information systems alignment: understanding the key issues. In: Proceedings of the 11th European Conference on Information Technology Evaluation, pp. 341–348 (2004)

18. Pollock, N.: When is a work-around? conflict & negotiation in computer systems development. Sci. Technol. Hum. Values **30**(4), 1–19 (2005)

19. Schekkerman, J.: How to Survive in the Jungle of Enterprise Architecture Frameworks: Creating or Choosing an Enterprise Architecture Framework. Trafford Publishing, Bloomington (2004)

20. Sousa, P., Pereira, C.M., Marques, J.A.: Enterprise architecture alignment heuristics. Microsoft Archit. J. **4**, 34–39 (2005)

21. TOG, The Open Group: TOGAF Version 9. The Open Group Architecture Framework (TOGAF). http://theopengroup.org/. Accessed 21 Jan 2015

22. Vom Brocke, J., Rosemann, M. (eds.): Handbook on Business Process Management 2: Strategic Alignment, Governance, People and Culture. Springer, Heidelberg (2014). https://doi.org/10.1007/978-3-642-45103-4

23. Wegmann, A., Balabko, P., Le, L.S., Regev, G., Rychkova, I.: A method and tool for business-IT alignment in enterprise architecture. In: Proceedings of the CAiSE 2005 Forum, pp. 113–118 (2005)

24. Wei, H., Wang, E.T.G., Ju, P.: Understanding misalignment and cascading change of ERP implementation: a stage view of process analysis. Eur. J. Inf. Syst. **14**(4), 324–334 (2005). https://doi.org/10.1057/palgrave.ejis.3000547

25. Zachman, J.A.: A framework for information systems architecture. IBM Syst. J. **26**(3), 276–292 (1987). https://doi.org/10.1147/sj.263.0276

On Blockchain

Das Contract - A Visual Domain Specific Language for Modeling Blockchain Smart Contracts

Marek Skotnica$^{(\boxtimes)}$ and Robert Pergl

Faculty of Information Technology,
Czech Technical University, Prague, Czech Republic
{marek.skotnica,robert.pergl}@fit.cvut.cz

Abstract. A Blockchain (BC) is a technology that introduces a decentralized, replicated, autonomous, and secure databases. A smart contract (SC) is a transaction embedded in the blockchain that contains executable code and its internal storage, offering immutable execution and record keeping. The SC has enormous potential in automating traditional paper contracts and encoding contract logic into program code. Thus, replacing the role of a notary and a central authority. It may dramatically reduce an effort with administration workload and enforcement of such contracts. In this paper, we propose a new visual domain specific language that can capture the SC in a user-friendly way and eliminate the errors associated with programming since the SC code is automatically generated from models. Finally, an open-source proof-of-concept environment for designing and generating the SC is introduced to demonstrate the feasibility of proposed concepts.

Keywords: Enterprise Engineering · DEMO methodology · Blockchain · Smart contract

1 Introduction

For thousands of years, contracts between people were conducted on paper or other material media and enforced by authorities. This approach requires all participants to believe in a central authority that enforces the contract obligation if necessary. However, still today, an enforcement process can take years to settle and can cost a significant amount of money in administration and attorney fees. Recent developments in a Blockchain (BC) technology have allowed creating contracts between people that are specified in a software code called Smart contract (SC). A SC is enforced by a network of computers which is guaranteed to execute the code adequately based on proven cryptographic algorithms. This was a breakthrough in computer science, however it seems that it has not delivered its full potential, yet – the most famous SC platform Ethereum [14] is still in the experimental phase and is not ready for a mass scale adoption. There are numerous challenges on the way towards the mass adoption of the SC technology.

© Springer Nature Switzerland AG 2020
D. Aveiro et al. (Eds.): EEWC 2019, LNBIP 374, pp. 149–166, 2020.
https://doi.org/10.1007/978-3-030-37933-9_10

This paper addresses one of them – a software code does not seem to be the best way to specify the contract between people for two reasons. First, non-technical people do not comprehend software code, and therefore they need to trust someone that will write the contracts for them. This is a similar situation to the ancient times when people were not generally able to read and write and thus had to put their trust in the experts of this special knowledge. Second, a semantic level of software code is too low and it is challenging to make a high-level comprehension and reasoning – there was already a case of a programming mistake in the SC which resulted in a loss of $50 million [36]. We argue that these issues can be addressed by applying modelling methods coming from the discipline of Enterprise Engineering (EE) [9];

EE builds on theories and models of social contracts. There are graphical representations used in practice with strong formal foundations guaranteeing that there is only one way to describe a particular contract, thus mitigating semantic misunderstanding.

In this paper, we propose a method of specifying SC using EE DEMO models and then generating executable SC to be run in a BC.

The paper is organized as follows: In Sect. 2, the research method and the research question are formulated. In Sect. 3, the underlying scientific foundations are briefly discussed. A vision of contract for the digital era is introduced in Sect. 4. A visual domain specific language for modelling blockchain smart contracts is introduced and demonstrated on a mortgage example in Sect. 5. In Sect. 6, the current results are summarized, and further research is proposed.

2   Research Approach

In our research, we applied the design science (DS) approach of Hevner [25,26], which is shown in Fig. 1. In the first cycle, a relevance of the problem is discussed in Sects. 1 and 4. The second cycle is described in Sects. 4 and 5. And finally, the relevant grounding into the existing knowledge base is in Sects. 3, 4.2 and 6.

The research question is: **Can enterprise engineering methods be applied to improve the state of the art of creating blockchain smart contracts in a high-level modelling language so that the language's expressiveness allows to model contracts between people or companies?**

3   Methodologies Used

3.1   Ontological Modelling

Ontological modelling allows to capture entities and their relations of domains in the real world. Therefore it is a great fit because we are capturing many different domains such as law, organisation design, and software engineering. There are several upper ontologies [31,58].

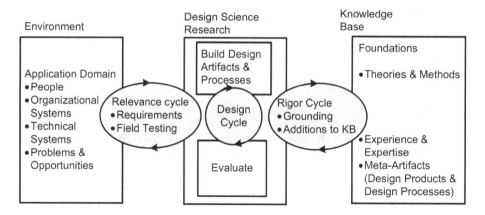

Fig. 1. Design science research cycles [25]

3.2 Enterprise Engineering

Enterprise Engineering (EE) is the scientific discipline focused on designing whole or a part of an enterprise. It examines all aspect of the enterprise from business processes, informational and technical resources to organisational structures. EE is built on four pillars: Enterprise Ontology, Enterprise Architecture, Enterprise Governance, which all together form Enterprise Design [9].

3.3 DEMO Methodology

DEMO stands for "Design and Engineering Methodology for Organizations". It is an enterprise modelling method based on Enterprise Engineering theories for designing organisations developed by Jan Dietz and others. DEMO is based on the Organisation Essence Revealing (OER) paradigm and the ψ-Theory (PSI, Performance in Social Interaction) of organisations [8].

3.4 The DEMO Machine

The DEMO Machine [48,49] is a theoretical computational concept that formalises a simulation of DEMO models. The underlying concepts also serve as a guide to implement executable artifacts based on DEMO models. We also mention a progress in formalisation of DEMO model execution [19].

3.5 Business Process Model and Notation (BPMN)

BPMN is a standard notation for business process modeling under the Object Management Group (OMG) [2,39]. In this paper we use UML Class diagram to define a metamodel of our proposed domain specific language.

3.6   Unified Modeling Language (UML)

Unified Modeling language (UML) [44] is a standardized modeling language enabling developers to specify, visualize, construct and document artifacts of a software system [54].

3.7   Blockchain

Blockchain (BC) is a technology introduced [34] by Satoshi Nakamoto[1] It is mostly known for its use with Bitcoin as it is its underlying technology. It is a new way of looking at transactions, assets exchange or even whole organizations. It introduces decentralized, autonomous, replicated and secure database. Based on cryptography offers trustless [42] network with no need of intermediary, resulting in major resource and also time saving. The possibilities of applying this technology are very broad and it could be effectively used in most of the parts of our world.

Smart Contracts. The idea of smart contracts (SC) [53] is to offer more complex solutions than just a sell/buy transactions. Smart contract is a transaction embedded in blockchain that contains enhanced logic – a contract that is executable, has its own data storage and can access other resources to evaluate its current state and perform actions – a contract made of code. "A smart contract is a set of commitments that are defined in digital form, including the agreement on how contract participants shall fulfill these commitments." [35].

The main characteristic of a programmable smart contract is, that it does not require trust between parties, as after its creation in blockchain, it would be able to execute itself immutably. The parties would not need to be in a further contact or use an intermediary, it would be autonomous instead. Smart contracts are not doing something that was not possible before, however they reduce the complexity of common problems and they help with automation [52].

4   Contracts for the Digital Era

The contracts are defined as *"An agreement between two or more parties creating obligations that are enforceable or otherwise recognizable at law."* [15]. The main goal of this section is to argue that the contracts can be done better than using only plain text. Especially the contracts in the modern digital world wherein the majority of countries the same law still applies for the online and offline world. By saying "can be done better" we mean that a large amount of the repetitive administrative work can be eliminated, the comprehension can be increased, and third-party involvement reduced (courts, distrainors, ...).

To limit our scope of interest, we will attempt to bridge the legal and technological worlds by providing a formal language to define smart contracts.

---

[1] Satoshi Nakamoto is probably a pseudonym for either one person or a group of people, the identity is currently unknown.

4.1   Towards Law Automation

Law is a broad and complex topic, so for this paper, we simplify it into two categories – substantive and procedural. *Substantive law* is a part of the law that creates, defines, and regulates the rights, duties, and powers of parties [15]. *Procedural law* are the rules that prescribe the steps for having a right or duty judicially enforced, as opposed to the law that defines the specific rights or duties themselves [15]. In other words, it describes a procedure that is taken in order to decide about substantive law.

In essence, the law needs to be very general to consider as many cases as possible. Sometimes, the cases which apply to a certain law does not exist at the time of writing the law such as internet criminality. This complexity and vagueness make it very challenging to maintain and automate. In most domains, plain text is still being used to describe the rules. There are notable exceptions in domains such as finance and regulatory reporting where a fully machine-readable XBRL format is used [7].

The vagueness of law is a required and important property in justice systems. However, when people or companies need to comply with the laws and design systems that will automate the associated work, they need a clear definition of how does the law apply in their case.

4.2   State of the Art

We reviewed the state of the art approaches law creation and found that most of the content is created and maintained in a xml formats such as [1,13,22,37]. Ontologies such as OWL [3] are used to create taxonomies. This is great for easier categorization and structure organization but a domain expert is required to interpret the content. A notable attempt to interpret EU law in charts was found in [55–57]. The authors created flowcharts from the EU law to help law students faster understand the complex documents. However, for the desired purposes of the paper - a fully executable model of a law, this is not sufficient.

A great efforts to model law and law processes were found in Nomos and VLPM 2.0 [4,38,46,47,59]. They specialize in modeling legal processes and have a great formal foundations. Sadly, both were discontinued and are not evolved anymore.

There are similar approaches that use BPMN [21,28,45] or UML [6,50,51] modelling languages. One paper was modelling a GDPR EU regulation with DEMO [20]. These approaches are is closest to our goal.

4.3   Contract Maturity Model

To measure the quality of the contracts, we do propose a contract maturity model. This model is focused on capturing the accuracy of a mutual under-standing in contract representation. A framework for a language evaluation pro-posed by Giancarlo Guizzardi [23] is used as a basis of this model. The Fig. 2 shows the relation between conceptualization, abstraction, modeling language and model [23]. In the world of law, the most used modelling language is plain text. Plain text has a great expressivity, but it can lead to ambiguity and undermine clarity.

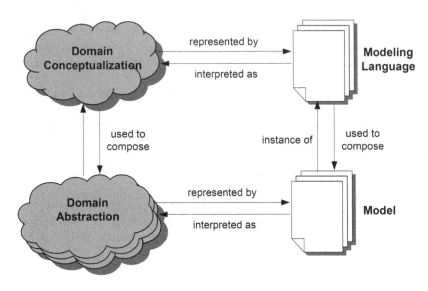

Fig. 2. Relation between conceptualization, abstraction, modeling language and model [23].

A Verbal Contract is the oldest form of contract between people. The terms of contracts are agreed upon in a natural language which is understood by both parties and stored in their brains. This form is great for a small number of people with shared domain conceptualizations who trust each other.

A Written Informal Contract is a version of a verbal contract which is written on a persistent medium in the form of a natural language. This simple act ensured that there is only one possible model of the contract. Sadly, the natural text can be interpreted differently by each participant because they may have different domain abstractions. In this type of contract, it is still possible to create illegal contracts because no legal framework is followed.

A Legally Binding Contract is a written contract which follows a legal framework. In this case, the legal framework and a natural language act together as a modelling language to allow the creation of a model. However, the law framework is usually defined in the form of a natural language, and it may be hard to create a model due to possibly multiple domain conceptualizations. This ambiguity makes it harder to compose a model and validate its compliance with a modeling language.

An Ontological Contract is a form of contract that controls the domain conceptualization and abstraction. The modelling language is represented by a domain conceptualization which allows only one possible interpretation. A composed model based on such modelling language has a clearly defined domain abstraction, and therefore the ambiguity can be controlled. This means that all involved parties work with a shared domain conceptualization and abstraction because it is stated explicitly.

Maturity	Name	Contract Form	Accuracy
1	Verbal contract	A mutual understanding	No written record of a contract
2	Written informal contract	Informal text	Typically ambiguous interpretation, possible errors, no legal framework
3	Legally binding contract	Legal text	Risks of ambiguous interpretation, possible errors, legal framework contains ambiguities itself
4	Ontological contract	Ontological model	Ambiguity effectively controlled

Fig. 3. A contract maturity model

4.4 The Proposed Approach

This paper builds on top of already published research [27] where a possible use of DEMO methodology to model blockchain smart contracts was explored and demonstrated on a mortgage case study. In this paper, we narrow the use-case to modelling legally binding contracts between two or more parties.

Our proposed approach is described in Fig. 4. It consists of three parts, in *Human Understanding* the contract is formally and legally specified. The *Technical Implementation* part shows an execution of the contract in the blockchain. In the *Digital Interaction* part, two or more parties are interacting with the smart contract through their digital devices.

Human Understanding part defines a contract between multiple parties that they need to agree on. Such a contract is a combination of legal text and formal ontological models. The legal text in some form specifies the legal validity of the formal model. The formal models need to be unambiguous, so only one possible interpretation is allowed. These formal models are specified in Sect. 5.

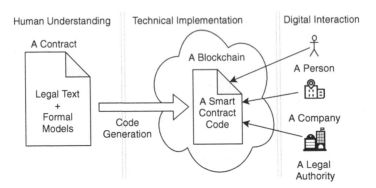

Fig. 4. A proposed concept architecture

Technical Implementation part specifies how formal models from the contract are transformed into a software executable code and uploaded into a blockchain as a smart contract. Guidelines on how to generate such code from the formal models were provided in [27].

Digital Interaction is a part where people, companies and legal authorities can interact with the agreed upon contracts. Since the contract is in a blockchain, the interaction is fully digital, and thanks to cryptography can also be legally binding. Blockchain by design also provides an audit trail of all actions performed by the parties and ensures that the agreed upon contract is executed correctly.

4.5   Possible Applications

The possible applications were described in [27]. The main domain of the possible applications is finance. Financial products such as mortgages, loans, trading, escrow can be in some way implemented. There is also a large potential in fields such as compliance, supply chain management, health care, real estate, manufacturing, and many more [16]. However, the technology is expected to reach its plateau in 2030 [16].

5   A Visual Smart Contract Language Specification

This section is focused on introducing a specification of *Formal Models* as it was introduced in Sect. 4.4. The formal language uses a combination of modified DEMO and BPMN models to describe a smart contract with high conceptual quality and enough expressiveness to model contracts between people.

The conceptual smart contract language is represented by a meta-model introduced in Sect. 5.1 and four visual models that provide multiple aspect views on top of the meta model. Finally, the language is demonstrated on a mortgage contract case from [27].

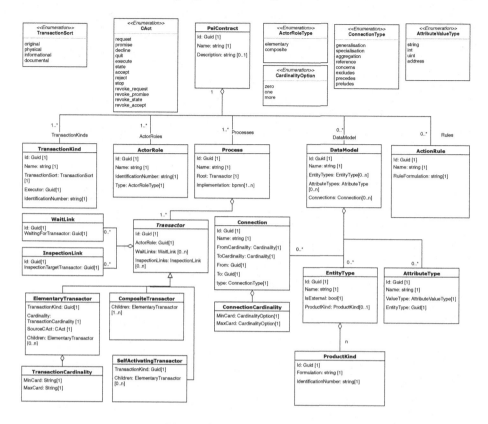

Fig. 5. A contract metamodel

An open-source web-based environment is currently being made to support modelling contracts in this notation. The source code is available at https://dev. azure.com/CCMiResearch/VSContract.

5.1 A Meta Model

A meta-model of the visual smart contract language is shown on Fig. 5. The meta model builds on existing DEMO Specification Language [10,33]. This meta model will serve as a formally defined part of a legal contract and contains all information needed to generate a blockchain smart contract. The contract is composed of transaction kinds, actor roles, processes, a data model, and action rules. All the diagrams defined in the following sections are a view on this meta model and define or reference some of its parts.

5.2 Contract Structure Diagram (CSD)

The CSD defines actor roles and transaction kinds in the same way as organization construction diagram from the DEMO 4 specification [12]. The only difference is that the metamodel allows specifying a source and target cActs on conditional links.

Definition: A Contract Structure Diagram is a DEMO OCD model as specified in [12] and further applies:

- A tree of transactors can be oriented horizontally or vertically.
- It is possible to specify target and source cAct of a wait link.
- It is possible to specify a source and a target cAct of an initiator link.

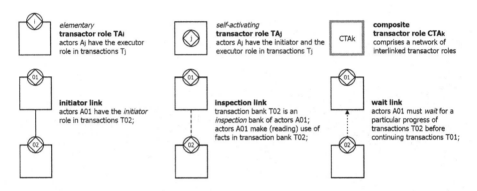

Fig. 6. A organization construction diagram [12]

5.3   Contract Process Diagram (CPD)

In the DEMO methodology the process is defined in the Process Structure Diagram (PSD) [12] and the order of steps is specified by a transaction axiom and a delta theory [11]. However, as argued in [48,49] a more information is required in order to create a fully executable software artefact such as a blockchain smart contract.

The most used process description notation is an OMG standard BPMN 2.0 [39]. Together with Decision Management Notation Tables (DMN) and the BPMN forms a great way to define a user-readable process description. Research on how to convert DEMO diagrams to BPMN was already published in [32]. However, it always generates the complete transaction axiom and does not allow a fine refinement to create a human-readable BPMN models. We do address this issue by allowing designers to create any BPMN process but require that it reflects the restrictions from the CSD.

For smart contract generation, some concepts such as timers cannot be implemented in blockchain and therefore will be restricted or implemented outside a smart contract.

Definition: A contract process diagram is represented by a set of BPMN and DMN models [39]. Further statements apply:

- The BPMN only uses a set of symbols that are supported in a target smart contract implementation.
- A BPMN activities can be associated with a transaction kind and a cAct.
- An order of BPMN activities and process execution need to respect a transaction and composition axioms.
- Conditional links specified in the CSD model need to be respected in the BPMN diagram.

5.4   Contract Data Model (CDM)

The contract data model is a diagram where entities, attributes, and properties are defined. Compared to the traditional UML data models, it contains a link to transaction kind products. We use DEMO object fact diagram for this purpose. The only difference is that it uses blockchain data types such as int and string instead of conceptual types such as money and year.

Definition: The data model is a DEMO OFD model as specified in [10] and further applies:

- Allowed data types are: int, string, uint, decimal, double, a blockchain address, and DateTime.

5.5   Contract Action Model

In a Contract Action Model (CAM) a logic which cannot be expressed by other models can be defined. This model is combination of DEMO Action Model [10] and a JSR-223 [43] like scripting ability which is used in BPMN engines for script tasks [5]. A visual coding block editor Google Blockly [17] will be used to compose rules. Blockly documentation claims that this editor is an intuitive, visual way to build code [18] which is in line with the requirements we described in Sect. 4.4. **Definition** A Contract Action Model is a set of action rules. An action rule is a block which contains following parts:

When This part identifies when the rule applies, it specifies a BPMN script task activity from a process model. **While** further specifies when a rule is triggered with a reference to a state of a child transaction. E.g. T02/Stated

- It should only allow selection of child and parent transaction types.
- This part is optional.

With specifies what data fields need to be entered to perform an act. E.g. mortgage.amount, mortgage.client (name, materialStatus, ...)

- Only parameters from the data model are allowed.
- This part is optional.

If statement allows to create boolean expressions and comparisons.Following comparisons are allowed:

- Transaction properties comparisons. E.g. `this.state == 'requested'`
- Data comparison. E.g. `client.age >= 18`

Then specifies what act is performed when the if is true. Following statements are allowed:

- Assignment of a calculated variable. E.g. `payment.amount = 555`.
- Perform a blockchain transaction.
- Perform other action supported by a target smart contract platform.

Else Optional, same as then part.

5.6 An Example

Our approach was already shown in [27] on a mortgage case study. Both the DEMO models and generated Ethereum Solidity smart contract are available on Github https://github.com/IamMarek/DemoBlockchain. This paper introduced enhanced DEMO diagrams which are suitable for specifying the smart contracts and contain enough information to generate smart contract code automatically. Therefore, we only provide the updated parts of the already existing mortgage case study.

A Contract Action Model is shown in Fig. 7. This model represents an ontological model of a mortgage contract. The main advantage of this contract is that it shows an essence of a social construct required for a mortgage to be conducted. Moreover, it shows the process roles and the coordination between all involved parties.

We can notice a significant reduction of space by including information from original OCD and OFD into just one diagram. Also, a position of elements is clearly defined in a tree structure that increases the readability of the mortgage process composition.

Contract Process Diagram is described in Fig. 8. This is an implementation model derived from the CAM ontological model. We made a conscious decision to leave out some tacit acts from a transaction axiom. The process can be directly translated into a smart contract source code.

Some additional process steps may occur in this diagram as it is required to contain technical implementation details such as communication with data sources.

Contract Action Diagram. An example rule created in a Blockly is shown in Fig. 9. This rule will be triggered on a first process step (T1/rq) as specified in the when part. The with part specifies a data fields which the step needs in order to be executed. The last part contains an if-then expression and enables the modeller to work with the smart contract properties, proceed to next process steps, or call smart contract-specific functions.

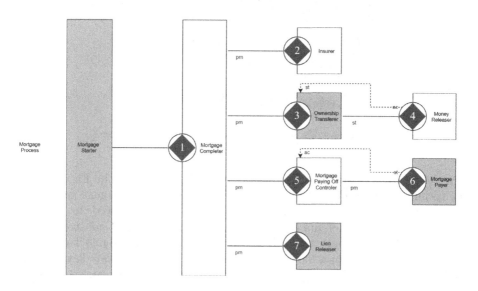

Fig. 7. A contract structure diagram for mortgage case

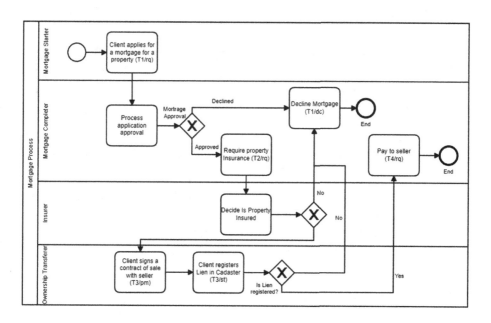

Fig. 8. A contract process diagram for mortgage case

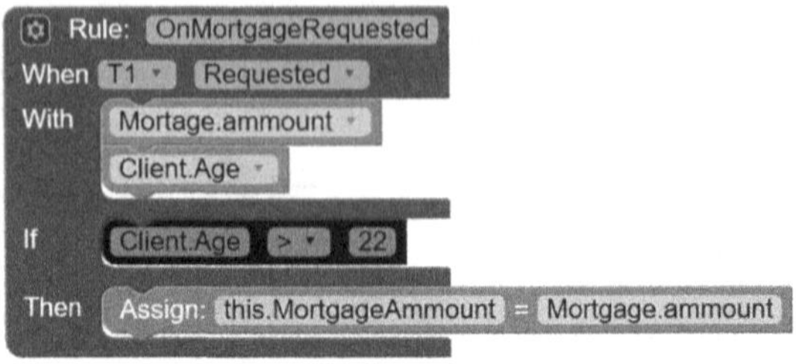

Rule: OnMortgageRequested
When T1 Requested
With Mortage.ammount
Client.Age
If Client.Age > 22
Then Assign: this.MortgageAmmount = Mortgage.ammount

Fig. 9. A contract action diagram for mortgage case

The Mortgage Solution Technological Architecture. The Fig. 10 shows the technological architecture of the mortgage case. The mortgage smart contract, which is generated from the DasContract, is deployed to a public blockchain such as Ethereum or Cardano. It assumes that the Cadastre is accessible from the blockchain through an oracle. All the participants have access to a blockchain through a blockchain wallet (keeping their private keys). In the wallet, they can see their cryptocurrency funds and available smart contracts.

Blockchain
IRS
Mortgage Smart Contract
Oracles
Cadastre
Homeowner
Insurer
Mortgage Holder

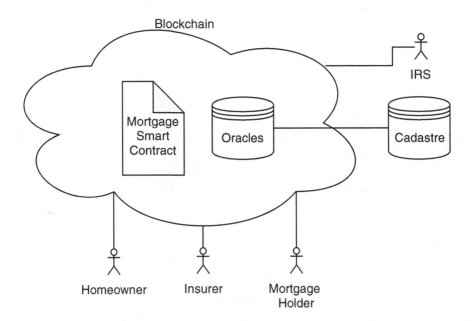

Fig. 10. The mortgage solution technological architecture

6   Conclusions

In this paper, we introduced a vision of contracts between people, companies, and legal authorities which can be partially automated and executed in blockchain smart contracts. It was argued, that the proposed concept can have a significant impact on how contracts are conducted. To pursue the goal, a visual domain specific language for modelling blockchain smart contracts was introduced and demonstrated on a mortgage case example. However, as Gartner claims [16], the blockchain technology is still very immature to support most of the potential use cases, and there is still a tremendous amount of research, implementation and adoption to be done.

Related Research. In Sect. 4.2 we already mentioned existing approaches to model law. As for the modelling law for the purposes of executing it in a blockchain smart contract, we are not aware of any visual language to describe all aspects of the smart contracts - process, data structures, and actions. However, there are already existing approaches that use BPMN [39] or Blockly [17]. An interesting project is Marlowe [29] which builds a domain specific language for the financial domain.

Further Research

- Automated generation of smart contracts on different platforms from the proposed language.
- A web-based editor to simplify the design of the proposed language.
- Case studies and usability studies to improve the proposed language design.
- Evolvability of the proposed contracts with Normalized Systems Theory [30].
- Explore whether the Contract Data Model from Sect. 5.4 can be enhanced or replaced by an OntoUML [23] which is based on Unified Foundation Ontology (UFO) [24] to achieve higher conceptual quality.
- Explore a possible extension of the proposed model by notions of social comments and claims (UFO-C), rights and duties (UFO-L) [24].
- Explore a possible extension of the proposed model by DMN [41] and CMMN [40] OMG standards.

Acknowledgement. This research has been supported by CTU SGS grant No. SGS18/120/OHK3/1T/18.

References

1. Metalex. http://metalex.eu/
2. Allweyer, T.: BPMN 2.0: introduction to the standard for business process modeling. BoD-Books on Demand (2016)
3. Bechhofer, S., et al.: OWL Web Ontology Language Reference. Technical report, W3C, February 2004. http://www.w3.org/TR/owl-ref/

4. Boer, A., Hoekstra, R., Winkels, R.: Metalex: legislation in xml. http://jurix.nl/pdf/j02-01.pdf
5. Camunda: Script task, 29 January 2019. https://docs.camunda.org/manual/7.8/reference/bpmn20/tasks/script-task/
6. Cherouana, A., Mahdaoui, L., Khadraoui, A.: BPM-based framework for e-government processes improvement: Legal requirements integration. Int. J. Intell. Inf. Database Syst. **10**, 21 (2017)
7. Debreceny, R., Gray, G.L.: The production and use of semantically rich accounting reports on the Internet: XML and XBRL. Int. J. Acc. Inf. Syst. **2**(1), 47–74 (2001)
8. Dietz, J.: Enterprise Ontology Theory and Methodology. Springer, Berlin (2006)
9. Dietz, J.: The discipline of enterprise engineering (2014). https://www.alexandria.unisg.ch/export/DL/224477.pdf. Accessed 25 Apr 2014
10. Dietz, J.: DEMOSL-Specification: Version 3.4 (2016). https://doi.org/10.5281/zenodo.47471
11. Dietz, J.: The delta theory - understanding discrete event systems, October 2017
12. Dietz, J.: The OMEGA theory - understanding the construction of organisations. Technical report (2017)
13. Estrella: Legal knowledge interchange format. http://www.estrellaproject.org/?page_id=5
14. Ethereum: Ethereum project. https://ethereum.org/. Accessed 29 Nov 2017
15. Garner, B.A.: Black's Law Dictionary: Deluxe, 9th edn. West, Eagan (2009)
16. Garther: The reality of blockchain. https://www.gartner.com/smarterwithgartner/the-reality-of-blockchain/. Accessed 29 Jan 2019
17. Google: Blockly. https://developers.google.com/blockly/. Accessed 29 Jan 2019
18. Google: Introduction to blockly. https://developers.google.com/blockly/guides/overview. Accessed 29 Jan 2019
19. Gouveia, D., Aveiro, D.: Colored Petri-Net for Implementing DEMO/PSI Transactions for N Actor Roles (N>=2) (2018)
20. Gouveia, D., Aveiro, D.: Modeling the system described by the EU general data protection regulation with DEMO. In: Aveiro, D., Guizzardi, G., Guerreiro, S., Guédria, W. (eds.) EEWC 2018. LNBIP, vol. 334, pp. 144–158. Springer, Cham (2019). https://doi.org/10.1007/978-3-030-06097-8_9
21. Governatori, G.: ICT Support for regulatory compliance of business processes (2014)
22. Group, A.N.: Akoma ntoso. http://www.akomantoso.org/
23. Guizzardi, G.: Ontological Foundations for Structural Conceptual Models, vol. 015. University of Twente, Enschede (2005)
24. Guizzardi, G., Wagner, G., Almeida, J.P.A., Guizzardi, R.S.S.: Towards ontological foundations for conceptual modeling: the unified foundational ontology (UFO) story. Appl. Ontol. **10**(3–4), 259–271 (2015)
25. Hevner, A.: A three cycle view of design science research. Scand. J. Inf. Syst. **19**(2) (2007). http://aisel.aisnet.org/sjis/vol19/iss2/4
26. Hevner, A.R., March, S.T., Park, J., Ram, S.: Design science in information systems research. MIS Q. **28**(1), 75–105 (2004)
27. Hornáčková, B., Skotnica, M., Pergl, R.: Exploring a role of blockchain smart contracts in enterprise engineering. In: Aveiro, D., Guizzardi, G., Guerreiro, S., Guédria, W. (eds.) EEWC 2018. LNBIP, vol. 334, pp. 113–127. Springer, Cham (2019). https://doi.org/10.1007/978-3-030-06097-8_7
28. Kühnel, S.: Toward cost-effective business process compliance: a research agenda, pp. 2379–2384 (2017)

29. Lamela Seijas, P., Thompson, S.: Marlowe: financial contracts on blockchain. In: Margaria, T., Steffen, B. (eds.) ISoLA 2018. LNCS, vol. 11247, pp. 356–375. Springer, Cham (2018). https://doi.org/10.1007/978-3-030-03427-6_27

30. Mannaert, H., De Bruyn, P., Verelst, J.: Exploring entropy in software systems: towards a precise definition and design rules. In: Proceedings of the Seventh International Conference on Systems (ICONS), Saint Gilles, Reunion Island, pp. 93–99 (2012)

31. Mascardi, V., Cordì, V., Rosso, P.: A comparison of upper ontologies. In: WOA (2007)

32. Mráz, O., Náplava, P., Pergl, R., Skotnica, M.: Converting DEMO PSI transaction pattern into BPMN: a complete method. In: Aveiro, D., Pergl, R., Guizzardi, G., Almeida, J.P., Magalhães, R., Lekkerkerk, H. (eds.) EEWC 2017. LNBIP, vol. 284, pp. 85–98. Springer, Cham (2017). https://doi.org/10.1007/978-3-319-57955-9_7

33. Mulder, M.A.T.: Validating the DEMO specification language. In: Aveiro, D., Guizzardi, G., Guerreiro, S., Guédria, W. (eds.) EEWC 2018. LNBIP, vol. 334, pp. 131–143. Springer, Cham (2019). https://doi.org/10.1007/978-3-030-06097-8_8

34. Nakamoto, S.: Bitcoin: a peer-to-peer electronic cash system (2009). http://www.bitcoin.org/bitcoin.pdf

35. NEO: Neo smart contract introduction. http://docs.neo.org/en-us/sc/introduction.html. Accessed 2 Jan 2018

36. Norta, A.: Designing a smart-contract application layer for transacting decentralized autonomous organizations. In: Singh, M., Gupta, P.K., Tyagi, V., Sharma, A., Ören, T., Grosky, W. (eds.) ICACDS 2016. CCIS, vol. 721, pp. 595–604. Springer, Singapore (2017). https://doi.org/10.1007/978-981-10-5427-3_61

37. OASIS: Legalxml. http://www.legalxml.org. Accessed 29 Jan 2019

38. Olbrich, S., Simon, C.: Process modelling towards e-government-visualisation and semantic modelling of legal regulations as executable process sets. Electron. J. E-gov. **6**(1) (2008)

39. OMG: Business Process Model and Notation (BPMN), version 2.0, January 2011. http://www.omg.org/spec/BPMN/2.0

40. OMG: Case Management Model and Notation (CMMN), version 1.1, December 2016. https://www.omg.org/spec/CMMN/1.1/

41. OMG: Decision Model and Notation (DMN), version 1.2, January 2019. https://www.omg.org/spec/DMN/1.2/

42. Preethi, K.: Eli5: What do we mean by "blockchains are trustless"? Medium. https://medium.com/@preethikasireddy/eli5-what-do-we-mean-by-blockchains-are-trustless-aa420635d5f6

43. Process, J.C.: Jsr 223: Scripting for the Javatm platform. https://www.jcp.org/en/jsr/detail?id=223. Accessed 29 Jan 2019

44. Rumbaugh, J., Jacobson, I., Booch, G.: Unified Modeling Language Reference Manual, 2nd edn. Pearson Higher Education, New York (2004)

45. Sadiq, S., Governatori, G., Namiri, K.: Modeling control objectives for business process compliance. In: Alonso, G., Dadam, P., Rosemann, M. (eds.) BPM 2007. LNCS, vol. 4714, pp. 149–164. Springer, Heidelberg (2007). https://doi.org/10.1007/978-3-540-75183-0_12

46. Siena, A.: Engineering law-compliant requirements: the nomos framework (2010)

47. Siena, A.: Engineering law-compliant requirements: the nomos framework. Ph.D. dissertation, University of Trento, March 2010

48. Skotnica, M., van Kervel, S.J.H., Pergl, R.: A DEMO machine - a formal foundation for execution of DEMO models. In: Aveiro, D., Pergl, R., Guizzardi, G., Almeida,

J.P., Magalhães, R., Lekkerkerk, H. (eds.) EEWC 2017. LNBIP, vol. 284, pp. 18–32. Springer, Cham (2017). https://doi.org/10.1007/978-3-319-57955-9_2

49. Skotnica, M., van Kervel, S.J.H., Pergl, R.: Towards the ontological foundations for the software executable DEMO action and fact models. In: Aveiro, D., Pergl, R., Gouveia, D. (eds.) EEWC 2016. LNBIP, vol. 252, pp. 151–165. Springer, Cham (2016). https://doi.org/10.1007/978-3-319-39567-8_10

50. Soltana, G., Fourneret, E., Adedjouma, M., Sabetzadeh, M., Briand, L.: Using UML for modeling procedural legal rules: approach and a study of Luxembourg's tax law. In: Dingel, J., Schulte, W., Ramos, I., Abrahão, S., Insfran, E. (eds.) MODELS 2014. LNCS, vol. 8767, pp. 450–466. Springer, Cham (2014). https://doi.org/10.1007/978-3-319-11653-2_28

51. Strahonja, V.: Modeling legislation by using UML state machine diagrams, pp. 624–627 (2006)

52. Swan, M.: Blockchain. O'Reilly Media Inc, Sebastopol (2015)

53. Szabo, N.: Smart contracts: building blocks for digital markets. www.fon.hum.uva.nl (1996). http://www.fon.hum.uva.nl/rob/Courses/InformationInSpeech/CDROM/Literature/LOTwinterschool2006/szabo.best.vwh.net/smart_contracts_2.html

54. Techopedia: Definition - what does unified modeling language (UML) mean? https://www.techopedia.com/definition/3243/unified-modeling-language-uml. Accessed 29 Jan 2019

55. Tobler, C.: Essential Eu Competition Law in Charts. HVG-ORAC Publishing House Ltd., Budapest (2011)

56. Tobler, C., Beglinger, J.: Essential Eu Law in Charts, 4th edn. HVG-ORAC Publishing House Ltd., Budapest (2018)

57. Tobler, C., Beglinger, J.: Essential EU Law in Text, 4th edn. HVG-ORAC Publishing House Ltd, Budapest (2018)

58. Verdonck, M., Gailly, F., de Cesare, S., Poels, G.: Ontology-driven conceptual modeling: systematic literature mapping and review. Appl. Ontol. 10(3–4), 197–227 (2015)

59. Xanthaki, H.: Drafting Legislation: Art and Technology of Rules for Regulation. Bloomsbury Publishing (2014). https://books.google.cz/books?id=AzLtBQAAQBAJ

Model-Driven Liaison of Organization Modeling Approaches and Blockchain Platforms

Eduard Babkin[(⊠)] and Nataliya Komleva

National Research University Higher School of Economics, Moscow, Russia
eababkin@hse.ru, nattscape@gmail.com

Abstract. In recent years, a number of relevant works actively studied connections between enterprise engineering modeling methods and blockchain models, however we may indicate the open problem of "a last mile": lacking principles, algorithms and tools for automatic generation of blockchain-related platform-specific models based on the organizational platform-independent models. In our research the objective was specified to develop a set of mapping rules and a corresponding software tool which facilitate automation of mapping between concepts of the ArchiMate enterprise architecture model and the HyperLedger Composer blockchain platform. The article describes the solution proposed and its evaluation in the test settings. According to the test evaluation, the development process was simplified.

Keywords: Model-driven engineering · Enterprise engineering · ArchiMate · DEMO · Blockchain · HyperLedger Composer

1 Introduction

In the domain of enterprise engineering [1], an organization is considered as a "complex socio-technical system that comprises interdependent resources of people, information, and technology" [2]. Business process modeling is a vital part of enterprise engineering [3, 4]. Modeling seeks to understand the internal work of the organization from beginning to end, which forms an idea of how the various divisions of the company work together, and also creates the basis for optimizing costs and improving business processes. A large number of different modeling approaches have been proposed in the enterprise engineering community. Among them we may distinguish DEMO [5] and ArchiMate [6] due to their maturity and great impact on advances of enterprise engineering.

Business process modeling is a key method for understanding the company's mechanisms. At the same time it contributes to reducing the distance between business and IT. Therefore, proper reflection of business process models in software design of information systems is an important aspect in practices of enterprise engineering. Advances in model-driven software engineering (MDE) [7–9] prove that an ability to automatically produce high quality platform-specific models (PSM) or artifacts for developing information systems on the basis of platform-independent models

© Springer Nature Switzerland AG 2020
D. Aveiro et al. (Eds.): EEWC 2019, LNBIP 374, pp. 167–186, 2020.
https://doi.org/10.1007/978-3-030-37933-9_11

(PIM) dramatically reduces time to market and leverages quality of complex organizational information systems. To the moment most of known model-based software development methods and tools produce software artifacts for traditional software technologies like Java EE beans, web-services, and embedded systems [9]. But the world of information technologies is rapidly developing, and that requires extending MDE approaches to technological novelties, such as the blockchain technology [10–14].

In recent years, a number of relevant works actively studied connections between enterprise engineering modeling methods (which produce PIMs) and blockchain models (both PIM and PSM). For example, Ellervee et al. [15] proposed a multi-layered reference model of a conceptual blockchain landscape using the ArchiMate modeling approach. A detailed conceptual mapping of three levels of Enterprise Ontology (ontological, infological, datalogical) to the platform-independent blockchain concepts was proposed by de Kruijff and Weigand [16]. Using DEMO as a PIM of organizations, Hornáčková et al. in [17] proposed principles for creating Ethereum Solidity smart contracts from DEMO transactions. In [18] Silva et al. proposed a UML meta-model for mapping between DEMO business transactions and elements of HyperLedger Composer.

However, we may indicate the open problem of "a last mile" (Fig. 1): lacking principles, algorithms and MDE tools for automatic generation of blockchain-related PSMs based on the organizational PIMs, in particular, there is no automatic tool to transfer ArchiMate models to HyperLedger Composer artifacts.

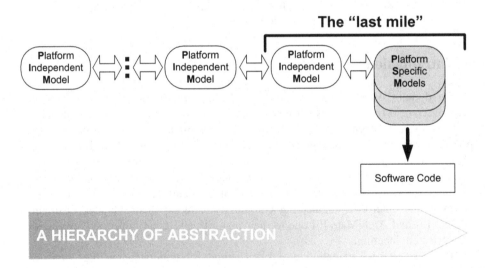

Fig. 1. The focus of the research

The aforementioned approaches still require manual software design of blockchain-related artifacts of information systems, which leads to increase of time and efforts needed due to additional testing and verification. Seebacher and Maleshkova offer conceptual motivation for solving that problem [19]. An example of a desired level of automation achieved by MDE tools may be found in [20], although the BPMN standard, used in that research, cannot be considered as a desired modeling approach.

To suggest a solution of that problem, we apply a method of comparative analysis to the language elements of a certain modeling approach in the scope of enterprise engineering (playing the role of PIM) and a blockchain platform selected (playing the role of PSM). Given the results of such analysis, we are able to design reusable mapping rules between the concepts of the modeling approach and software elements of the blockchain platform. The mapping rules produced can be embodied in the form of a new MDE tool, which can automatically generate software elements of the blockchain platform on the basis of a particular organizational business model. In terms of the design science research methodology, our result may be described as a working system of constructs, models, and methods, which may be applied in practice (Implementation).

Following that research outline, we made a selection between DEMO and Archi-Mate for the role of PIM, as well as studied several blockchain candidates for the role of PSM. As a result, we propose a set of mapping rules and a corresponding software tool that facilitate automation of mapping between concepts of the ArchiMate model and the blockchain platform HyperLedger Composer [21]. The software MDE tool performs a partial transfer of the artifacts of the ArchiMate model previously exported from the Archi modeling environment to the concepts of HyperLedger Composer.

These results were evaluated using an ArchiMate educational model ArchiSurance. The evaluation outcomes allow us to prove correctness of our approach to transferring the organization's platform-independent models to the blockchain platforms. We observed simplification of the development process, as well as determined the directions of further work.

In this article, Sect. 2 provides readers with the results of selection of a target blockchain technology (PSM) and a source process modelling approach (PIM) accepted for our research. In Sect. 3 our method of mapping between concepts of the ArchiMate and the HyperLedger Composer is described, including proposed mapping rules and overview of tooling. Section 4 presents results of practical evaluation of our approach for the ArchiSurance model. In the conclusion we outline major results, compare them with known results and open issues for further research.

2   Selection of PSM and PIM

Application of MDE methods requires selection of particular programming languages and software frameworks, which will provide concepts of PSM, as well as choosing a certain modeling approach for PIM. In our research an origin of PSM should be selected among alternative implementations of blockchain technologies. We also need to make a choice between ArchiMate and DEMO modeling approaches for PIM.

2.1   A Problem of Proper Choice of the Blockchain Platform

In principle, software engineering determines blockchain as a continuous sequential chain of blocks (a linked list) that contains some information [10, 12, 13]. The stack of blockchain technologies appeared along with Bitcoin cryptocurrency and the peak of its popularity came at the end of 2017.

Due to the novelty of the technology, it provides a wide range of possibilities for studying and soon we can expect a large number of scientific papers and practical projects on this topic (Fig. 2).

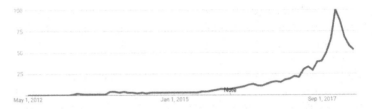

Fig. 2. Raising of interest to blockchain according to Google

Currently, the blockchain term is mistakenly associated only with cryptocurrencies. However, the blockchain technology can be applied to any interconnected block chains in various fields - banking, medical, and agricultural [12]. An important concept of the blockchain, without which it is impossible to imagine its existence, is a transaction - the transfer of an asset from one participant to another. This principle implies several key features of the blockchain technology [10]:

- Decentralization. The blockchain system is distributed and decentralized. It exists thanks to many networked computers. In contrast to the usual client-server archi-tecture, all blockchain operations are carried out directly between the participants of this network. It turns out that each participant is a server and thus supports the work of the entire network;
- Security. Storing the history of the transferred data is one of the key ideas of the blockchain. The transaction history is stored in an unchangeable structural chain and is available only for addition, which makes it protected from fraud. To create new blocks, it is necessary to reach a consensus of blockchain nodes, which allows you to record only legitimate transactions and makes it difficult to replace data. Despite the fact that this principle slows down the speed of adding new transactions, it leads to the fact that data manipulation becomes difficult and ineffective, because it requires compromising data on all computers;
- Transparency. Blockchain allows different stakeholders to store transaction history, which is available to each user. As a result, the blockchain can be compared with an open distributed accounting system (register) or a ledger. Openness and trans-parency are key blockchain ideas. The openness of the platform/system solves the problem of double-spending, because each user can check any transaction and prevent, for example, a double withdrawal of funds. However, this approach is at odds with the idea of privacy, which implies that information about transactions and

the accounts and funds involved in them will be transferred in a hidden form. From this inconsistency, a conflict arises between the transparency of the system and the high requirements for confidentiality.

Aforementioned properties of blockchain make it highly relevant for design and developing next generations of information systems, in particular for the cases of semi-autonomous and distributed organizations.

There are multiple differences between practical implementations of the blockchain technology. The selection of a proper blockchain platform depends on the organization's goals, because with all the advantages in transparency and security, the organization simultaneously gets significant drawbacks in privacy and speed. There are several ways to solve these conflicts. To choose between transparency and privacy, it is necessary to decide who should be granted access: each user or a limited number of users. In this regard, the following blockchain types are distinguished:

- Public blockchain - gives everyone access to "read" data of the blockchain platform and gives the right to create new transactions.
- Private blockchain - provides access for reading, as well as the right to create new transactions only for a pre-determined group of users or nodes.

When choosing between security and speed, there are two options. The first is permisionless blockchain which provides everyone with write access. The second is permisioned blockchain which grants access only to a limited and predefined group of users or nodes that are identified by the system as "trusted". As a result, only this group has the right to write access.

As part of this work, it is planned to pay special attention to the private blockchain. Due to the fact that we are going to introduce a blockchain into an organization, only a dedicated, reliable group of users should have access.

Currently, there are many blockchain platforms, some of which work exclusively with cryptocurrencies, and some have gone further and are seeking to introduce technology into the business domain. We have performed a study of several popular platforms supporting both public and private blockchain technologies such as Ethereum [22], HyperLedger Sawtooth [23], HyperLedger Iroha [24, 28], HyperLedger Fabric [25], Multichain [26], HydraChain [27], HyperLedger Composer [29]. Analysis shows that observed solutions have particular specific features, targeting to different applications domains:

- Ethereum is a platform for creating decentralized blockchain-based online services that operate on the basis of smart contracts. Smart contracts allow a designer to make an exchange of something directly, bypassing the intermediary. They define the rules, and also allow the designer to automatically fulfill these obligations. The organization that works through smart contracts is called the DAO (Decentralized Autonomous Organization) or DAC (Decentralized Autonomous Corporation);
- HyperLedger is an open source project that includes several more projects: HyperLedger Sawtooth is a set of modules developed by Intel using the PoeT (Proof of Elapsed Time) consensus algorithm; HyperLedger Iroha is a project with Japanese roots, creating an easily joining framework for the blockchain; HyperLedger Fabric is a flexible plug-in created under the guidance of IBM;

- Multichain - a platform for creating and deploying private networks both within one and within several organizations. It aims to introduce the blockchain technology in the financial sector for private financial transactions;
- HydraChain is an extension for the Ethereum platform that supports the creation of scalable blockchain-based applications that meet organizational and regulatory requirements.

If we consider the popularity of platforms among developers, we can see a significant value of Ethereum. However, this comparison is not entirely correct, since Ethereum uses a public blockchain. At the same time among the solutions for private blockchain, HyperLedger products (Fabric, Sawtooth, Iroha) lead.

For the purposes of our research, we made a selection of HyperLedger Composer (HLC) - this tool allows designers to deploy an organization model on the blockchain platform. Consider the basic principles that must be followed by a business model. HyperLedger Composer is a set of tools that simplify the development of blockchain applications [29]. In particular, this framework allows a developer to integrate an existing business system into a blockchain platform with minimal time costs. It also provides integration with HyperLedger Fabric, which ensures that transactions will be validated according to the rules established for members of a particular business network.

An important difference is that HyperLedger Fabric and Composer do not depend on cryptocurrency or mining, which ensures their stable development. Cryptocurrencies, for example, rely on financial incentives for participants to solve complex mathematical problems that require considerable time, computing power, and energy. In HyperLedger Fabric, participants work together for a common value: transfer patient data safely or ensure food safety. These systems require far fewer resources, which makes them much more efficient for business [13].

The main entities of HLC, like any other blockchain platform, are assets, participants, and transactions. Consider each concept in detail. An asset is everything that has value and can be transferred from a participant to a participant as part of a business agreement. This may be a house, a toolbox or a contract for the supply of equipment. Participant is a person who participates in a business model. He/she can produce goods, deliver them or receive them. Transactions model business logic (or smart contracts) using highly generic concepts: A HLC transaction represents the interaction between two participants in the business model, necessarily involving in itself some object as an asset (Fig. 3).

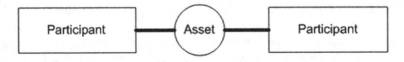

Fig. 3. HyperLedger business model

In addition to primary modeling concepts HLC also define some auxiliary elements for modeling software implementations: access control, events, concepts. Access control is used to grant or limit access to an asset. In a business model, not every member has access to all assets. For example, one client should not have access to the personal data of other clients. Event specifies a domain-specific notification. Concept corresponds to all other concepts which cannot be attributed to other groups. The concept may be, for example, the postal address.

HLC provides its own entity modeling language - CTO. In addition, designers should use JavaScript to program the business-logic of smart contracts.

2.2   Selection of the Business Process Modeling Approach for PIM

As a part of this work, the task was set to choose an approach for platform-independent modeling of organizational processes that would be easily used in our solution for the problem of automatic generation of blockchain-related PSM from the organizational PIMs.

ArchiMate [6] is a modern enterprise architecture modeling language developed by The Open Group and complementary to the TOGAF (The Open Group Architecture Framework), which is the leading framework for enterprise architecture. Enterprise architecture seeks to fully encompass the organization and is used as an important tool for organizational change.

The key features of the language are: compatibility of ArchiMate concepts with concepts of languages at other levels of modeling, a strong level of detail that facilitates a deeper understanding and analysis of the model. However, this language does not replace such well known modeling languages as BPMN and UML, but it complements them.

In the ArchiMate language, three types of elements are distinguished: an active structural element, an element of behavior, and a passive structural element (Fig. 4). An active structure element is considered to be an entity capable of performing specified actions. These entities include both business executives and devices that perform certain actions. The passive structure element (passive structure element) is an entity on which certain actions are performed. These entities can include both a data object and an information object. The behavioral element determines who performs the action. As a rule, this element is assigned to active structural elements.

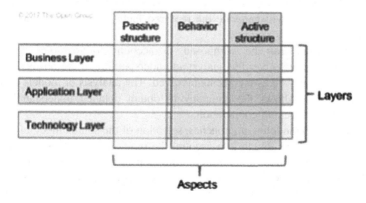

Fig. 4. Layers and elements in ArchiMate

To describe the enterprise in the language, there are three layers in accordance with the principles of TOGAF. Each layer contains specific elements for this layer, based on basic concepts, but specified specifically for this layer. Each layer contains executors of activities, activities and objects of activities:

- the business layer describes what the enterprise and its surroundings do and how it develops. This layer describes the products and services provided for external customers, business objects, as well as business processes and business roles that perform these processes;
- the application layer aims to describe existing applications, functionality, and existing communication between applications. This layer describes the application services that support the business layer, as well as the data objects that the application uses;
- the technology layer describes the implementation of application components or data objects. This includes devices, equipment and software on which applications run, as well as artifacts that form the physical and infrastructure services that are necessary for the operation of applications (processing and storage of information).

Between these layers, there is a "use" type relationship, which shows how the higher layer uses elements of the lower layer, and "implementation" showing how the elements of the lower layers implement the elements of the higher layers.

DEMO (Design & Engineering Methodology for Organizations) is a formal methodology for design and engineering of organizations [5]. The DEMO methodology is based on the PSI (ψ) theory (Performance in Social Interaction), which combines ontological work, and includes 4 axioms and 1 theorem: construction axiom (construction axiom), transactional axiom (transaction axiom), abstraction axiom (abstraction axiom) and an organizational theorem that combines systems of three interconnected levels:

- B-organization (business level);
- I-organization (informational level);
- D-organization (data level).

In DEMO, the basic pattern of a business transaction is composed of the three phases. During the actagenic phase a client requests a fact from the supplier agent. The action execution which will generate the required fact. A factagenic phase leads the client to accept the results reported.

Basic transactions can be composed to account for complex transactions. The DEMO methodology gives the analyst an understanding of the business processes of the organization, as well as the agents involved. The analysis of models built on the DEMO methodology allows the company to obtain detailed understanding of the processes of governance and cooperation.

Among these two modeling approaches, selection of the source modeling technique was done in several steps taking into account the pragmatic research priorities.

First of all, since we use the method of comparative analysis of language elements from PIM and PSM in our study, DEMO and ArchiMate were analyzed in terms of coincidence with HLC concepts. DEMO operates with such concepts as actor and transaction which almost completely correspond to entities of HLC with the exception that DEMO lacks a direct counterpart of the asset that is transferred from a participant to a participant during each transaction. However, the elements of the state model can be used in that role. ArchiMate is a more complex and multi-layered language, the basic concepts of which include "element" and "relation". But since the elements are of three levels, as a result, we have about 80 entities, which is almost 16 times more than the number of HLC entities. The analysis suggested that both modeling approaches have enough expressive power for mapping to HLC concepts.

Secondly, we evaluated availability of a convenient modeling editor with rich export capabilities. That factor plays a critical role for successful accomplishment of the research tasks. There are free online editors for DEMO and ArchiMate, however they are inconvenient due to the slow speed of work and problems with the export and import of models. Only commercial DEMO editors satisfy our requirements, however, there is Archi open-source modeling editor for ArchiMate, which perfectly fits our purposes [30]. In particular, in the Archi editor a designer can find examples of three fictional organizations - ArchiSurance, ArchiMetal, Open Day, as well as Archi allows the designer to export models in multiple variations of xml, csv.

In many cases, an issue of soundness and rigor of semantics in the modeling approaches has great impact on the selection results. However, in our study, that aspect was studied from a slightly different view point. Undoubtedly, the DEMO modeling approach is based on the set of strong and formal theories and is accompanied by a solid modeling methodology. However, the following challenge was found: strength and deep scientific foundational theories of DEMO imply a highly abstract level of ontological models. In order to match the ontological models with transient business peculiarities and existing software frameworks, a modeler should produce a considerable number of intermediates: infological and datalogical models. To the best of our knowledge, a comparable with ArchiSurance set of such hierarchically structured models does not exist in a machine-readable form, but its design is out of the scope of that project. At the same time even early comparative study of DEMO and ArchiMate [31] determines connection points among them and suggests to use DEMO as a "front-end approach". Moreover, recent researches like [32] demonstrate applicability of formal methods for expressing the semantics of ArchiMate models. These results take "the doors open" for reusability of our results.

In a conclusion, after comparing *pro* and *contra* arguments, the ArchiMate language was selected for developing and evaluation of the trial version of our MDE approach due to great modeling and export capabilities of the Archi 3.0 program.

3 Proposed Mapping Approach

Development of our approach includes design of correspondence rules and implementation of a corresponding MDE tool for producing PSMs on the basis of PIMs.

3.1 Analysis of Correspondence

To map the concepts of an ArchiMate model into the concepts of HyperLedger Composer (HLC), inconsistency between ArchiMate artifacts and HLC concepts should be taken into account. In the HLC, we may select only 5 main concepts, while ArchiMate provides as many as 76. In order to find correspondences between two domains, English terminology and parts of speech used in its context were studied. Some concepts of ArchiMate can be interpreted unambiguously - their names already provide a hint. Thus, the concepts containing Event (TechnologyEvent, BusinessEvent) directly correspond to the HLC event, Access (AccessRelationship) to HLC access, Actor/Role (BusinessActor) to the HLC participant, and everything that contains Process (BusinessProcess) to the HLC transaction. As Table 1 shows, relationship types in ArchiMate, with the exception of AccessRelationship, also apply to the HLC transaction. On the other hand, the relationship in ArchiMate may not be particularly significant for the HyperLedger Composer. In most cases, they represent the link between the participant and the transaction.

Table 1. Analysis of the relationships group

ArchiMate	HLC
Aggregation	*relationships*
Assignment	*relationships*
Association	*relationships*
Flow	*relationships*
Grouping	*relationships*
Influence	*relationships*
Junction	*relationships*
Realization	*relationships*
Relationship	*relationships*
Serving	*relationships*
Specialization	*relationships*
Triggering	*relationships*

We are also interested in cases where the relationship itself becomes a transaction and has its own name. These cases are rare, so let's move on to a detailed analysis of other entities. The following matches (Table 2) were selected for them.

Table 2. Analysis of the assets group

ArchiMate	Part of speech	HLC
ApplicationInterface	Noun	asset
Artifact	Noun	asset
Assessment	Noun	asset
BusinessInterface	Noun	asset
BusinessObject	Noun	asset
Capability	Noun	asset
CommunicationNetwork	Noun	asset
Constraint	Noun	asset
Contract	Noun	asset
CourseOfAction	Noun	asset
DataObject	Noun	asset

Despite the large number of assets of the type "asset", some of them are not useful in the HLC context – for example, goal, driver, meaning can not be transferred from one participant to another. Other concepts that cannot play the role of an asset include location, gap, plateau, value, but still they play an important role.

As our analysis shows (Table 3), the group of participants in $\sim$ 90% of cases is represented by nouns.

Table 3. Analysis of the participants group

ArchiMate	Part of speech	HLC
ApplicationCollaboration	Noun	participant
ApplicationComponent	Noun	participant
ApplicationService	Gerund	participant
BusinessActor	Noun	participant
BusinessCollaboration	Noun	participant
BusinessRole	Noun	participant
BusinessService	Gerund	participant
Device	Noun	participant
Stakeholder	Noun	participant
TechnologyCollaboration	Noun	participant
TechnologyService	Noun	participant

The nouns group was separated from the previous keywords – such as actor, role. Transactions (Table 4) are represented mainly by verbs with such keywords as process, function, interaction.

Table 4. Analysis of the transaction group

ArchiMate	Part of speech	HLC
ApplicationFunction	gerund	transaction
ApplicationInteraction	verb	transaction
ApplicationProcess	verb	transaction
BusinessFunction	gerund	transaction
BusinessInteraction	verb	transaction
BusinessProcess	verb	transaction
CommunicationPath	gerund	transaction
TechnologyInteraction	verb	transaction
TechnologyProcess	verb	transaction

Event and access (Tables 5 and 6) are related to the event and access keywords. The rules for member access to assets can be defined in the ACL file.

Table 5. Analysis of the events group

ArchiMate	HLC
ApplicationEvent	event
BusinessEvent	event
ImplementationEvent	event
TechnologyEvent	event

Table 6. Analysis of the access group

ArchiMate	HLC
AccessRelationship	access

Based on the results obtained, the most numerous groups of concepts can be distinguished (Fig. 5). Their description should be given maximum attention and as much as possible to automate their generation.

Fig. 5. Ratio of each concept's category

In order to ensure the correctness of the mapping rules proposed, an additional check was carried out, in which each concept was analyzed manually. Based on the xml-model of the ArchiSurance organization, a sample was generated containing the name of the entity, its type in ArchiMate and the intended type in HLC. The test showed the following results:

1. Asset - 100% (all 43 concepts are indeed an asset);
2. Transaction ∼ 95% (21 out of 22 are true);
3. Member ∼ 89% (only 47 of 53 entities are members);
4. Event - 50% (1 of 2).

No access concepts were found.

From the obtained results it can be concluded that the proposed mapping rules (Tables 1, 2, 3, 4, 5 and 6) reliably reflect the peculiarities of mapping from one domain to another for assets, and with minor errors for transactions and participants. In the case of events and access concepts, it is necessary to analyze more data in order to draw conclusions.

3.2   Tooling Support of the Mapping Proposed

Based on the mapping rules between the ArchiMate and HLC, a specific tool should be developed to automate transfer of the organization model from one environment to another. First of all, consider the principle by which the blockchain network is deployed and draw up requirements for the software solution.

As already noted, HLC uses its own modeling language - CTO. It is a key artifact for creating a model because all relevant entities are specified in the .cto file. Automated generation of such a file should be the most important task for the intended software tool. Let's take a closer look at the structure of the .cto file and define the requirements:

- models must have a unique namespace;
- any asset and participant must be identified using the statement "identified by";
- the concept is indicated by a lowercase letter "o", the reference by "->";
- in the .cto file, mentioning the transaction is enough, the business logic is designed separately in the file logic.js.

Based on the requirements, the tool should generate two kinds of the artifacts:a .cto file; a logic.js file.

To automate the transfer of ArchiMate artifacts into the HLC concepts, a software tool was created in accordance with the requirements above and the mapping rules developed (Tables 1, 2, 3, 4, 5 and 6). Python was chosen as the implementation language due to its lightness, cross-platform, and ability to work with xml and csv. The software tool also simplifies the development of the business logic: the tool generates the .cto file, which contains the main participants, assets, and transactions of the business network, as well as the logic.js file where the business logic should be specified. For input data, the tool receives the .csv file with an organization model generated from ArchiMate.

Due to the different specifics of the data models under the study, currently the tool only simplifies the transfer of the organization model to the HLC environment, but does not accomplish it by 100%. Business analysts are invited to write their own logic in JavaScript, as well as supplement the model with additional characteristics.

4 Practical Evaluation

As an example illustrating application of our approach, a ArchiMate model of the fictitious insurance company ArchiSurance was taken (Fig. 6). The complete model contains a large number of elements - 120 (43 of them are assets), so a manual transfer is time and quality expensive, a designer can easily miss one of the elements.

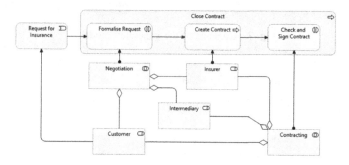

Fig. 6. The model taken for evaluation

Using our tool and the .csv file exported from the Archi editor, a test engineer obtains the generated set of HLC artifacts (cto-file) (Figs. 7 and 8). Some amount of manual work is required to define business-logic and edit the logic.js file. As the editing will be completed, the test engineer needs to re-run our tool with the –bna option to create a complete HLC archive for deployment.

In our case, as a result of the conversion, a code with a length of 732 characters was obtained, which was later extended to 862. Thus, the tool allows a developer to automate generation of 84.9% of the code, and the remaining 14.1% is the code of the business logic which should be defined manually. If a designer should specify business-logics of transactions in more detail, what is recommended to do, the amount of manual work will increase to 33.6%.

```
namespace test
asset Request for Insurance
identified by
InsuranceNumber {
o String InsuranceNumber
o String description
--> Customer customer
}
asset Contract identified by
ContractId {
o String ContractId
--> Customer customer
}
participant Customer
identified by CustomerId {
o String CustomerId
o String firstName
o String lastName
}
```

```
participant Insurer
identified by InsurerId {
o String InsurerId
o String firstName
o String lastName
}
participant Intermediary
identified by IntermediaryId
{
o String IntermediaryId
o String firstName
        o String lastName
}
transaction Close contract {
}
transaction Formalise
Request { }
transaction Check and Sign
Contract {
}
transaction Create Contract
{ }
transaction Negotiation { }
transaction Contracting { }
```

Fig. 7. Contents of the generated model.

Fig. 8. The file structure of an automatically generated .bna file

As Fig. 7 shows, the number of elements of the ArchiMate model fully corresponds to the number of elements in the .cto file. This amount can be reduced. For example, the transaction "Close contract" combines three other transactions. This violates the rule of the participant-transaction-participant, which means that the transaction must be changed or redesigned. Despite some inaccuracy in automation, it is a convenient and optimal solution compared to manual creating a .cto file from scratch.

To check the artifacts generated in the real blockchain environment the deployment test of the bna-file designed was performed on the blockchain platform HyperLedger Composer using HyperLedger Fabric. For clarity, we consider the test case in which the insured event occurs, and the company pays money to the customer's account.

Let's reduce this case to one transaction (Pay) (Fig. 9). To do this, you must also reduce the .cto file to two participants - the client and the insurance company and the Pay transaction.

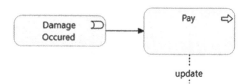

Fig. 9. A transaction analyzed

As an asset, a bank account was additionally created, on which the company's money are deposited (Fig. 10):

```
namespace archi
asset BankAccount identified
by accountId {
o String accountId
--> Customer owner
--> ArchiSurance company
o Double accountbalance
}
participant ArchiSurance
identified by companyId {
o String companyId
}
```

```
participant Customer
identified by
InsuranceNumber {
o String InsuranceNumber
o String FirstName
o String LastName
}
transaction Pay {
--> BankAccount from
--> BankAccount to
  o Double
  }
```

Fig. 10. A test CTO-model.

Corresponding business-logic was written for the .cto file (logic.js) (Fig. 11). The @param parameter allows a designer to associate the Pay transaction with the pay-Money Javascript function. In the script designed a money transfer between two bank accounts was implemented according to standard transaction rules.

```
/**
 * @param {archi.Pay} payMoney
 * @transaction
 */
function payMoney(payMoney) {
if (payMoney.from.accountbalance < payMoney.to.accountbalance) {
throw new Error ("Not enough money");
}
payMoney.from.accountbalance -= payMoney.amount;
payMoney.to.accountbalance += payMoney.amount;
return getAssetRegistry('archi.BankAccount')
.then (function (assetRegistry) {
return assetRegistry.update(payMoney.from);
})
.then (function () {
return getAssetRegistry('archi.BankAccount');
})
```

Fig. 11. The business-logic in logic.js.

After archiving to the .bna file, a new business network was successfully deployed. HLC allows a designer to create a server that uses the RESTful API - an architecture style used to present data in a simple and convenient way. The server contains all the entities of the created model (Fig. 12). Using such REST-interfaces a test engineer is able to manually create the participants using the POST request to the server, substituting the necessary data into a template that we defined in advance in the .cto file. If the participant is added successfully, the server's response with the HTTP code "200" will be returned.

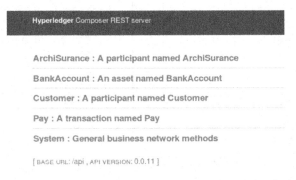

Fig. 12. Representation of data instances corresponding to the CTO-model

Thus, any number of participants can be added to the network. The test engineer can check their number using the HTTP GET request. You may notice from Fig. 13

that each participant in the system is determined by additional data—concepts that are not in the ArchiMate model—they allow you to identify the user in the system. To these data, in addition to the name and insurance number, you can add a type of insurance, insurance status, etc. In this model, each participant was additionally associated with a bank account from which the transfer of funds should take place. You can make sure that the company's account is equal to 1,000,000 units, while the client's account is zero. Of course, we do not have direct access to the amount of funds in the client's account, therefore the "accountbalance" parameter can be interpreted as the amount of money that the company has already paid to the client.

Model Pay transactions can be launched using the HTTP POST requests. That transaction requires the account number and total amount for the transfer. The transaction identifier is generated automatically and can be used to review the transactions history which is secured by the Blockchain technology.

```
{
  "$class": "archi.Pay",
  "from": "000",
  "to": "001",
  "amount": 10000,
  "transactionId": "68b27173dbbb4c510c10aa3157a860c6d04ce8268992d0fbdbed751885e4a1ac",
  "timestamp": "2018-05-06T16:53:42.756Z"
}
```

Fig. 13. Information about a successfully accomplished POST transaction

To verify the success of the transaction, the test engineer can re-send a HTTP GET request to the server (Fig. 14).

```
[
  {
    "$class": "archi.BankAccount",
    "accountId": "000",
    "owner": "resource:archi.Customer#archisurance",
    "company": "resource:archi.ArchiSurance#ArchiSurance",
    "accountbalance": 990000
  },
  {
    "$class": "archi.BankAccount",
    "accountId": "001",
    "owner": "resource:archi.Customer#nkomleva",
    "company": "resource:archi.ArchiSurance#N/A",
    "accountbalance": 10000
  }
]
```

Fig. 14. Information about a successfully accomplished GET transaction

The amount of funds in the company's account has decreased, as has the value of the amount paid to the client by the insurance company. All tests performed approved validity of the automatically generated HLC artifacts.

5   Conclusion

Our work aimed at the solving the problem of automatic generation of blockchain-related Platform-specific models and other artifacts based on the organizational Platform-independent models. That problem can be called the problem of "last mile" in the model-driven engineering, and becomes certainly challenging for emerging software technologies like Blockchain. We looked at several organization modeling methods (ArchiMate, DEMO), studied the features of blockchain platforms. We applied outcomes of that study in practice, exploring the possibility of model-driven liaison of ArchiMate process modeling approach and the HyperLedger Composer blockchain technology. As a result, a mapping methodology and a corresponding software tool were created for semi-automated mapping that allows a system designer to transfer ArchiMate artifacts to the concepts of HyperLedger Composer and, thereby, automate the creation of a new blockchain-enabled information system.

In the course of the research, the feasibility of transferring the organization's business processes to blockchain platforms was confirmed. Test cases show that our approach simplifies this process. In addition, during data conversion, it is possible to analyze critically the current processes in the organization, which can serve as a good start for the reengineering of business processes.

In comparison with other known MDE approaches to automatic generation of blockchain artifacts [18, 20], our solution permits using a complete organizational model in ArchiMate language instead of partial BPMN models. At the same time our results open opportunities to extend latest applications of DEMO for blockchain analysis [17, 18] by mechanisms for automatic generation of HyperLedger artifacts.

Unfortunately, during the transfer, we lost many of the advantages of ArchiMate: nesting of elements, the multi-level system, the advantages of the relationship between the elements, since they do not fit into the principles of blockchain platforms. However, these advantages are not important at the stage of software implementation.

The further development of this approach is planned in the direction of improving the proposed mapping rules for generating ready-made models for the blockchain platform and minimizing manual work. It is also recommended to examine in detail the issue of security of the resulting platform and automated check of business-logic correctness.

References

1. Dietz, J.L., et al.: The discipline of enterprise engineering. Int. J. Organ. Des. Eng. 3(1), 86–114 (2016)
2. Giachetti, R.E.: Design of Enterprise Systems: Theory, Architecture, and Methods. CRC Press, Boca Raton (2016)

3. Sandkuhl, K., et al.: From expert discipline to common practice: a vision and research agenda for extending the reach of enterprise modeling. Bus. Inf. Syst. Eng. **60**(1), 69–80 (2018)
4. van Gils, B., Proper, H.A.: Enterprise modelling in the age of digital transformation. In: Buchmann, R.A., Karagiannis, D., Kirikova, M. (eds.) PoEM 2018. LNBIP, vol. 335, pp. 257–273. Springer, Cham (2018). https://doi.org/10.1007/978-3-030-02302-7_16
5. Dietz, J.L.G.: Enterprise Ontology: Theory and Methodology. Springer, Heidelberg (2006). https://doi.org/10.1007/3-540-33149-2
6. Van Haren Publishing, Zaltbommel: The Open Group: Open Group Standard. ArchiMate 2.1 Specificattion (2013)
7. Beydeda, S., Book, M., Gruhn, V. (eds.): Model-Driven Software Development, vol. 15. Springer, Heidelberg (2005). https://doi.org/10.1007/3-540-28554-7
8. Brambilla, M., Cabot, J., Wimmer, M.: Model-driven software engineering in practice. Synth. Lect. Softw. Eng. **3**(1), 1–207 (2017)
9. Liebel, G., Badreddin, O., Heldal, R.: Model driven software engineering in education: a multi-case study on perception of tools and UML. In: 2017 IEEE 30th Conference on Software Engineering Education and Training (CSEE&T). IEEE (2017)
10. Drescher, D.: Blockchain Basics: A Non-Technical Introduction in 25 Steps, 1st edn. Apress, Frankfurt am Main (2017)
11. Hughes, A., Park, A., Kietzmann, J., Archer-Brown, C.: Beyond bitcoin: what blockchain and distributed ledger technologies mean for firms. Bus. Horizons **62**(3), 273–281 (2019)
12. Glaser, F., Hawlitschek, F., Notheisen, B.: Blockchain as a platform. In: Treiblmaier, H., Beck, R. (eds.) Business Transformation through Blockchain, pp. 121–143. Springer, Cham (2019). https://doi.org/10.1007/978-3-319-98911-2_4
13. Mendling, J., Weber, J.I., Van Der Aalst, W.: Blockchains for business process management – challenges and opportunities. J. ACM Trans. Manag. Inf. Syst. (TMIS) **9**(1), Article No. 4 (2018)
14. Zheng, Z., Xie, S., Dai, H.N., Chen, X., Wang, H.: Blockchain challenges and opportunities: a survey. Int. J. Web Grid Serv. **14**(4), 352–375 (2018)
15. Ellervee, A., Matulevicius, R., Mayer, N.: A comprehensive reference model for blockchain-based distributed ledger technology. In: ER Forum/Demos, pp. 306–319 (2017)
16. de Kruijff, J., Weigand, H.: Understanding the blockchain using enterprise ontology. In: Dubois, E., Pohl, K. (eds.) CAiSE 2017. LNCS, vol. 10253, pp. 29–43. Springer, Cham (2017). https://doi.org/10.1007/978-3-319-59536-8_3
17. Hornáčková, B., Skotnica, M., Pergl, R.: Exploring a role of blockchain smart contracts in enterprise engineering. In: Aveiro, D., Guizzardi, G., Guerreiro, S., Guédria, W. (eds.) EEWC 2018. LNBIP, vol. 334, pp. 113–127. Springer, Cham (2019). https://doi.org/10.1007/978-3-030-06097-8_7
18. Silva, D., Guerreiro, S., Sousa, P.: Decentralized enforcement of business process control using blockchain. In: Aveiro, D., Guizzardi, G., Guerreiro, S., Guédria, W. (eds.) EEWC 2018. LNBIP, vol. 334, pp. 69–87. Springer, Cham (2019). https://doi.org/10.1007/978-3-030-06097-8_5
19. Seebacher, S., Maleshkova, M.: A model-driven approach for the description of blockchain business networks. In: Proceedings of the 51st Hawaii International Conference on System Sciences (2018)
20. Tran, A., Lu, Q., Weber, I.: Lorikeet: a model-driven engineering tool for blockchain-based business process execution and asset management. BPM Demo Track (2018)
21. Androulaki, E., Barger, A., Bortnikov, V.: HyperLedger fabric: a distributed operating system for permissioned blockchains. In: Proceedings of the Thirteenth EuroSys Conference, pp. 1–15. ACM (2018)

22. Ethereum. https://www.ethereum.org. Accessed 10 May 2019
23. Sawtooth. https://www.hyperLedger.org/projects/sawtooth. Accessed 10 May 2019
24. Iroha. http://iroha.tech/en/. Accessed 10 May 2019
25. HyperLedger Fabric. http://hyperLedger-fabric.readthedocs.io/en/latest/. Accessed 10 May 2019
26. Multichain. https://www.multichain.com/. Accessed 10 May 2019
27. Hydra Chain. https://github.com/HydraChain/hydrachain. Accessed 10 May 2019
28. HyperLedger. https://www.hyperLedger.org/. Accessed 10 May 2019
29. HyperLedger Composer. https://HyperLedger.github.io/composer/. Accessed 10 May 2019
30. Archi Editor. https://www.ArchiMatetool.com/. Accessed 10 May 2019
31. EttemaJan, R., Dietz, L.G.: ArchiMate and DEMO – Mates to Date? Advances in Enterprise Engineering III (2009)
32. Klimek, R., Szwed, P.: Verification of ArchiMate process specifications based on deductive temporal reasoning. In: 2013 Federated Conference on Computer Science and Information Systems, pp. 1109–1116. IEEE (2013)

Author Index

Printed in the United States
By Bookmasters